The Hangman's Scrapbook

The Hangman's Scrapbook

The Life and Executions of John Ellis

Neil R. Storey

PEN & SWORD
HISTORY

First published in Great Britain in 2024 by
Pen & Sword History
An imprint of Pen & Sword Books Limited
Yorkshire – Philadelphia

ISBN 978 1 39903 166 0

A CIP catalogue record for this book is
available from the British Library

Typeset by Mac Style
Printed in the UK by CPI Group (UK) Ltd, Croydon, CR0 4YY.

Pen & Sword Books Limited incorporates the imprints of After
the Battle, Atlas, Archaeology, Aviation, Discovery, Family History,
Fiction, History, Maritime, Military, Military Classics, Politics,
Select, Transport, True Crime, Air World, Frontline Publishing, Leo
Cooper, Remember When, Seaforth Publishing, The Praetorian Press,
Wharncliffe Local History, Wharncliffe Transport, Wharncliffe True
Crime and White Owl.

For a complete list of Pen & Sword titles please contact

PEN & SWORD BOOKS LIMITED
47 Church Street, Barnsley, South Yorkshire, S70 2AS, England
E-mail: enquiries@pen-and-sword.co.uk
Website: www.pen-and-sword.co.uk
or
PEN AND SWORD BOOKS
1950 Lawrence Rd, Havertown, PA 19083, USA
E-mail: uspen-and-sword@casematepublishers.com
Website: www.penandswordbooks.com

For Rob Clack, my friend and fellow crime historian.

My last message to everyone is 'Sursum corda', and for the rest, my good will to those who have taken my life, equally to all those who tried to save it. All are my brothers now.

Sir Roger Casement

Contents

Introduction

The worst thing you can do with a man is hang him. The next worst thing is to make him a hangman.

Ellis family saying

John Ellis was an upstanding family man, shopkeeper and well-liked member of his local community in Rochdale, Lancashire. A very ordinary looking man, he was of average height, slight build with a very fine, large, chestnut-coloured moustache that had a natural curl at the ends. When out and about he always wore a neat, charcoal-coloured three-piece suit with a fresh starched collar and tie, and a watch and chain on his waistcoat, all crowned off with a bowler hat. To look at him he was the epitome of an Edwardian small business owner and men who dressed like him could be found in every British town and city in those days. There really was nothing about him that stood out. Personally, he was a typical Northern man of upper working-class status. He lived in a modest home of his own with his wife where they raised five children. He enjoyed watching local sporting events and held office in Buersil Lodge as part of the Royal Antediluvian Order of Buffaloes. Ellis was also a keen breeder of dogs and prize chickens. In fact, he was well known for being a keen animal lover with an aversion to harming anything. But that inoffensive looking man who you would have passed on the street without giving him a second glance was Britain's senior hangman – the man at the top of the Home Office list of persons trained to carry out executions for over twenty years and a man responsible for sending over 200 men and women to their death on the gallows in Britain and Ireland.

During his years as executioner, between 1901 and 1924, Ellis hanged some of the most infamous killers of the twentieth century including Dr Crippen, Samuel Dougal 'The Moat Farm Murderer', John Dickman 'The Railway Murderer', George Smith 'The Brides in the Bath' murderer, and poisoners Frederick Seddon and Major Herbert Rowse Armstrong. He also executed Henry Jacoby, who was just 18 years old and one of the youngest men to hang at Pentonville. He hanged Sir Roger Casement, and members of the Irish Republican Army (IRA) for treason and carried out the execution of Edith Thompson, one of the most controversial executions in the history of capital punishment.

John Ellis was born at 18 Broad Lane in the Balderstone district of Rochdale, Lancashire, on 4 October 1874. He was the eldest of six children (four girls and two boys) to Joseph James 'Joe' Ellis and Sarah Ann Ellis. John's father, Joe, worked on his own account as a hairdresser from a shop on Oldham Road, Rochdale, near the Swan with Two Necks pub.

Joe was a well-respected local tradesman and an upstanding Christian. John described his father as a 'stern disciplinarian' who was determined his children were all raised with strong Christian values. Young John, known to many of his pals as Jack, was educated at the Red School, a Methodist chapel and day school a short distance away from Joe Ellis's hairdressers on Oldham Road.

Joe had been keen to see his first-born son join him in the family business but young John did not fancy the life of a barber. John was an adventurous lad and at the age of 16 he ran away from home ... twice. Each time he travelled the roads around the north making what money he could by singing. After the second attempt did not work out, John could not face returning to his parent's home again and he went to live with one of his aunts, concluding he would be better served finding employment at one of the local cotton mills. John's local mill was the Eagle Mill in Balderstone and it was there he worked as a stripper and grinder for the next seven years. While at the mill John met Annie Beaton Whitworth, the woman he would marry at the parish church of St Leonard, Middleton, Lancaster on 20 April 1895 when he was aged 20 and she was 22 years old. Both stated their occupation on the marriage register as 'cotton operative'.

Sadly, John suffered an accident at work which damaged his spine and left him with long term back problems. He had no other option than to find work that was not so physically demanding. Fortunately, he soon found another position at Tweedales & Smalley, a large textile machinery manufacturer in Castleton, Rochdale. It was when John was employed at Tweedales that the notion first entered his head that he should become a hangman. It all began with a flippant remark during a breaktime conversation with fellow workers about a recent execution. Ellis chirped up 'It is just the kind of job that would suit me. I should like to be a hangman'. Everybody present laughed. In fact Ellis would freely admit he almost laughed himself, but that moment was something of an epiphany for John and he set about making enquiries as to how he may realise what he would later describe as his 'calling'. John could never state any particular reason for why he was so keen to become a hangman. He was far from a gruesome sort of man and would simply state: 'I wanted to be one – and that was that!'

Perhaps mindful that obtaining time off to carry out his duties as hangman could be problematical for an employee of a mill, John also made the decision to return to his family trade of hairdressing and started his own business as a hairdresser, newsagent and stationer at 451 Oldham Road, where he also sold umbrellas, toy dolls and postcards of local views, actors and entertainers. Clearly John liked variety in his working life and soon after he had established his business he diversified again and began the formal application process to become a public executioner.

Ellis made his application discreetly, knowing full well that becoming a hangman would be greeted with repugnance by his wife, his parents and in-laws who would undoubtedly attempt to dissuade him from pursuing the matter. After due process and a successful interview with Mr Robert Dickson Cruickshank, the Governor of Strangeways Prison in Manchester, Ellis was given his chance when he received his invitation to attend a week's training as executioner at Newgate Prison in London, commencing on 14 March 1901. It was only after he received this invitation that John mentioned his intentions to his family. It came as quite a shock to them when he broke the news – firstly to his wife, who took quite some persuading that there was nothing disgraceful in such work. His mother's reaction was etched bold in his memory:

Gracious John! Whatever put such an idea into your head?...What will people say about us?

John tried to pacify her by explaining that executioners were part of the law of the land and that somebody had to do the work. To which she retorted: 'Let someone else do it, then'.

John remained resolute. He was off to Newgate! Under the tutelage of the Chief Warder, Scott, John proved himself both competent and efficient on the scaffold and his name was added to the Home Office list of approved executioners and assistants on 8 May 1901. He attended his first execution as assistant to William Billington for the executions of John Miller and his nephew, John Robert Miller, at HMP Newcastle on 7 December 1901. Ellis learned well and progressed to carry out his first hanging as senior executioner when he sent John Davis through the gallows trap for the murder of Jane Harrison at HMP Warwick on 1 January 1907.

Ellis would serve in the capacities of Assistant and Chief Executioner for a total of twenty-three years and would be involved in over 200 executions. British executioners tended to keep their own 'little black books' in which they recorded brief details of the name, prison, date, height, weight and 'drop' of those they executed, Ellis's is mentioned in one of the last interviews he gave to reporter Frederick Bowman who recorded:

I found that he [Ellis] *talked 'drop' as easily as other men talk shop. He used his little black book – of which I wrote at the time – to do it. His little black book was the private ledger of his very private business. In it, with a tidy method which was as neat as his own person – he straggled only in his heavy moustache – he had written the details of those executions which he had performed or at which he had attended as assistant. Besides the names of all the men and women who marched in procession down its pages was a business like, and, I have no doubt, necessary statement of their physical and mental peculiarity, their height, their weight, their demeanour – and the 'drop' that he had to give them at the end. There was also a record of their last words. 'Anything interesting!' said Ellis, succinctly and informatively. Ellis snapped its covers together and deposited it in his pocket with one action. 'No, no, no' he said, and there was an excusable asperity in his tone. 'You can't have that … you can't have that.'*

After over two decades as executioner Ellis had many stories to tell but the question that also has to be considered is how heavily were these experiences playing on his mind?

When he resigned in 1924 some spoke of nerves finally getting to him and the spectres of those he had executed haunting his dreams. Some commentators, however, were far more scathing, suggesting Ellis resigned because he could not enter into a lucrative deal with a newspaper to publish his memoirs as serving executioner because the terms of his appointment would not permit him to do so.

Ellis did have a remarkable memory and using cuttings and material he had assembled over the years he dictated his memoirs which were serialised and published in *Thompson's Weekly*. After each account was published he carefully cut it out of the paper then pasted it onto foolscap paper which he kept in a 'Pilot' brand letter file with smart black covers and a patent lock fastening system, a forerunner of the lever arch binders we know today. At the rear of the file he also pasted pages of the newspaper serialisations of his former assistant, William Willis, and his Victorian predecessor, James Berry of Bradford, who was in office as Britain's No. 1 executioner from 1884 until he resigned in 1891.

Ellis clearly envisaged his scrapbook collection of cuttings becoming a book and he dictated additional information which was annotated in ink by hand in the margin for several of the newspaper accounts. In a few instances Ellis's recollections of particular murderers and executions extend over several sheets of foolscap. Notably, there are three pages dedicated to the execution of Seddon, the poisoner who Ellis described as 'the most impudently calm murderer' he ever executed. That said, the man he considered 'the worst' he had ever encountered on the scaffold was former Army officer Frederick Rothwell Holt, 'The Sandhills Murderer', who murdered his girlfriend, Elsie 'Kitty' Breaks, by shooting her three times in the sand dunes at Lytham St Anne's near Blackpool in 1919. Holt was the only condemned person ever to threaten Ellis while carrying out his duty. Ellis would vividly recall:

When I was putting the cap on him he glared at me. Queer eyes he had, too! I remember them now. 'Don't forget', he said to me, 'I'll see you again'.

Ellis's longest hand-written account, however, covers a column beside the printed account and a further three pages in which he recollects the execution that would become his most controversial, and the one that probably haunted him most of all – that of 29-year-old Mrs Edith Thompson who was convicted of being complicit in the murder of husband by her younger lover, Frederick Bywaters, in 1923.

With over 200 executions to his credit, John Ellis chose the most notable personages and the most infamous and remarkable executions for inclusion in his memoirs. Ellis candidly relates his impressions of those he hanged and how not everything always went as smoothly as he hoped. He did, however, sidestep some issues of personal controversy, notably the jealously that festered in Henry Pierrepoint towards Ellis as he saw himself being passed over and his former assistant receiving a number of engagements instead of him. The situation came to a head when Henry Pierrepoint was given the execution of murderer, Frederick Foreman, at Chelmsford Prison in 1910, with Ellis as his assistant. When Pierrepoint arrived he had clearly been drinking and when the pair met in the prison gatehouse something snapped in Pierrepoint. He called Ellis an 'Irish bastard' and punched him in the face and violently assaulted him. Fortunately a warder soon intervened and ended the matter. Pierrepoint and Ellis carried out the execution the following morning, but Ellis wrote to the prison to complain about Pierrepoint's behaviour. The matter was brought to the attention of the Home Secretary. As a consequence, Henry Pierrepoint was removed from the Home Office list of approved executioners, and John Ellis was exonerated of all blame and was promoted to No. 1 senior executioner. In his autobiography *Executioner Pierrepoint* (1974), Albert Pierrepoint (son of Henry Pierrepoint) recalled:

I know that my father held a strong feeling against Ellis. I have heard him express it but not give the reason. 'If I ever meet Ellis', I have heard him say, 'I'll kill him – it doesn't matter if it is in the church.'

There is also one glaring omission from amongst the most notable figures Ellis executed in Ellis's memoirs, that of the diplomat and Irish nationalist Sir Roger

Casement. Casement had opened negotiations to garner German military aid for the Easter Rising in 1916. Shortly after he arrived back in Ireland from Germany, Casement was arrested by the Royal Irish Constabulary and charged with high treason, sabotage and espionage. Brought to London to stand trial, Casement was found guilty of high treason and was executed by John Ellis at Pentonville Prison, London, on 3 August 1916. The execution of Sir Roger Casement and Ellis's subsequent executions of a total of ten members of the Irish Republican Army left Ellis in mortal fear of reprisals for the rest of his life so it is hardly surprising he chose to avoid mention of it in his memoirs.

There is no mention of any extraordinary incident taking place at Casement's execution in credible reports. One of Ellis's few published accounts of the execution appeared in H. Montgomery Hyde's *Famous Trials: Roger Casement* (1964):

> 'The impression will ever remain on my mind of the composure of his noble countenance, the smile of contentment and happiness, as he helped my assistant ... the steady martial tread of his six feet four inches and soldierly appearance adding to the solemn echo of his prompt and coherent answers to the Roman Catholic chaplain ... Roger Casement appeared to me the bravest man it fell to my unhappy lot to execute.'

Ellis echoed this view in a comment to Frederick Bowman who knew and corresponded with Ellis over many years: 'Casement may have been a traitor but he died like a soldier'. This comment certainly rings true for Ellis who, no matter who the condemned was or what crime they had committed, would always relate his impression of the people he hanged as he experienced them.

Tragically, it seems the memories of incidents during his work as a hangman began to haunt the mind of John Ellis, particularly the execution of Edith Thompson, after which a warder would claim that Ellis told him that he would never hang another woman. This was clearly compounded when only months later that same year he conducted the execution of child murderer, Susan Newell, at Duke Street Prison, Glasgow on 10 October 1923. As a matter of courtesy to a woman Ellis only lightly pinioned her wrists together. When she arrived on the gallows trap she angrily objected to having a white cap placed over her head. This outburst caused Ellis to falter and in that moment Newell managed to free her arms from the strap. Ellis's assistant, William Willis, spotted what had happened and managed to adjust the strap and restore the restraint as Ellis ditched the hood, placed the noose over her head, adjusted the rope around her neck, shot over to the lever and sent her on her way.

Ellis realised he was losing his nerve and his mind was troubled more than ever. He conducted what would prove to be his last execution, that of Sheffield murderer John Eastwood, at Armley Prison in Leeds on 28 December 1923 and resigned the following year. Only a few months later, on 25 August 1924, Ellis attempted to take his own life by somewhat ironically shooting himself with the automatic pistol he had purchased for his personal protection in the event of a revenge attack against him by assassins from the IRA.

Fortunately for Ellis, the bullet he tried to kill himself with lodged in his jaw and he survived, but he was ordered to appear before Rochdale Magistrates Court for what was then the criminal offence of attempting to commit suicide. The hearing drew large crowds and police had to maintain order as far more people attempted to enter the court than capacity would allow. Hundreds were turned away, so they lingered outside.

When the Magistrate asked Ellis if he had any reason to give for why he had attempted suicide he replied: 'No reason at all'. The Magistrate clearly sympathised with the former hangman and after asking Ellis to make a solemn promise not to repeat what he had done and after receiving Ellis's promise by return he discharged him.

John then returned to his work at his barber's shop where there were often a few people loitering around outside to catch a glimpse of him. Strangers would regularly drop in, sometimes having travelled many miles across the country, to have a shave or haircut whether they really needed it or not. They just wanted to be able to say they had met and had been under the blades of the former executioner. By all accounts he was a very fine barber if the letters and postcards of some of those who met him are anything to go by. His shop was neat and clean, he put his customers at ease and was so skilled he did not nick the skin of those he shaved, even those suffering from boils or pimples.

Ellis, however, could just not settle into day-to-day shop work. He was asked to play the role of hangman William Marwood in a play about Charles Peace which opened at Gravesend in December 1927. The audiences roared their approval but its run was curtailed after the press declared it to be in bad taste. Questions were raised on the matter in the House of Commons and the run of the play was terminated after its first week. Ellis purchased the gallows from the show and briefly toured as a side show demonstrating his method of execution on a good wage at Southall Fairground, but his health was deteriorating and he broke down with congestion of the lungs and could not carry on. He would try again but his health was failing and he had to give up the shows.

By 1932 Ellis, now 58 years old, was in poor health. He had been suffering increasingly dark bouts of depression and had taken to drinking to excess which frequently fuelled angry outbursts. On Tuesday 20 September 1932 he took his own life at his home at 3 Kitchen Lane, Balderstone Fold, Rochdale. At the inquest his wife, Mrs Annie Ellis, said that her husband was regular in his habits. On the Tuesday morning he got up as usual, but 'seemed a bit strange'. He had not taken any breakfast and did not return home as usual. She continued:

> *About five o'clock he came home and had something to eat, then went to the parlour for a smoke, as usual. He had had some drink, but was not drunk. About 7.15 he had a cup of tea and a little to eat. Suddenly my husband rushed into the kitchen, pulling at his collar and tie. My daughter Ivy and I were there, and he seized a razor from a pot shelf, and shouted: 'I will cut your head off'.*

Annie then fled the house and ran to her son Joe's home just down the road.

Ellis's daughter, Ivy, had heard the shouting and came downstairs to discover her father standing in the kitchen clutching a razor with a strange expression on his face. Ellis turned on his daughter and holding the razor close to her face snarled 'If I can't cut your mother's head off, I'll cut yours off'. Ivy could smell he had been drinking and pushed him away. He glared at her, then went into the front room leaving the poor girl cowering in the kitchen.

When Annie arrived at Joe's house she found her son, Austin, had dropped by to see his brother and on seeing the state his mother was in and hearing her blurt out what had happened, he rushed out. He was heading towards his parent's home with Annie close behind when he saw his father on the front door step. As they drew close, they could see his neck was bleeding and he had a wild look in his eyes.

As they continued to approach he went back inside. Austin followed him inside and into the front room which he entered just in time to see his father draw the razor blade across his throat, stagger, and fall hard face down onto the floor. Austin wanted to shield his mother from this horrific sight and managed to persuade her to return to Joe's house as he called for a doctor. Dr Harris soon arrived and found John in a spreading pool of blood. Nothing could be done; he had delivered two deep cuts of about five inches in length to his own throat and life was declared extinct.

At the inquest the Deputy Coroner, Mr J. M. Chadwick, sought to discover from witnesses if Ellis was suffering from personal worries or if the work Ellis had done in his capacity as public executioner had in any way affected his brain. Annie said apart from ill health her husband 'had no real worries'. When he enquired if she had ever witnessed him in a similar condition to how he was on the night of his suicide, she replied: 'No. It struck me that he had suddenly gone mad'. A verdict of suicide while of unsound mind was recorded.

Conjecture over what had driven Ellis to commit suicide continued long after the inquest. William Billington, under whom Ellis first served as assistant executioner, remarked in the course of a conversation with a reporter that 'somehow this hanging job never brings anybody much luck' and that he 'wondered how Ellis had stuck to the job for so long because he was always so nervous and anxious, wondering whether everything would turn out all right'. Others who knew Ellis spoke of how none of his grim official duties had given him greater anxiety than when he was called to perform the execution of a total of ten members of the Irish Republican Army at Mountjoy Prison, Dublin, in 1926 (he hanged six of them in one day) and how he was left in constant fear of reprisals.

The comments made by Ellis's son, Austin, to a reporter after his father's death, however, are probably the greatest insight that we have into the mental state of the former hangman:

Dad hadn't had a proper night's sleep for many years. We all knew what the trouble was. He was haunted. I don't think it was the memory of the two hundred and odd executions he had taken part in, but the recollection of the hanging of two women that drove him to suicide. He was a quiet man, who would sit in a corner and listen to the conversation of other people. But he became a nervous wreck. It was definitely his old job that drove him to his death.

John Ellis's funeral service was held at a packed St Mary's Church, with his coffin borne by his fellow members of the Buersil Lodge of the Royal Antediluvian Order of Buffaloes. The cortege then proceeded to Rochdale Cemetery for the committal and thus John Ellis was laid to rest with dignity.

Despite negotiations believed to have been in progress, no contract had been agreed for the publication of Ellis's memoirs. An undated page from *Empire News*, the majority of which is dedicated to the suicide and life of Ellis, was slipped inside the cover of his scrapbook by a member of his family. John's widow and family then drew a veil over the life of the husband and father who was our nation's executioner for over twenty years. Ellis's grandchildren were not told of their grandfather's work as an executioner and when they eventually found out in maturity it came as quite a shock to them.

What happened to John Ellis's scrapbook immediately after his death is unknown. Perhaps it was given away or sold along with some of Ellis's effects. Or perhaps it was put away in a case in an attic, as can happen with family memorabilia, where it was forgotten about and then sold on years later when the attic was cleared. The scrapbook is believed to have once been in the collection of popular true crime author, Bernard O'Donnell. After O'Donnell's death in 1969 much of his crime collection was rapidly disposed of and the Ellis scrapbook was lost again for over forty years until it was purchased with a number of other crime books and ephemera by a book dealer and subsequently sold to me.

Executioners James Berry and Albert Pierrepoint, and assistant executioner, Syd Dernley, all published their memoirs in book form. An excellent edited version of John Ellis's memoirs based on those published in *Thompson's Weekly News* was published by Forum Press in their True Crime Library series under the title of *Diary of a Hangman* in 1996, but now long out of print it has become hard to obtain and is an expensive second hand book in its own right.

British executioners tended to keep their own legers recording brief details of those they executed. John Ellis certainly maintained just such a leger too but he is believed to be the only British executioner to have kept an additional scrapbook of his personal accounts of those he executed and their crimes. As such, it is a unique volume in the annals of British crime and punishment.

The contents of John Ellis's lost scrapbook, its cuttings, manuscript texts and annotations have now been diligently transcribed complete with his own turns of phrase, opinions and thoughts. At last we can read the book Ellis envisaged in which he tells the story of his life and notable executions in his own words. And in doing so we gain a remarkable insight into the life, work and philosophy one of Britain's most notable and yet least known No. 1 executioners.

Neil R. Storey
Norwich
2024

Chapter 1

How I Became a Hangman

Though it is many years ago since I first applied for the post of hangman, I can still vividly remember the horror with which my wife and my parents received the news that I was to go to London at the request of the Home Office to take a course of instruction at Newgate in the method of conducting an execution. Up to that moment I had successfully concealed all the preliminary negotiations, and the sensation created in my family circle was a painful one when at last they learned of the new profession I proposed entering.

It is a matter of pride to me that, by conscientious regard for my duty, the humane innovations I have made to rob a criminal's last moments of many old time terrors, and my flat refusal ever to pander to morbidly curious folk or sensation mongers, I have earned the goodwill of all who at one time were prejudiced against me because of my profession.

My mother and other relatives gradually lost their repugnance, and even my wife at last came to accept the thing as commonplace. But I may say that she and I never discussed executions, and, as a matter of fact, I never talked of them to anybody. From the beginning I adopted a discreet silence as the keynote of my official career, and when I wrote my life story for *Thompson's Weekly News* I opened my lips for the first time as to the things I have witnessed and heard on the scaffold.

Many a time have I been pestered by those who thought to learn some spicy news about the last words and acts of a man whose crime had formed a topic of discussion for months. It was often difficult to evade such curiosity and remain polite, for my private work first as a hairdresser and then as a publican left me easily open to attack by the would-be gossips, and after every execution of a well-known murderer my house would be packed with people from far and near, all hoping to shake the hangman by the hand, and perhaps learn some titbit of what happened behind the vague screen which officialdom always draws around such affairs. They were invariably disappointed in their quest. I was ready enough to be pleasant to everybody but I conceived it as part of my duty to keep my lips sealed as far as my work as executioner was concerned.

Those who came had a further disappointment which is best conveyed by the remark of a man who had walked several miles to see me on the Sunday after I hanged Sir Roger Casement. 'What!' he exclaimed, 'Is that the hangman!'

His accent on the 'that' was as significant as it was forcible. It was almost unnecessary for him to add that he had expected to see 'some big six-footer', for the tone of his first remark explained his feelings fully. That was a common experience, for I am by no means a giant in stature and an injury to my spine, which I sustained some years ago, still detracts from an appearance of robustness.

Comments upon my slight build were of frequent occurrence. People, so I imagine, believed it was an executioner's ordinary experience to have to drag resisting and struggling wretches to the noose-end, and wondered how a man so mild looking as myself could manage it.

But as a subject of speculation this topic of 'how' I did it was easily beaten by the question 'why' I did it. Dozens and dozens of times have I been asked, just as my mother and my wife asked me at the beginning, 'What on earth made you want to be a hangman!'

And I have been forced to confess 'I don't know!'

The idea of becoming a hangman was born in my mind in the most casual manner possible. I was one of a group of fellow workmen occupying an idle half-hour in the textile machine workers' workshop, where I then earned my living, with gossiping about an execution which had taken place the day previously.

'It is just the kind of job that would suit me,' I remarked suddenly, 'I should like to be a hangman.'

Everybody laughed. For I was only a young fellow of 22 and by no means an imposing figure physically. I almost laughed myself, as up to that moment such a wish had never framed itself in my mind. But once formed it stayed there, and though I said nothing to anybody I quietly set about making inquiries to discover how to respond to what seemed to me to be almost 'a call'.

At that time I had been married two years; my wife hailing from Thornham, near Rochdale, her mother being a native of Dumbarton. Knowing what opposition I should meet from her and from my father and mother, I kept my own counsel. It was well that I did so, for my father was always a stern disciplinarian with the members of his family and as a child I had been somewhat adventurous. So it was not likely that he would view my new venture very kindly.

He kept a hairdresser's shop in Rochdale, and was highly respected there, and he had a thorough scorn of anything appertaining to the hangman's art.

It is a curious fact that next door to my father's house was a shoemaker's shop and the man who kept it worked for years on an idea he had for a new patent scaffold. He fitted up a full-sized model in his back room and spent a small fortune on it. But it never came to anything. Nobody was ever allowed to see it for the inventor was terrified lest somebody should steal his idea. As a boy I heard many tales and legends concerning this model scaffold, but I cannot say they had any influence on my subsequent choice of a career.

I was a pretty adventurous youngster. I hated the trade of barber, but when I left school my father set me to lathering in the shop. This did not suit my tastes at all, so I planned with two other lads that we would all run away.

An opportunity came one August day in 1890, which I quickly communicated to my co-conspirators. At that time I was approaching my 16th birthday, having been born at Broad Land, Rochdale, on 4 October 1874. Well, my father had gone to Manchester on business leaving me in charge of the place and I let the other boys know that this might be the very chance we were waiting for.

I was sent out on an errand that afternoon and meeting the other boys we stayed out until it was too late for me to dare to go home, even if I had wanted to. The three of us, therefore, hid ourselves in the slaughterhouse loft of the next-door butcher's shop, and from there I distinctly saw my father, when he came home and missed me, enter the butcher's and ask – 'Is our Johnny in?'

Naturally the butcher could only say I had not returned, and they all seemed in a most anxious state.

Then the boys who were with me got funky and decided that they would go home. Their departure filled me with disgust, but I was determined to 'stick it' so I went to a stable and slept there until four o'clock in the morning, when I arose and made off towards Burnley. On the road I met my uncle going to his work, but in the dim light he passed me without recognition, much to my relief. At Burnley I put up at a lodging-house, and fell in with some lads who were considerably sharper than I was. I had come away with nearly a sovereign, which I had been saving up for the Wakes, but when they had finished with me I had only 2s 6d left.

I tried to get work at a barber's shop as lather boy, but I found they knew my father and were telephoning him, so I left hurriedly. Returning to my lodging house, I heard my father had already put the police on my track, and, in great fright I went off to see if I could secure work at the trackway depot. There I again heard the detectives were again inquiring after me, so, realising that the place was getting too hot to hold me, I set off on the road.

As I tramped along I was to meet another wayfarer, a man whose first question was 'Have you any money?' Having learned a little wisdom I said, 'No, only a penny'. Whereupon he seemed quite satisfied and told me he would teach me how to earn some. His method was for me to sing to passers-by and I soon collected several coppers in this way. In fact, I more or less supported myself in this way during all my travels. Together we gradually tramped north. We went through Colne and Nelson and on to Leeds, York, and Darlington. Then we circled the north, visiting Sunderland, Shields, and Newcastle. A bad dream ended my tramp for the time being. While at Newcastle I dreamt that my mother was dead, and this affected me so much that I wrote home to see if it were true. The reply was reassuring, and I was begged to return, money being sent me to pay my fare.

Like the prodigal, I went back to the home of my father, but I cannot recall that any fatted calf was prepared for me. However, I was at home for not more than a fortnight when the spirit again moved me to venture forth into the world. Two other boys having heard of my adventures tempted me to lead them in a similar tramp again, and, agreeing, we all went off to Bury.

But they lost their pluck when it got dark and though I threatened in my juvenile way to kill them if they left me in the lurch, after asking me to go with them, they nevertheless deserted me the next day.

This time I was positively afraid to go home, and as a matter of fact I never did return to live with my parents after that. For a time I lived with my aunt and went to work at a spinning mill. At the end of seven years' service there I met with a bad accident which laid me up for twelve months, and left me with a lifelong physical weakness. I had, however, one stroke of luck at the mills, for it was there I met my wife. We were married when I was only 20 years of age.

After a time I got work again at Messrs Tweedale & Smalley, the big textile machine makers at Castleton, and it was while working there that the conversation already mentioned occurred, and the idea of becoming a hangman, which had then entered my head so idly for the first time, was pursued with quiet determination until I got my own way.

It would be useless for me to attempt to ascribe any particular reason actuating me in my desire to adopt such an unusual profession as that of a hangman. I simply wanted to be one – and that was all! It wasn't any love for the gruesome, for I was not attracted by things of that nature. Perhaps it may be difficult to believe, but it is nevertheless true that never in my life have I been able to steel myself to drown a kitten or kill a fowl.

Only once did I try to drown a kitten and I was upset for the rest of the day. After that, whenever things like that had to be done in our house, either Mrs Ellis or somebody else had to do them. Yet I have never had the slightest uneasiness over executing that sentence of the law upon a murderer.

Still, despite my helplessness when faced with the drowning of a kitten, I stuck to my secret project of becoming a hangman and at last made a definite move in the matter. Before doing so I threw out a sort of 'feeler' on the subject to my wife, but she objected so strongly that I dropped the subject – or rather, pretended to – for I was determined to take up the work.

The results of my accident at the mill kept making themselves felt so much that I became quite unfit for heavy labour and had to leave the Castleton works, after which I opened up in business as a hairdresser at 451 Oldham Road, Rochdale.

It was from that address that I wrote to the High Sheriff of Lancashire, telling him I would like to be an executioner and asking how I could obtain such a position. In reply he advised me to write to Messrs Wilson, Wright & Wilson of Preston who acted as Under-Sheriffs, and they in their turn told me to apply to the Governor of Strangeways Prison, Manchester.

That gentleman (Major R.D. Cruikshank) answered, fixing an appointment and requesting me to bring some testimonials. That was on 14 March 1901. With the latter purpose in mind I visited three well-known gentlemen in the district where I lived (one of them the vicar) and though they all willingly agreed to help me, they were all amazed at my project and laughed at my answer of 'I don't know' to their inevitable question, 'Why are you going in for such a job?'

Armed with my credentials I went to Strangeways Prison. Never shall I forget that day, for it was snowing hard and they kept me standing for an hour in the bitterly cold space between the two outer gates and the entrance before I could interview with the Governor. This off-handed treatment contrasted oddly with my next visit to Strangeways, for on that occasion they showed me in at once, and gave me a chair in front of a warm fire, and treated me in general like a distinguished visitor. But I was a full-fledged executioner then, which no doubt accounted for the change in treatment.

My weary wait came to an end at last, and I was shown into the Governor's room. Major Cruikshank was a somewhat stern-looking figure, but he had great natural kindness, and I afterwards had many things to thank him for. Almost his first words were in the forms of that old, old question – 'Why do you want to be an executioner?' and once more I made the reply – 'I don't know'.

The Governor seemed somewhat taken aback, but he conversed in a kindly way. 'Of course, Billington is not dead or retired yet', he pointed out, referring to old James Billington. 'No', said I, 'but he cannot go on for ever. Someone will have to take his place some day.'

Then he tried another tack. 'The job is not a gold mine', he said. 'You will have to act as assistant for some time before you can hope to get a post as senior. And, you know, an assistant only gets £2 2s and his expenses for each execution.' All this did not deter me in the least, and when he saw I was really serious in the matter he said he would report to the Prison Commissioners, and in due course I might expect to hear from them.

Up to this time, it must be remembered, nobody in my family knew what I was doing, but the bombshell burst when I had a letter from the Home Office instructing me to go to Newgate Gaol for a week's training as an executioner.

The cat had to be let out of the bag now and it was no easy task to persuade my wife that there was no disgrace in such work. It was still more difficult to talk round my father and mother. Both of them were intensely shocked when

I expressed my intentions. 'Gracious, John', said my mother, 'whatever put such an idea into your head?'

It was the old question again, and I could only give the same unsatisfying reply. My mother was particularly upset. 'What will people say about us?' she cried, and was deaf to all my arguments in favour of the course I was pursuing. It was in vain for me to point out that executioners were part of the law of the land, and that somebody had to carry out the work. 'Let someone else do it, then', was all I was told. They remained unconvinced when the time came for me to go to London, but I went nevertheless. Nothing could shake my resolve to see the thing through, and I felt that in time they would see the matter in the same light as I did.

I may as well say at this point that, although their opposition lasted vigorously for some time afterwards, it faded eventually, and I can honestly say that, with the exception of only one thing, I have never seen cause in either my domestic or my public life to regret the step I then insisted on taking. That exception has relation to my failure to secure admission as a Freemason, but I will deal with this later on.

Never before had I been to London and my confusion at its vastness when I arrived there was not diminished by my haunting fear that people would discover me as an embryo hangman. That dread was so strong in me that for some time I couldn't summon up sufficient pluck to ask anybody how to reach Newgate Prison. At last I asked a policemen outside Euston Station, and he looked at me so quizzically that I felt sure my secret was discovered. 'Newgate?' he echoed. 'I never knew there was such a place!'

I went off abashed. The bobby had, of course, taken advantage of an obvious provincial and 'pulled my leg', but I at that time took him quite seriously. My spirits went down into my boots. Often since then have I smiled at the misery I felt and the unreasoning fear I had that all the passers-by were looking at me and saying to themselves with scorn, 'That man is going to be a hangman!'

Newgate Prison, found at last, looked the most miserable place both outside and inside that I had ever seen in my life. So gloomy was it that artificial lights were burning there day and night, and taking all in all, I felt a most lonesome person when I was shown into a big, white-washed chamber which they told me was called the Hangman's Room. That room had been occupied by hangmen for as long as Newgate had stood and I could almost imagine the ghosts of Calcraft, Marwood, and Berry flitting about the murky place. Their names and initials were all carved on the walls.

Sleep did not come easily that night. Under the influence of my surroundings all sorts of fevered imaginings ran riot in my brain, and it was with great relief that I eventually arose and prepared to begin to learn my new trade. They took me to see the scaffold soon after breakfast and I cannot pretend to have viewed it with any great confidence. I stepped into that chamber of death with a shudder. Chief Warder Scott, who I found was always in charge of candidates for employment as executioners pointed phlegmatically to a yawning hole in the centre of the floor, explaining, 'That is the drop'.

He instructed some warders to put a couple of planks over this hole and invited me to stand on them. The air of the place appalled me, but I dare not show my feelings, and though I would rather have done anything than stand on those planks, I did so.

Looking down I saw a pit 12 feet deep and realised that it was in that lower space that the actual tragedy of an execution was accomplished. The grimness of it all made me feel anything but comfortable and a terror possessed me lest the planks should give way and precipitate me into that dreadful pit.

Chief Warder Scott noticed my nervousness and spoke most kindly to me, and gradually I recovered my self-possession. Then Assistant Warder Shepherd appeared with what looked like the limp body of a man under his arm. 'This is what you will have to practice on', he said. It was a dummy, made of straw, fully clothed like a man. I never expected to see anything so startlingly realistic, but I was now beginning to control myself, and under the guidance of the officers I put straps on the dummy's wrists and ankles, and placed the noosed rope round its neck.

The dummy was placed standing upon the two trap doors, which had now been pulled up to close the aperture covering that 12 ft pit, and at a given signal I pulled the scaffold lever for the first time in my life.

It all happened just as if a real man was being executed. The doors fell downwards with a thud and the dummy disappeared. The sight was almost too realistic to be pleasant, but I had now nerved myself up to be disconcerted by nothing, and I noted with pride a significant glance pass from Mr Scott to Mr Shepherd, as if to say, 'He will do!'

For the rest of the week I practised on that dummy, and learned all the minute intricacies of calculating drops, measuring them off, the right and wrong ways of fixing the noose and the pinioning straps, and all the other numerous details about which the layman never dreams. For hanging a man is not such a simple process as it seems, nowadays every care is taken that the most humane means shall be adopted to lessen the misery of the condemned.

It may be of interest to state here that the scaffold on which I learned to do my work is still in use. When Newgate was demolished, the scaffold was removed to Pentonville and upon it I executed such famous characters as Dr Crippen, Seddon, and Sir Roger Casement. It still remains one of the finest scaffolds in Great Britain, and if necessary, four men could be executed at one time upon it.

During the week I had one or two prowls round London, but I rarely went far from Newgate in case of losing myself. I did actually get lost one dinner hour. I had turned to the right after leaving the prison and in my innocence I thought if I kept on turning to the right I would surely come back to the prison again. But in practise this theory went utterly wrong, for the more I turned to the right, the more hopelessly lost I got. It was very late before I at last found the prison again and as I was still a bit afraid of the officers, I expected to get into trouble. Instead of that they merely laughed at the story of my wanderings and were very sympathetic.

All the fear of the execution shed and its ritual vanished after my first morning there. I had made up my mind to learn quickly and thoroughly and banished every other thought. On my last day, Colonel Milman, the governor, put me through a final mock execution as a test, and I had that dummy hanging in three-quarters of a minute after I had pinioned it in the condemned cell.

I returned to Rochdale encouraged by the remarks of subordinate officers who were confident I had passed with flying colours, but was anxious to hear what those in authority would have to say about me. Even my wife, who had formerly objected so strongly now turned round and wanted to hear that I had succeeded. Intimation came at length on May 9, 1901, that my name had been added to the list of executioners and assistants, and I was happy. It came as a shock to find that months slipped by after that without an engagement coming my way, and I grew very impatient and disheartened.

Just as I was beginning to give up hope of ever getting a job I was surprised to receive word from the Governor of Newcastle Gaol that I would be required to act as assistant at a double execution which would take place there on December 1 1901. The condemned men were John Miller, proprietor of the roundabouts on the shore at Cullercoats, and his nephew, John Robert Miller. They had murdered a Mr Joseph Ferguson as a result of some family feud, the details of which were never clearly revealed.

The victim, Ferguson, had married the widow of the elder Miller's brother. The lady apparently obtained considerable wealth when her first husband died, and when she married Ferguson she made a will bequeathing it all to him. This presumably angered the Millers, and one evening the uncle and nephew burst into Ferguson's house and stabbed him to death before his wife's eyes. Blow after blow was rained on his prostrate body, and subsequent medical examination showed that he had sustained no fewer than eight terrible wounds.

The murderers were safely under arrest before nightfall, and the nephew at once confessed to the crime, but alleged he acted under his uncle's persuasion and influence. At the trial his counsel brought this forward in the young man's defence and also declared that he was intoxicated at the time, and not quite mentally sound.

On the uncle's behalf it was urged that he had taken no actual part in the stabbing but the Judge badly crumpled this defence by remarking, 'If the elder man wanted to stop the murder he could have done so after the first blow was struck. He scant raised a finger, but stood by and saw it done'.

Both were condemned without hope of mercy, and, as I have already said, I was engaged as executioner's assistant.

In high feather I went to Rochdale Station to catch the Newcastle train on the morning of December 6 for I was instructed that I must be in the prison at four o'clock on the afternoon preceding the execution, and would not be allowed to leave the building till all was over. My train was already there and I was allotted a compartment when I heard the engine driver fling a remark to some of the people on the platform.

In a moment there was a crowd gathered round a little fat man who was out on the platform stretching his legs before the train resumed its journey. I asked one of the onlookers whom it was and got a surprising reply. 'That is Billington, the hangman', he said. 'He is going to execute the Millers at Newcastle.'

It struck me that this was particularly opportune, and I decided to make myself known to my colleague.

'I am going with you to Newcastle', I said stepping up to him in front of all that crowd and displaying considerably more boldness than I felt. He wheeled round on me in the most disconcerting fashion and replied with forcible emphasis in his broad Lancashire dialect – 'Tha's doin' nowt o' t' kind!'

'Oh yes, I am', I replied. 'I am going to the same place as you are whether I go with you or not.'

He looked at me in silence for several moments. Then he asked —

'Well, where am I going then?'

'To Newcastle Prison', I answered, 'and I have been engaged as your assistant.'

At that, I produced the Governor's letter, and convinced him of my bona fides, and he then invited me into his carriage and we got in. No doubt the watching crowd thought the incident had a certain amount of spice in it for they observed us closely and kept round our window until the train left the station.

My companion proved to be William Billington. His father, the famous James Billington, had originally been engaged for this job, but had caught a cold while carrying out an execution at Manchester and so the Commissioners had agreed to his passing the appointment over to his son William. When he had told me this, Billington seemed to freeze up, and as I, being a stranger, did not like to talk very much, there was very little conversation between us after that until we got to our journey's end.

On arrival at Newcastle Billington asked me to go for some refreshment, and we entered a public-house close to the gaol. We found, seated in it, three women of striking appearance. They were all dressed in furs and their fingers were covered with rings. Their identity was not revealed to me, but we could make shrewd guesses from their behaviour that they were connected with the condemned men.

They were all weeping as if their hearts were broken, and kept sobbing out: 'Oh poor John!' and 'They have to go to-morrow,' and things of that kind.

When we realised who they were Billington said quietly – 'Come on, we will clear out of this.' And I wasn't sorry to get away. I felt touched on the raw by the poor women's overflowing distress.

We were in the prison within a very few moments and as the outer gates clanged behind us, I put all these and other distracting thoughts away and resolved to concentrate on the business in hand. The Governor has us brought before him and told us that an alteration had been made in the arrangements. Originally it had been intended to hang both men at once, but there had been a hint of trouble between the uncle and nephew, for the latter persisted in viewing himself as the victim of his elder relative's plot. The young man kept declaring he had no feeling against Mr Ferguson himself, but that his uncle had taken advantage of his intoxicated condition and put him up to committing the murder. Consequently, said the Governor, it was feared they might cause an unpleasant scene when they stood side by side on the scaffold, so two separate executions had been decided upon. The younger man would be executed at 8.00am and the uncle at 9.30am.

We signified our understanding of these arrangements, and moved off to have a peep at the condemned men. This was not a matter of idle curiosity, but was a regular part of our duty, as the condition of the man's neck and general physique guided us in fixing the length of the drop. Young John Robert Miller was kept in the hospital, as there was only one condemned cell, and that was occupied by his uncle. We were told that young Miller had maintained a very truculent air since he was sentenced to death, but on the afternoon we arrived he began to show signs of mental collapse. He had often before yelled defiant threats against his uncle, but his behaviour now become less rational than ever.

It seemed to me that he had gone clean out of his mind. My bed was on the same floor as the place where he was kept, and it was little sleep I had that night. His screams and cries disturbed me through all those dark hours and as I was also excited at the strange situation I was in, it turned out to be one of the most wakeful nights of my life. I was glad when morning came and I could be free for a time of those awful screams from the condemned man. The older man, I might add, was awaiting death with much more calmness.

It was, of course, still quite dark when I had to get up, and this coupled with the fact that I had never seen an actual execution before combined in creating a feeling of strong uneasiness within me. In my fevered imaginings I pictured all sorts of things going wrong, but the calm, easy nonchalance of 'Billy' Billington acted as a tonic. I did not mean that he or anybody else should see anything in me that could be construed as showing the white feather.

With an air of being perfectly familiar with everything, as if this were my hundredth instead of my first execution, I went with him to the execution shed and helped to put everything in readiness. The sandbag – of a weight somewhat heavier that the condemned men – which had been suspended all night to test the rope and take out all the stretch – was hauled up, and the rope was coiled up, with the noose placed ready for its human burden.

We pulled up the trapdoors, dropped them with a pull of the lever to see that they were working properly, pulled them up again, and placed upon them a mark where the condemned men should stand. Satisfied that all was well, we returned to the gaol; and as we entered it received a signal to go in at once and pinion young Miller.

Now that the supreme seconds had arrived, I was surprised to find all my qualms and fears had miraculously disappeared. I knew it was possible we should have trouble with the raving young fellow, but somehow I was now as calm as the proverbial cucumber. A change had also come over the poor doomed fellow. He had dropped his screaming, and stood looking with dull moroseness at the door as we pushed it open and entered.

In a trice his arms were behind him and his wrists were pinioned, and he made not the slightest resistance. 'Billy' Billington saw to it that all was loose and open round the condemned man's neck, and we were now ready for the walk to the scaffold.

This again produced no incident. For a moment as we moved along, Billington and I immediately behind the doomed fellow, the strangeness of the scene came home to me. It was a weird sensation to gaze on this fine young man in front of us and know that in a very few seconds he would be no more. But I declined to allow myself any morbid broodings. I was there to do my duty to the State just as were the gaol Governor and the other high officials.

When we got him on the trapdoors young Miller gazed around with a dazed expression as if not quite aware what it was all about. 'What are all these people here for?' he asked, pointing at the chaplain and the magistrates and the officials who made up a small knot of people a few yards away. Then, to everybody's astonishment, he calmly turned his back on the scaffold and began to walk back towards his cell. He only made a few steps in this direction, for Billington and I at once caught him gently but firmly by the sleeve and pulled him up. With the docility of a child he allowed himself to be led back to the fatal spot, and this time he never left it alive.

Working at top speed I strapped his feet while Billington slipped the noose over Miller's head and tightened it. On went the white cap, and with a warning cry to me Billington sprang for the lever and pulled it.

Miller disappeared at once. The trap doors had opened beneath his feet, and almost simultaneously with their thudding against the sides of the pit, the murderer was hanging inert and dead at the rope's end.

After many experiments with straw dummies I had at last seen a real man go down to his doom. True to the resolutions I had formed, I suppressed all feeling in the matter, though it was difficult, and tried like Billington, to look upon the execution merely as something accomplished that had to be done. The pale faces of the other officials showed how real was the strain on one's heart strings, which I was trying to avoid, and the Governor was frankly somewhat upset. As it happened, it was his first execution too and he invited us into his office to join him in a glass of brandy. But the morning's grim work was not yet over. We still had another man to deal with. Young Miller's body was left hanging for the hour enjoined by law, and then Billington and I got everything into readiness for the elder man.

The strain of the longer wait for death told slightly upon the elder man, but we had not the slightest trouble with him, and within a short time he had passed without a single incident or hitch. Our work was done. My first execution was accomplished. That morning had begun with something akin to terror within me, and it ended with the birth of a new personality.

My early nervous anticipation had gone. So, too, had my habit of allowing the fate of the doomed men to weigh heavily upon my spirits. That morning ended with me having found complete control of myself. I was still full of pity for the unhappy condemned men, but it now found expression in the desire to get them out of their misery as quickly and painlessly as possible.

Looking back over the intervening executions between that day and this, I can honestly say that the ideals that I set myself that morning have been my ruling principles throughout my official career. Consequently, despite all the sensations that frequently attended the carrying out of my duties and made it difficult for me to remember that I was for the time being not an independent man but an official instrument of the law, I have never faltered from the determination made that day of my first execution to subordinate everything else in my life to the one aim of shortening the misery of condemned persons. And I sincerely claim that the methods I have introduced have robbed executions of many of their old-time terrors, and in that sense I hope I shall receive credit for honest services to humanity in an uncommon side-track of our civilisation.

My efforts have always been to try to obtain executions without 'incidents', but despite all precautions these have very frequently occurred. I was also frequently entrusted with official news of the secrets behind a condemned man's crime and his behaviour in prison, and hope to relate many hitherto unrevealed things and it is of these I hope to tell in the reminiscences of mine.

Chapter 2

Last Victim of the Newgate Scaffold

(George Woolfe, Newgate, 1902)

Among the various little records of my career I number my participation in the very last execution that ever took place at Newgate. We are fast forgetting that famous old prison, and one is apt to think of it as a place that merely figures in musty volumes of a past age. Yet this last execution at the grim old building took place as comparatively recently as the year 1902.

My readers may perhaps remember that event because the man who was the Newgate scaffold's last victim was George Woolfe, who was concerned in a mysterious murder that evoked considerable sensations and was everywhere spoken of as the Tottenham Marsh tragedy. I myself, however, chiefly remember the occasion because 'Billy' Billington and I broke the record for quick executions, though it had to be admitted that Woolfe himself contributed largely, if unconsciously, to the result.

Those who remember the furore that arose over the Tottenham Marsh tragedy may recall the doubts that were expressed to the end – and even to this day in some quarters – as to the possibility of Woolfe's innocence.

It would therefore be profitable before I tell how we performed that last execution under Newgate's roof to remind my readers of the chief facts and theories about this murder, of which, with his last breath on the scaffold, Woolfe protested his innocence.

Boys playing football on Tottenham Marshes made the initial discovery of the body of a dead woman in a ditch. Murder stood revealed! Police and doctors were summoned. The latter found seventeen wounds on the body, and the former established the woman's identity as Charlotte Cheeseman, a 21-year-old stripper in a cigar factory, who lived with her married sister.

The medical man decided that the murder had taken place on the Saturday night, the body having been found on Sunday morning. Their post-mortem examination also revealed the fact that the most serious wounds had been caused by some strong, sharp-cutting instrument.

The problem that now presented itself was – Who was the murderer? The police started inquiring into the dead girl's history in the hope of discovering a clue, and found that on the last afternoon of her life she had gone out to meet her sweetheart who was a former soldier called George Woolfe. They had been 'keeping company' for two or three years. About Christmas time one of their inevitable lovers' tiffs grew into a rather severe quarrel. Woolfe had got jealous of some other man, who had been paying attentions to Charlotte, and they had 'strong' words on the subject.

It blew over, though, for the couple had undoubtedly a strong attachment for each other. Indeed, from January 11 until the night of the crime (25 January) they went out together every evening taking the strolls so dear to lovers.

On Sunday morning, 26 January, Woolfe went round to Charlotte's house and asked her sister if she was at home. 'No', came the staggering reply, 'She has not been home all night!'

Woolfe appeared very astonished at her reply; 'I missed her last night', he said and went off looking worried.

Again in the afternoon and in the evening he presented himself at the house but they had no news to give him of his missing sweetheart. Had they but known it, her dead body had been lying all that day unidentified at the mortuary.

A day or two later, simultaneously almost with the discovery of the dead girl's name and address, a new mystery stood revealed. Her lover, George Woolfe, had disappeared! He had left his home at Hoxton (where he lived with his parents) ostensibly to go to work, and had never afterwards returned. Where – and why – had he gone? Had another tragedy occurred? Or was he fleeing from the possibility of arrest? In connection with the last-named query, it must be borne in mind that when he disappeared on the Monday (27 January) there was nothing whatsoever to connect him with the murder; indeed, there were plenty of things lending all against any suspicion of him. His sudden vanishing into space, however, focussed attention upon him, and set up the theory that if he could be found some progress might be made with the solution of the mystery of Charlotte Cheeseman's murder.

Everybody was talking about the tragedy, and wondering as to the whereabouts of the missing man. All sorts of people found themselves under suspicion, and in this connection a certain scrap of conversation which afterwards came to light as having transpired between two soldiers in the barracks of the Surrey Militia contains considerable significance. It occurred a week after the discovery of the crime, and one of the soldiers, sitting with a pal called Slater, coming across an account of the Tottenham Marsh mystery in the Sunday paper, suddenly turned to Slater and cried:

'Look here!' – 'Murder at Tottenham. You come from that way, don't you?'

'Yes – what of it?' came the reply.

'Well, listen to this', said the soldier with the paper, and he then read out an account of the affair. Slater sat listening with his brows wrinkling ominously, and when his chum had finished, exclaimed in sudden heat —

'You don't think it was me that did it, do you? You don't think I am as bad as that?'

The other, surprised and not a little startled at the sudden outburst, hastened to soothe his companion.

'Oh no', he averred. 'Don't you think that.'

But he thought it queer all the same. He had better reason for wonderment than he imagined at first, for four days later the barracks was invaded by a squad of resolute-looking men who turned out to be detectives.

They had discovered that the man he knew as 'Slater' was none other than George Woolfe! The public announcement that Woolfe had been found contained a further surprise. He had been arrested and charged with the murder of Charlotte Cheeseman!

There now began a long legal tussle. On the one hand the authorities had nothing but a string of circumstantial incidents to secure a conviction upon, while Woolfe on his side had what appeared to be a good alibi and plausible answers to other points raised by the prosecution. It was a pretty even battle. Take the evidence for the prosecution first. A barman at a public-house swore that he served the couple with refreshments between 9 and 9.30 on the tragic night, and a tram conductor also declared the lovers were on his car that evening about nine o'clock. The former identified Woolfe from twelve other persons, and the latter picked him out of a crowd of twenty-two.

The next news of them being seen together came from men in the neighbourhood of the Marshes themselves. One man, a signalman, saw a young couple cross a railway bridge and go in the direction of the Marshes, and an engine-driver also saw what were evidently two lovers strolling in the same direction. Neither of them could positively say that the man and woman were George Woolfe and Charlotte Cheeseman, but in their description of them they spoke of the woman being slightly the taller of the two, which were exactly the relative heights of the principal figures in the case.

From that time until nearly midnight there was a hiatus in the evidence for the prosecution. They were, however, satisfied in producing testimony that the couple were together up till 10.30. What happened afterwards they could only conjecture, but they put it that Woolfe murdered the girl and then returned to Hoxton about midnight. They also argued that his flight, his enlistment under a false name, and his refusal to come forward and tell the police what he knew about the affair when he saw in the paper they were advertising for him, all went together as strong circumstantial evidence against him. Furthermore, his face was seen to be scratched on the Sunday, and as the doctors said the woman had fought for her life it was declared that it was she who had inflicted those scratches.

These theories of the prosecution were violently attacked by the counsel for the defence, and even their facts were challenged. Woolfe himself went into the witness box and spun off a story, which, if true, supplied a plausible alibi and an answer to other points raised against him.

He admitted having been with the ill-fated girl on Saturday afternoon and again early in the evening. She then wanted him to take her back to the theatre, but he said he could not do so as he was hard up. He left her in the street for a moment or two about 7.15, and when he returned she had gone, and he never saw her again. Failing to find her, he went to the World's Fair, where he stayed from eight o'clock till 10.35 – which covered the period when he was said to have been seen by the barmen and the tram conductor, and by the signalman and engine-driver.

He produced witnesses, who declared they had seen him at the places he mentioned at times when the prosecution witnesses swore they had seen him elsewhere. The scratches on his face he explained were received in a fight he had that night about 11.50 with a man near his father's house at Hoxton. He brought witnesses who said they had not seen the scratches on his face prior to the fight, but saw them afterwards. Here, again, there was a conflict of evidence, for the man with whom he had been fighting testified that, although he struck Woolfe, he did not scratch him.

Woolfe gave some sort of explanation of his enlistment under a false name, and swore that the first he knew of the murder was when his soldier comrade at the barracks had read the newspaper account to him. When he discovered from this that the police were wanting him he got frightened, and dared not return home.

Under cross-examination he said he did not know Tottenham Marshes at all. He also told the Court that he was very fond of Charlotte, and intended to marry her. His counsel, in his final appeal to the jury dwelt upon the fact that no motive had been adduced for such a cruel murder. Epitomising the case, Mr A. Hutton pointed out that the contention of the prosecution was that Woolfe was in the company of Charlotte Cheeseman up to 10.30, and this, coupled with his having enlisted on the following Monday, indicated that it was he who murdered her.

These deductions were rebutted by the defence. It was denied that Woolfe was in the murdered girl's company after 7.15, and the reason why he enlisted was not to hide himself, but merely to carry out an intention he was known to have had several days previously. The case went to the jury, who took three-quarters of an hour to reach a conclusion. Their verdict at the end of that time was 'Guilty!'

'I can assure you', exclaimed Woolfe, before being sentenced to death, 'that I would commit no crime, let alone such an atrocious crime as this. I am innocent of it.'

Was he speaking the truth? I put this question to myself when I received notice from the Governor of Newgate Gaol to hold myself in readiness to act with William Billington as Woolfe's executioner on 6 May 1902. Nowadays a convicted man has an opportunity to appeal, but in Woolfe's time there was no such institution as a Court of Criminal Appeal. Weighing the thing up for myself, I felt that the verdict, although obtained by purely circumstantial evidence, was a just one. One or two points came into my mind that were not touched upon at the trial. Woolfe said he could not take his sweetheart to the theatre because he was too hard up, but he admitted that he got drunk after drinking steadily all the evening. If he had no money for the theatre how could he afford an evening of steady drinking?

Again, when he heard of the murder of the girl he loved would he, if he were innocent, calmy go on living in hiding under a false name? He knew he had witnesses who would swear to his having been in their company at the time of the murder, so he need not have worried about the suspicions against him. Would not an innocent man have come forward and helped the police by all in his power to find the man who had so foully done to death the girl whom he was going to marry? No, his behaviour was altogether that of a guilty man, and as such I had no compunction in presenting myself at Newgate on the afternoon of March 5 to help to administer the punishment that British law measures out to a murderer.

During the journey to London from my home in Lancashire I got talking with a clergyman in my compartment or perhaps I ought more correctly to say he got talking with me. He was rather inquisitive about me, though not offensively so. 'What is your business?' he queried after conversation had started up.

I told him I was a hairdresser. 'And are you going to London on business?' he went on.

'Yes', was my non-committal reply, for I fancied that a man of his cloth would be shocked at knowing I was going there as hangman. But he wasn't satisfied.

'What sort of business?' he persisted.

There was no help for it now. I had to tell him. After that he remained courteous but not quite so talkative. I am afraid I had killed his interest in me.

Subsequently, after narrating the story of this little encounter to other friends in London, I discovered the possible identity of my clerical companion. He had told me he lived in St Paul's Churchyard, and this, coupled with my description of his physical build, etc., led my hearers to the conclusion that I had been talking to no less a personage than the famous Venerable Archdeacon Sinclair. I wonder what he really thought of me?

On arrival at Newgate I was shown to the Hangman's Room, which at once brought forth memories of my previous visit to the ancient gaol about eighteen months previously. I was then there on probation to learn the duties of a hangman, and, though I lived and slept in the Hangman's Room, I did no more than perform execution after execution upon a harmless straw dummy! But now I was to sleep in that famous chamber with the prospect of arising to hang a real condemned murderer. The contrast set me thinking.

After tea came a talk with the doctor and then I went off to have a look at the man in the condemned cell. He was a boyish-looking fellow, only 21 years of age, and of slight build. In fact, he tipped the beam at the comparatively light weight of 9 ½ st. and stood no taller than 5 ft, 5 ½ in. If ever a man looked untroubled by approaching doom, Woolfe was he. He hadn't a care on his face when we gazed in at him, and he was chatting away quite freely with the warders sitting with him.

The task of watching a condemned man day and night is one that no warder likes, but Woolfe made his attendants quite easy in their minds about him. Rarely would his talk touch upon Charlotte Cheeseman, but when he did he constantly renewed his protestations of innocence. He maintained this attitude to the end, but I have to warn my readers against attaching too much importance to such declarations in the condemned cell.

There is hardly a convicted murderer who does not swear he is innocent. The object in view is simple enough. They are hoping and angling for a reprieve. 'While there is life there is hope' may be taken as their guiding rule, and so long as there is a chance of escaping the gallows they keep on declaring their guiltlessness in the hope of instilling in the minds of the authorities a fear of a grave miscarriage of justice.

Such protestations of innocence are especially effective in cases of conviction upon purely circumstantial evidence, such as this Tottenham Marsh affair, and I must say I myself would not have been surprised if the Home Office had intervened at the last moment, convinced though I was, of Woolfe's guilt.

However, the only word that came from the Home Secretary was to the effect that Woolfe must pay the penalty, a decision which Woolfe received with the calm courage of a stoic. I believe there was even a hint of relief in his manner, as though he were glad that he knew the worst.

One can easily credit this, for there can be no doubt that the period of uncertainty during which the condemned man is a prey to all sorts of hopes and fears as to his ultimate fate are among the worst agonies that befall a man under sentence of death. These gnawing anxieties during the two or three weeks that elapse between the declaration of his sentence and its carrying out are the murderer's heaviest punishment – not the swift, painless snapping of the life-link on the scaffold.

I must say I could hardly help liking young Woolfe from what I saw and heard of him. He was a proved murderer, that was true, but who shall sit in judgement upon what may have been provocation? At any rate he was no braggart. He behaved throughout with most seemly modesty, and never altered this behaviour even when he saw Billington and I enter his cell a few minutes before eight o'clock on the morning of 6 May.

At the back of our minds there was the idea to get this execution over in record time, and for my part I know I was determined to make it go off as quickly as possible, because I wanted to see poor Woolfe put out of his misery without the least waste of time. For time is agony to a man waiting for death. Woolfe said nothing as we pinioned him, but as he stepped out of his cell he was obviously listening hard to the prayers of the chaplain, whose voice was the only sound that broke the stillness of that ancient prison.

Presently the condemned man's impatience got the better of him. He had apparently quite unconsciously become imbued with the same desire as Billington and myself. He wanted it over and done with quickly. He had started on his walk to the scaffold with straight, firm steps, but now he exchanged for short, quick ones. He began to walk like a man who has an important appointment and fears to be late, and I can assure you we had our work cut out to keep up with him. In a surprisingly short space of time – for Woolfe took no heed of the restraining hands laid on his coat sleeve – we had reached the scaffold. It now remained for us to do our part in relieving the poor wretch of the life he was evidently so anxious to give up.

The last grim details were adjusted with extraordinary celerity. A few instants sufficed for strapping his legs and fixing on the noose and white cap. Then came the tragic climax. Almost before those in the rear of the procession had got near enough to see what was happening the bolt was drawn and Woolfe was dangling dead in the pit.

The chaplain continued his prayers for a moment or so, but I caught sight of the doctor taking a surreptitious peep at his watch. Approaching him, I put the question – 'How long have we been sir?' 'You have done your work very quickly', he replied. 'You have been only 25 seconds!' 'Well', said I, 'we have the young fellow himself to thank for that, for he walked so quickly and manfully.'

A record was achieved, and the officials very likely were pleased that the affair had been carried out so quickly. The unassuming George Woolfe had 'gone out', leaving his name one always to be remembered, not only because of the Tottenham Marsh Mystery, but because he was the last man to be executed under Newgate's roof. The time-stained walls of that grim edifice, whose name was synonymous with the blackest part of a century's crime, were never again to witness another execution.

Shortly after that the building was in the housebreaker's hands, and I saw it in course of demolition when I passed through London on my way home after the execution of Dougal, the Moat Farm murderer, in the following year. I then secured a piece of one of the wooden beams in the Hangman's Room, and still treasure this in the form of a walking stick.

Chapter 3

The Last Moment Confession of the Moat Farm Murderer

(Samuel Herbert Dougal, Chelmsford, 1903)

Picture to yourself a doomed man standing on the fatal trapdoor, with the rope round his neck, the white cap over his face, and his arms strapped behind him; imagine the hangman springing to the lever to complete the law's sentence; and then think of the sensation that would be caused by the sudden, imperative cry of – 'Stop!' If you can bring such a scene before your mind's eye you will have some dim perception of what happened on the morning when Samuel Herbert Dougal paid the penalty for the murder of Miss Holland – that care which is known and spoken of even to-day as the Moat Farm Mystery.

Never in modern times has there been such a scene at an execution. Ordinarily nothing in any shape or form is allowed to interrupt the smooth carrying out of the law's decree. Yet here was the astonishing command – 'Stop!' – and the voice was that of the chaplain, of all men.

Everybody stood thunderstruck. Then the Rev. J. Blakemore addressed the man standing there awaiting death.

'Dougal, are you guilty or not guilty?'

There was no answer. The white-capped figure gave no sign. A second time came that appeal in a slightly louder voice.

'Dougal, are you guilty or not guilty?'

Still there was no response. The white-capped figure remained as motionless and silent as before. A third time came the question, almost shouted.

'Dougal, are you guilty or not guilty?'

This time the man on the edge of doom stirred slightly. He was speaking.

'Guilty sir!'

The confession was in such a low tone I doubt if anybody but we, the executioners, heard it.

The chaplain was satisfied. With a motion of the hand he signalled to us to go on with our grim work, and within a fraction of a second Dougal was dead.

The incident was unique in criminal history, and forthwith became the topic of discussion all over the kingdom. There were reporters present at the execution, but I've never yet read a description of it that accurately told what occurred. For that reason I am particularly gratified at now being able to put on record the precise happenings of that extraordinary occasion, and I shall presently narrate the chaplain's own reasons for causing this unexampled scene.

This explanation has never before been given to the public. As a matter of fact, it was not until thirteen years after Dougal's execution that it was given to me by the Rev. Mr Blakemore himself. I will go into this matter presently. For a moment let me tell how Dougal came to be standing on the scaffold that morning in July, 1903.

One of the most extraordinary things to life is the way in which men of vile character are often able to captivate pure women of high intelligence. It was this feature that fascinated me in all that I read and heard about the Moat Farm case. Dougal's record before he met the gentle Miss Holland, whom he afterwards murdered, reveals him as one of those utterly unscrupulous scoundrels who prey upon women until they have exhausted their little fortune, after which they are callously thrown aside.

Miss Holland was by no means the first victim to his doubtful charms; indeed it is believed that she was not his first but his third victim in the murder sense. Thrice had he been married before he met her, and two of his wives had died in Canada. Naturally he said nothing about his previous wives when he met Miss Camille C. Holland through the medium of a matrimonial advertisement. Neither did he tell her that his third wife was still living, or that he had once been convicted of forgery at the Old Bailey.

No, to her he posed as a retired Army officer, and his big powerful frame and handsome jovial countenance decorated with a pointed beard quite took the heart of the slightly eccentric spinster. In reality, I might add, he had actually been in the Army, but his rank on retirement was that of Quartermaster-Sergeant.

Miss Holland was 56 years of age at the time, and was possessed of a snug little fortune of about £6000, which had been carefully invested. The daughter of an officer of high rank in the British Army, she was a woman of great refinement, an artist and musician, though with the reputation among her friends of being just a trifle eccentric. In her early youth she had had a tragic love affair. Her lover had been drowned, but she constantly wore an engraved amethyst ring of his, which had been washed ashore and picked up. It is worthwhile remembering this ring, for it played a part in the drama that developed later on.

In April of 1899 Dougal, having persuaded Miss Holland to allow him to act as her manager in the purchase of a place known as the Moat Farm, in

Clavering, Essex, took her there to live with him. Dougal had chosen this house with a wonderful eye to its possibilities in his fell plans.

It was situated in one of the most desolate spots in the British Isles and was just such a house as one would associate with dark deeds. Built in Elizabethan times on the dungeons and fortifications of an ancient castle, I could well imagine that it would have its appeal to a lady of Miss Holland's romantic nature and artistic perceptions; but to a man with murder in his heart it would at once suggest itself as eminently suitable for his nefarious purpose.

The Moat which gave the farm its name stretched all round the house. It was lined with bulrushes and its grim and stagnant waters added to the prevailing gloom and air of desolation. The only access to the house was by a small bridge, resting upon two brick arches and leading to the front door. One has only to mention that the main road – a very unfrequented thoroughfare – was a mile and a quarter away, and the nearest house a mile distant, to give the reader a still more vivid impression of the loneliness of the farm, which, however, has undergone considerable changes since the murder.

It was in this desolate place that Dougal and Miss Holland – who were known in the neighbourhood as 'Mr and Mrs Dougal' – went to live. They had only been there about three weeks when Miss Holland mysteriously disappeared, though Dougal always had a plausible story ready to account for her absence. The servant to the house knew that 'Mr and Mrs Dougal' had set out in the trap one evening and that Dougal had returned alone, saying her mistress had 'gone to London'. That evening Dougal went out several times, ostensibly to visit the station to meet her on her return, but she failed to turn up. Next morning he told the girl he had just received a letter from 'Mrs Dougal'.

'She says she is going to have a little holiday', he explained pleasantly, 'and is sending a lady friend to the farm.'

The servant girl was very perturbed in mind over her mistress' absence, for Dougal's conduct on previous occasions had led her to complain to 'Mrs Dougal'. So fearing to be left alone in the house with him, she left that morning.

The 'lady friend' referred to, arrived in due course. Nobody in the neighbourhood suspected whom she was, but in reality she was his third wife, who had come back to him. She remained at the farm until 1902, then Dougal, with colossal impudence, petitioned for a divorce against her, and indeed obtained decree. But, thanks to the intervention of the King's Proctor – the official whose duty it is to watch divorce cases in the interest of public morality – the decree was nullified, it having been discovered that Dougal's own life had not been such as to entitle him to relief. This was one of the most audacious actions in Dougal's astonishing career.

The real Mrs Dougal here passes out of the story, but she should be remembered as one of the probable motives in the case.

For four years after Miss Holland had left the district nobody heard anything about her, but she was presumably alive for cheques signed by her were frequently being cashed at the bank by Dougal. Nevertheless, as might have been expected in such a rural district, all kinds of weird stories were afloat concerning Miss Holland or 'Mrs Dougal', as she was called.

Rumours went so far that Superintendent Pryke, of the Essex County Constabulary, went to the Moat Farm and made inquiries about the missing lady, who was said to be concealed in a cupboard. The superintendent said he would like to make a search, and to this Dougal readily assented. Of course, the officer found nothing, but Dougal was mistaken in thinking that he had easily cleared himself of all suspicion.

Those frequent cheques, signed 'Camille C. Holland', came at last to be closely examined and it was decided they were forged. Shortly afterwards it was proved that a number of letters to Miss Holland's stockbrokers and signatures to certain cheques were cleverly executed forgeries, and, on the strength of these facts, a warrant was issued for the arrest of Dougal on a charge of forgery. But Dougal had not been feeling too comfortable since the visit of the police to the farm; and apparently decided that the time had come for him to leave the district. Accordingly he cashed a large cheque at the Birkbeck Bank, drawing nearly the whole amount in notes. Then he bolted and for some days the police lost trace of him. His arrest, however, was not long delayed, taking place exactly a fortnight after Superintendent Pryke's visit.

The police acted promptly. When they learned that their quarry had withdrawn a big cheque from the Birkbeck Bank, the numbers of the notes were obtained, and they were stopped. He went to the Bank of England on the afternoon of March 18, 1903, with the purpose of cashing these notes, and within a few minutes was confronted by a detective with the warrant for his arrest. Dougal denied all knowledge of forgery but consented to go with the detective to the office of the Old Jewry. When almost at the gates of the office Dougal made a desperate attempt to escape, but he dashed down a cul-de-sac and was recaptured without difficulty. This wild dash for liberty constituted the last free moments of Dougal's life. Never again did he appear in public without the handcuffs upon his wrists.

When Dougal first passed in the custody of the police it was never anticipated by them that he would ever go on trial for murder. The warrant against him was for forgery, and if it had not been for the undaunted courage and persistence of Detective-Inspector Bower, of Scotland Yard, it is doubtful if the Moat Farm mystery would ever have been solved.

The forgery charge for the time being satisfied the law's requirements. But suspicion gradually grew to a feeling of certainty that Miss Holland's disappearance could not be accounted for by Dougal's nonchalant story.

He was wearing that ring of hers when arrested – that ring of her dead lover's which never left her finger. And in the Moat House were found boxes which Dougal himself had told Superintendent Pryke she had taken away with her.

Detective-Inspector Bower, of Scotland Yard, now took the case in hand in conjunction with the local police, and from the beginning he held the theory that Dougal had murdered Miss Holland. This was all right as a theory, but how was it to be proved when there was even no positive knowledge that the woman was dead? Feeling certain that the Moat House itself held the key to the mystery, Detective Bower got to work there. The house itself revealed nothing, and naturally the next proceeding was to drain and drag the moat.

I should explain perhaps that there were really two moats, the larger one surrounding the house and being connected to a subsidiary moat round one side of which was the ditch, which Dougal had caused to have filled in.

This was the most disagreeable task police officers ever had. The waters were inconceivably foul, and several men who were engaged in the work fell ill. After they had been at work three days they were greatly excited when they came upon a number of bones. When they had all been brought to view, however, an examination quickly showed that they were those of an animal, apparently a calf or small cow. The dragging of the moat was completed without any discovery of importance.

All the time the police were carrying on these investigations at the Moat Farm they were subject to considerable criticism and even more ridicule, and as the weeks passed and no discovery of importance was made, Dougal, through his solicitor, expressed his intention of applying for a writ against the police to recover damages for the injury done to the Moat Farm. When the search had continued for about a month the police were further discouraged by an intimation received from the Treasury, which had charge of the prosecution of Dougal, that if nothing were discovered during the course of the next three weeks they would order the digging to be stopped and proceed with the prosecution of Dougal on a charge of forgery. But Detective Bower, who, in the course of his career solved several most baffling murder mysteries, including the Southport tragedy, the Slough crime, and a famous Eastbourne murder, was not easily cast down.

Though the moat had revealed nothing that could possibly incriminate Dougal, Detective Bower held to his opinion that the secret still lay buried in the lonely Essex farmhouse. By a lucky chance it came to the detective's knowledge that there had formerly been a big ditch on the farm. Though no trace of it existed at this time its position was soon located. Here digging was at once commenced, but without result. So they hunted up the man who had filled in the ditch, and he declared that the bottom had not yet been reached. So digging was continued, and on April 27, 1903 – exactly four years later to the very day of Miss Holland's arrival at the Moat Farm – Sergeant Scott turned up a woman's shoe – and murder was out! Spades were at once thrown down, and carefully the men removed the soil until the body was revealed to view. It was fully dressed, and the underlinen was quite clean. A ghastly hole in the skull at the back of the head indicated only too plainly how the luckless Miss Holland had met her death.

The chain of evidence to link Dougal to the dead body was gradually completed. It then appeared quite clearly that Dougal had shot Miss Holland dead that evening when he told the servant she had gone to London, and his subsequent absences from the house that night were for the purpose of interring her in her shallow grave.

His very statements to the servant to account for Miss Holland's departure 'came home to roost' at the trial, and were shown to be lies.

He had told her that her mistress had taken the train to London, and would be returning the same night. But it was proved by the railway officials that Miss Holland had not travelled that evening, and that it would have been impossible for her to go to London and return the same night – as no trains ran.

Finally, Dougal capped his inventions by informing the servant girl at seven in the morning that he had received a letter from Miss Holland stating that she had decided to remain in London. Now, the postal officials showed conclusively that it was impossible for any letter from London to have reached the Moat Farm by that time. Had Miss Holland gone to London by evening train she could not have posted a letter in time for the first delivery at Clavering. In face of all this Dougal continued to protest his innocence, but the jury's verdict and the Judge's sentence of death merely reflected what everybody in the kingdom believed. Nobody believed him. Thus was Samuel Herbert Dougal delivered into the hands of the hangman. He made a theatrical appeal from the condemned cell to be allowed to be 'shot like a soldier', and it is hardly necessary to add that his impudent request was treated as it deserved.

At that time I kept a barber's shop in Rochdale, and had not yet risen to the dignity of senior executioner. But I had already received several commissions to act as assistant. Only the week before Dougal was to die I was in Chelmsford Prison (where he was lying awaiting execution) in order to help to hang another soldier named Charles Howell for a murder committed at Colchester.

On this occasion I was on my way to the scaffold to put things in order the night before Howell was to die, and as we passed along a corridor in the centre of the prison the warder in attendance pointed to a cell door and remarked,

'That's Dougal in there.'

So we stopped for a moment to have a look at him, for the Moat Farm mystery was on everybody's tongue just then. This was July 6. 1903, and Dougal's execution had been fixed for 14 July. His cell was guarded by a grating and an outer door. This door was open, but the grating, although closed, gave us an opportunity of peering in at Miss Holland's murderer.

Dougal was lying asleep on his bed. He looked quite peaceful.

'How is he taking it?' I queried of the warder.

'Very well indeed', he replied. 'He gives no trouble, and does not seem to be at all upset about his position.'

The reason for this was not hard to find, Dougal honestly expected to be reprieved.

When I returned to Chelmsford the following week – Howell's execution having gone off without incident – with instructions to act as assistant to William Billington I heard that Dougal had maintained this air of composure for several days after our surreptitious peep at him.

He had appealed to the Home Secretary on the ground that the shooting of Miss Holland was 'an accident'. This was before the establishment of the Court of Criminal Appeal, but it is certain that even if it had been in existence at that time the Judges would have taken the same view as the Home Secretary did. Yet Dougal was confident he would not be hanged, and, buoyed up by this, he betrayed not the slightest emotion.

Then came the Saturday before his execution (which was fixed for a Tuesday), and with it the intimation from the Home Office that there would be no reprieve. At once the callous culprit broke down. For the rest of the day he sat silent, eating but little, and with his eyes fixed on a stony manner on nothing in particular. Later he gave way to tears, and professed to be heart-broken at the idea of leaving his little girl, aged about twelve years, the daughter of his third wife.

As the Tuesday drew nearer, he paced up and down his cell like an animal at bay but although he gave the prison officials some anxiety at times owing to his behaviour, he was always very gracious towards them, and thanked them for all they did for him. He listened eagerly enough to the ministrations of the chaplain, but, as I will show presently, even yet he hardly realised the extreme peril of facing his Maker with an unconfessed murder on his soul. The Rev. Mr Blakemore laboured patiently to prepare him to meet death properly, but always failed when it came to the extreme point.

On our arrival in the prison about 3.30 on the afternoon of July 13, the Governor told us that Dougal (whose age was given as 56 years) stood 5 ft. 9 ½ in. in height and weighed 161 lb. Upon this, after a second peep at Dougal, we decided upon a drop of 6 ft. 8 in., and the scaffold and rope were prepared accordingly. On the execution morning I was called at six o'clock, had a cup of tea, and went to the scaffold to put the final arrangements in order. It was feared that Dougal's nerve might fail him at the last, therefore the precaution was taken to place planks across the pit mouth, upon which warders could stand beside the doomed man to give him support if required.

'You had better be getting ready for the pinioning', came the advice of a warder at about three minutes to eight, and we accordingly went to the corridor outside Dougal's cell. I have never seen such a crowd of officials at an execution as were gathered there that morning. Among them one was pointed out to me as Inspector Fox, the man who arrested Dougal. He had asked for and been granted special permission to witness the execution.

Dougal had been sitting just before we entered, but he rose upon the door being opened, flashed his fiery eyes at his visitors and settled them upon us. They bore a look of weariness and anxiety. His face was haggard, but the beard and moustaches were well groomed, and the hair was still well parted, with small curls on each side at the front. He was dressed in the dark blue coat and vest he wore at his trial and the same dark striped trousers. He wore patent leather button boots, and his shirt was a clean white starched linen one.

We went straight up to him and pinioned his wrists behind his back. He made no resistance. Just previously a warder had poured out some brandy into a tin can for Dougal to drink. It stiffened him up, and he had himself well in hand as he stepped forth to take his last walk.

To do him justice, I must say he moved along like a soldier, with head erect and body braced. He never faltered and as he stood on the trapdoors I could see that the emergency planks could have been done without. Nevertheless, two warders took up their stations upon them. 'Billy' Billington was just on the point of pulling the lever when the chaplain's command – 'Stop!' – rang out. I can even now visualise the look of blank astonishment on his face. I myself wondered what was to happen next. Had a reprieve been received after all? Then came the thrice repeated demand. 'Dougal, are you guilty or not guilty?' just as I have already described it.

Dougal did not live more than a fraction of a second after he had made that hesitating confession 'Guilty, sir!' I think Billington would have pulled the lever then whether the chaplain had signalled or not. 'Billy' was indeed very upset about the incident, as he told me very frankly afterwards, and if it had not been for the paralysing effect of the shock of the chaplain's cry to stop it is conceivable that Billington would have ignored him and pulled the lever. In that case the world would have been robbed of the satisfaction of knowing Dougal had confessed his crime, but it must be understood that it is the executioner's duty to put the law's victims to death with the minimum of agonising delay.

On our way back to Lancashire – for Billington came from Bolton – we had to change stations at London, and took the opportunity to go to Newgate Prison, which was then in the process of demolition. I may add that I had officiated at the last execution that took place within its walls. We secured several relics of the historic building, and I still possess a walking stick made out of one of the beams taken from the Hangman's Room, and for which I was offered £5 by a man in the train on my way home.

And now for the explanation of the Rev. Mr Blakemore's strange action, which at the time was even made the subject of questions in the House of Commons. The sequel that brought me this explanation occurred thirteen years later when, on 16 August 1916, I hanged William Allan Butler at Birmingham. The crime for which he suffered calls for little comment. It was a matter of jealousy. Under this influence Butler had stabbed to death a married woman living apart from her husband, and went to his execution quite unrepentant. The chaplain could make no impression on him whatsoever. It struck me as grimly appropriate when I alighted from the train at Winson Green Station to see facing me big posters of the local cinema theatre announcing as its star picture, 'The Final Judgement.'

Butler's execution in itself brought out nothing worthy of special mention. But after it was all over the chaplain accosted me. 'I recognise you, Mr Ellis', he said, 'Do you remember me?'

I told him I seemed to know his face, but could not exactly place the occasion when we had met.

'Don't you remember the Dougal case?' he asked.

'Yes, very well indeed.'

'Well it was I who was chaplain at Chelmsford that day', he declared, and then I recognised him. It was the Rev. Mr Blakemore, who had created that strange scene on the scaffold.

After thirteen years here was I face to face once more with one of the chief actors in the final act of the Moat Farm drama. In the course of our subsequent conversation he made clear to me many things in that case which had hitherto puzzled me, and especially the reasons that lay behind his strange behaviour towards the condemned man. He told me that Dougal had been a very difficult man to handle, he made two or three purported 'confessions', which duly appeared in the public prints, but he always ascribed Miss Holland's death to an accident.

The reverend gentleman felt convinced in his own mind that Dougal was prevaricating. That he was really her murderer he felt convinced, but he always failed to get Dougal to admit his guilt. Time after time during his attendance in the condemned cell, Mr Blakemore tried to bring Dougal to a realisation of the awfulness of his position. He strove his utmost to move Dougal to a state of penitence before he went before the final Judge. Dougal, however, constantly maintained his innocence. Occasionally Dougal would be so touched by what the chaplain was saying that he would promise to confess. Yet when it came to the point of carrying out his promise, he invariably drew back and shut his mouth.

Mr Blakemore was in despair. He saw the man's soul craving for purification, but always prevented by some intangible barrier of pride or something of that kind from obtaining the solace it required. Matters stood thus on the execution morning. The two selves that had been fighting a battle within Dougal's soul under the ministrations of the Rev. Mr Blakemore had still not come to a decision. This was a victory for the man's evil self. In this condition Dougal stepped forth to the scaffold. The confession of his guilt which had several times been trembling upon his lips, remaining unsaid. And in a few moments he would be dead.

Mr Blakemore told me that when he led the grim procession from the cell to the scaffold he had not the slightest idea of doing what he afterwards did. He merely chanted the prayers for the dead as he was bound in duty to do. It was not until Dougal actually stood on the drop that something flashed across Mr Blakemore's mind to make one last effort to save the man's soul. He stood on the brink of eternity with his terrible sin still not admitted. Could he secure a confession at that perilous juncture? He resolved to try. Almost without realising the shock it would cause everybody he cried, 'Stop!' and then had made his appeal to the doomed man – Dougal, are you guilty or not guilty?' It was a daring thing to do, but it succeeded. At the third appeal, as I have already described, the battle that had been going on inside the wretch with the rope round his neck was won. His better self had triumphed on the edge of doom. He admitted his guilt.

Mr Blakemore told me that the incident had caused him infinite worry, for many folk had resented his interference with the speedy execution of the law's decree. But he himself felt he had been justified, and this view was shared by the majority of the hundreds of correspondents who took the trouble to write to him on the subject. The Home Secretary himself wrote asking him for an explanation of why he had spoken to the condemned man on the scaffold. Mr Blakemore made a frank report upon his reasons for the course he took. And shortly afterwards he was removed from Chelmsford to Winson Green Prison, Birmingham. As a matter of fact, this removal proved to be something in the nature of a promotion, so evidently his superiors had agreed with the motives that had prompted him. The most gratifying of all the letters that Mr Blakemore received on the subject was one from Dougal's wife. She congratulated the chaplain on securing that confession from her erring husband, for, as she said, she 'knew how stubborn he was'.

That, then, is the inner history of the most sensational episode in the famous Moat Farm case. Dougal's conviction was admittedly secured on a chain of circumstantial evidence, and it might always have been open to a few to have questioned the law's right to take the man's life on the evidence alone. But his last moment confession removed all possible doubts and stamped him as one of the most crafty calculating deceivers of women this country has known.

Chapter 4

The First Time I Saw a Condemned Woman

(John Gallagher and Emily Swann, Armley, Leeds, 1903)

Only three times in the whole of my career have I officiated at the execution of women. I have been engaged many times by Under Sheriffs following upon a woman's condemnation for murder, but this particular one which I am about to describe was the first of the only three cases in which a reprieve was not granted. It happened in the earlier years of my work as executioner, and I presume that since then the 'powers that be' have taken a different view of the subject of hanging women. Whether that be so or not, I am quite sure that some of the women who were afterwards reprieved were very little better than Mrs Swann. I do not say this because I think these other women ought to have gone to the scaffold, but because I think it was a pity that Mrs Swann did not have the same good fortune.

It is worthy of note, too, that each of the three women whom it was my lot to execute caused a scene of some kind. Mrs Thompson collapsed completely, and had to be carried unconscious to the scaffold. Mrs Swann, of whom I am about to speak in detail, fell to pieces pitifully just before execution, and then suddenly regained her nerve, and actually made smiling remarks as she stood on the trap-doors, while Mrs Newell showed temper because I tried to put the white cap over her head at the last moment, and startled the officials very much, who had been expecting a much more feminine breakdown.

One of the women whom I was engaged to execute was a spy. The public never knew at that time that such a woman existed, nor were they informed that she had been tried and condemned. Everything was done in secrecy.

Since then they have learned a little more about her, for her name was Eva de Bournonville, though they may not know that I still possess the officials papers instructing me to present myself at Holloway Prison on February 7, 1916, to execute this woman who had been condemned as a spy. She appealed, and the case was again heard behind closed doors. Once more she failed to secure the verdict, and I was informed that I must carry out the postponed execution on February 23. But higher authorities intervened to prevent the carrying out of the death sentence, and she was reprieved.

She remained in prison for six years, and then, in February 1922, I heard that the girl who had so narrowly escaped the gallows had been taken out of Walton Gaol, Liverpool, and sent to Newcastle where she was placed on board a ship by deportation order. I presume she was packed off to her native country of Sweden, and I never heard anything definite about her afterwards.

The affair which sent Mrs Emily Swann and John Gallagher to the scaffold together in Armley Gaol, Leeds, was, however, of a very different character. They earned the capital sentence by being jointly concerned in killing the woman's husband. 'The Wombwell Murder' was the title given to this tragedy, it having occurred in that district of Yorkshire. The victim, William Swann, was a glassblower, and John Gallagher was a 30-year-old miner who lodged in the house with Mr and Mrs Swann.

Whether William Swann ill-treated his wife because he thought she was too intimate with Gallagher, or whether Emily Swann went to Gallagher for protection after her husband ill-treated her, I cannot say. The facts certainly were that Emily Swann was brutally beaten at times by her husband, and that she and Gallagher were very friendly. Only the parties themselves could really say which state was a consequence of the other and they are all dead now.

Anyway, Gallagher had to leave the Swann's house at Wombwell after a series of quarrels. He frequently revisited it afterwards, and it was rarely that there was not a fight or a disturbance on such occasions.

In June 1903, Gallagher decided to leave Wombwell and go to Bradford, but it was destined that a terrible event was to occur before he could carry that resolve into practise.

On the afternoon of June 6 Mrs Swann walked into the house of a neighbour with a shawl over her head. Throwing it back in dramatic fashion as she entered, she cried out —

'See what our Bill has done!'

She pointed to her eyes. They were black with bruises. 'Bill' was, of course, her husband.

Gallagher happened to be present, and, seeing the woman's injuries, he at once jumped up and shouted —

'I will go and give him something for himself for that.'

Rushing out of the house, followed by Emily Swann, he was seen by a neighbour to enter the house of the Swanns, shouting as he disappeared through the doorway —

'I will coffin him before morning!'

The sound of a struggle soon issued from within, and above the racket the neighbour heard Mrs Swann say. 'Give it to him Johnny!' This at any rate showed that Emily Swann was tacitly agreeing with the punishment her husband was evidently receiving.

There was about ten minutes of this sort of thing, and then Gallagher came out and returned to the house he had left. 'I have broken four of his ribs, and I will break four more', he announced. After a short stay he arose to take his leave when he again broke into prophecy. 'I'll finish him out before I go to Bradford', said he.

Once more the neighbour saw Gallagher go back to the Swann's house, exclaiming – 'I will murder the pig before morning. If he can't kick a man he shan't kick a woman.'

Further sounds of scuffling reached this neighbour's ear and again came the voice of Mrs Swann – 'Give it to him, Johnny.'

After about another ten minutes of this sort of thing, things cooled down, and Gallagher and Mrs Swann appeared at the door holding each other's hands with every sign of affection. Yet, behind them, in that shambles of a room, lay William Swann – dead! They went over to their friends to announce the news.

The police soon had the matter in hand, and before she was many hours older Emily Swann was under arrest. Gallagher could not be found anywhere. For weeks he was searched for, without avail. He had, in fact, two months liberty before he got into the clutches of the police at Middlesbrough at the house of a relative of his. It appeared that he had spent the intervening period in tramping miserably up and down the country, and when he got to Middlesbrough he was starving and absolutely broken up.

The man and woman were placed on trial together, and counsel for their defence, while admitting that the affection between them was of a misdirected order, contended that Gallagher had merely gone to the house to administer to a brutal husband the chastisement he deserved for his cruel treatment of his wife. There was no proof, they declared, that either Gallagher or Mrs Swann desired William Swann's death.

Such arguments failed to convince the jury. The Judge advised them that there was proof of deliberate intention in Gallagher's remark, 'I'll finish him out before I go to Bradford', which was made between the two fights, after which he had gone back and carried out his threat. 'As for the woman', said his Lordship, 'it is my duty to tell the jury that one does not commit murder only with one's hands. If one person instigates another to commit murder, and that other person does it, the instigator is also guilty of murder.'

The Judge had a secret up his sleeve as he spoke thus, but he did not reveal it until after the jury had found their verdict.

For half an hour the jury deliberated, and then returned to Court with a verdict of 'Guilty' against both parties in the dock. Those who looked for Mrs Swann to faint or create a scene at this point were amazed to find her receiving that terrible verdict with the utmost calmness.

'I am innocent!' she said in an even tone. 'I am not afraid of immediate death because I am innocent and will go to God.'

His Lordship then made his revelation of a vital piece of evidence which had been withheld from the jury. 'The counsel for the prosecution thought it would press unfairly on the woman', explained the Judge, 'and so it was not given.' But I will state it now. When Gallagher was taken into custody he said the woman hit William Swann and beat him with a poker, and that he (Gallagher) did not touch the dead man, although he was present.

'That statement', explained his Lordship, 'was not direct evidence against the woman, but from the proved position of the poker I am convinced that the statement was partly true, and that Mrs Swann did really take part in the actual killing.' Considerable sensation was aroused by this revelation. It was still another example of the even-handed justice of our legal system, which declines to take unfair advantage of an accused person. It was also a matter for satisfaction that even without that vital evidence the jury had still been convinced of the woman's guilt.

As for Mrs Swann, her equanimity remained, despite what had just been said. Even the passing of the death sentence failed to move her, and she smiled all round the Court and kissed her hand to somebody in the gallery as they led her below. For some reason that I cannot understand a rumour got about that the jury had recommended Mrs Swann to mercy. That was not the case. They found her guilty without qualification, and the attempt that was afterwards made to get up a petition for reprieve failed.

William Billington (whom we called 'Billy') and I were engaged to carry out the double execution on December 29, 1903, and when we arrived at Armley Gaol on the previous afternoon (which was a Monday) the official refusal of a reprieve had just been received and communicated to the condemned couple. I was told that Gallagher had never anticipated anything else, but the woman had alternated from fits of hysteria to bouts of optimism. When they told her of the Home Office decision it absolutely staggered her, and she wore a look of absolute misery when I peeped in at her that evening. She was a little, stumpy, round-faced woman of 42 years of age, and was only 4 ft. 10 ½ in. in height, and 122 lb, in weight. As I looked at her I could not forbear a sympathetic thought for her in her terrible position. I had never seen a condemned woman before, and must admit that I, too, could hardly believe that the authorities would allow her to go to the scaffold.

She had been the mother of eleven children, and came of very respectable folk, who naturally felt the disgrace very severely. Her mother was over eighty years of age, and the tragedy was almost her death-blow. When news of the Home Secretary's decision reached the family they sent a last, despairing telegram to the King himself, appealing for an exercise of the Royal clemency, but His Majesty declined to interfere. Mrs Swann must die. It was hard, but then her complicity in that terrible murder was an inexcusable thing. She was warned to make her peace with the Supreme Judge by the chaplain, for her human Judges could not save her because of the necessity for upholding the sanctity of human life against the danger of murder. Indeed, both the condemned displayed religious penitence. In this connection I was told that the first occasion on which they met each other after their trial was in the prison chapel.

This happened on Christmas Day. There was a special service in the chapel for this occasion, and they took Gallagher and Mrs Swann to a curtained pew under the charge of their individual warders and wardresses. The doomed couple looked at each other for a moment, but did not speak. Then they devoted themselves to following the service and afterwards were taken back to their own cells to eat their Christmas dinners.

It is a curious commentary on the force of habit, but it is nevertheless the fact, that they both enjoyed that meal as it there were no such thing as death on the gallows looming but four days ahead.

Still, I do not want to convey an impression that they were callous to their position, for in that respect both had altered from their behaviour at the trial. Their behaviour in the condemned cell was quite contrite and proper to their position.

Gallagher was the more resigned of the two, Mrs Swann being much worried about the disgrace she was bringing on her family. A topic she often brought into her conversation with her attendant wardresses.

Gallagher, I ought to add, was of fair height (5 ft. 5 ¾ inches) and was considerably younger than the woman for whom he had conceived such a misplaced affection, being only 30. He was a sparely-built fellow and weighed several pounds short of 10 st. He was calm enough when we went in to pinion him on the fatal morning about a minute or so to nine o'clock. The condemned couple were, of course, in separate cells, and we went first to the man. Having got him ready for the scaffold, we left to pinion the woman, the officers in the meantime walking Gallagher on a little in order to get him out of sight of the woman when she came forth on her last walk.

A distressing thing was to happen before that point was reached. As we walked towards her cell I said to an officer by my side —

'How is she keeping up?'

He hesitated a moment before replying. And then said —

'If you look through the inspection hole you will see her all in a heap on the floor.'

It was true enough. I peeped into the cell, and saw as distressing a sight as it was ever my lot to witness. It was all very similar to that ghastly occasion several years later when Mrs Thompson was the victim.

Mrs Swann's self-possession had been failing for days, and had suddenly gone altogether. The realisation that death was inevitable in a matter of minutes had bowled her over completely. There she lay on the floor, moaning pitifully and practically unconscious. Two wardresses, manifestly upset, were trying in vain to pacify her and get her to stand up. The poor woman came out of her faint, but was too dazed to understand what was required of her.

Her moans continued, and they seemed to lacerate my very heartstrings. Turning to one of the officers, I said

'Give her some brandy as quickly as possible.'

The suggestion was instantly acted upon. He procured some spirits and the wardresses induced the woman to take a drink.

The effect was miraculous. She gulped down the brandy hardly knowing what she was doing, but it put new life into her. Courage returned to her, and in about two minutes the woman who had been prostrate with fear and dismay was more or less normal.

It was now possible for us to enter and complete the necessary pinioning of her arms behind her back, an operation that would have been absolutely out of the question only a few moments previously.

It was now the turn of the wardresses to break down. They had got quite attached to Emily Swann, and as she stepped forth towards the scaffold they burst into tears. But Mrs Swann was actually smiling now!

We did not let the weeping wardresses come near the scaffold. We were walking behind the doomed woman, and took charge of her when we got within a few yards of the place of execution.

Here Gallagher stood quietly awaiting us, surrounded by warders, and it was at this point that Mrs Swann first saw him. Gallagher, however, had no opportunity of seeing her, for he was standing with his back to us as we arrived, and 'Billy' Billington put the white cap over his head at once.

Another white cap then descended over Mrs Swann's head, and the two were placed in position under the beam. Mrs Swann had previously seen the two significant nooses dangling from it, but the sight failed to disturb her new-found balance. She seemed quite calm now. We were putting the rope round Gallagher's neck when the woman suddenly called out —

'Good morning, John!'

Gallagher started violently under our hands. He had no idea up to that moment that Emily Swann was standing beside him. Pulling himself together, he answered back —

'Good morning, love!'

By this time the other rope was round her neck, but again she spoke —

'Good-bye. God bless you!'

The reader may easily imagine the astonishment evoked by this extraordinary conversation between two persons, one of them a woman, standing with pinioned arms and legs, faces blotted out by shapeless white bags, and with ropes fixed round their necks. How much more of this kind of talk might have followed it is impossible to say, but with one quick pull on the lever both tongues were stilted for ever. The doctor certified that they died instantaneously, and it may also satisfy the public to know that Dr Exley, the medical officer present at the execution, assured the Coroner and jury at the subsequent inquest that death was 'perfectly painless in both cases'.

Chapter 5

Three Who Met Death with a Smile

(Samuel Holden, Birmingham 1904; William Joseph Foy, Cardiff, 1909; and James Honeyands, Exeter, 1914)

Three times in my long career I came in contact with condemned men who were so little afraid of death that they calmly smoked cigarettes on their way to the scaffold, and actually went through the terrible trapdoors with the 'fag-ends' still between their lips! This sort of thing argued courage of an exceedingly high order, for it would be no disgrace for the pluckiest man to feel a tremor of nervousness at the prospect of being hurled to death as a punishment for committing murder.

In the majority of cases, I am sure, that nervousness displayed is not due to physical fear, but rather to a very natural quailing at the prospect of what may await on the other side of the border line that divides life from death.

Possibly the act of smoking a cigarette may be thought to indicate just a little too much insensibility to the soul's future, but I would rather not enter into a discussion on that point.

The first time I ever had this kind of experience was in 1904, when Samuel Holden paid the extreme penalty at Birmingham for the murder of the woman he loved – Susan Humphries. Of Samuel Holden's crime little need be said. It was of a by no means uncommon order – the outcome of a combination of drink and passion – but it was at least remarkable in that the fatal stabs were actually witnessed by a woman looing through her window on the opposite side of the road. Rare indeed are the murders wherein any other than the principles and their accomplices (if any) have an opportunity of seeing the fatal deed accomplished.

Samuel Holden did his duty well in the South African War, and returned with four clasps to his medal. And then, foolish fellow, he made an association that had dire consequences. Susan Humphries had many good qualities, no doubt, but she was not the partner for a man such as he. Instead of rescuing him from his loose habits she followed him into them, and what happened on July 2, 1904, was merely the logical outcome of a life like theirs.

On that day there was another of their innumerable quarrels, and it is quite possible to believe Holden's statement that the woman provoked him. The sound of their angry voices brought to her window a woman who lived on the opposite side of the road to their house in Coventry Street, Birmingham, and to her horror she distinctly saw Holden lift his arm and deliberately stab Susan Humphries. Three times did that murderous hand descend, and when the alarm was raised and the house broken into Susan was past all mortal aid. She died on the way to the hospital.

By the 30th of the same month Holden was before the Lord Chief Justice on the murder charge. His counsel pleaded for a manslaughter verdict on the grounds that the attack had been made under great provocation as a result of a spontaneous quarrel, but the Lord Chief Justice put the clear issue before the jury in his summing up. He told them that, although Holden's previous life entitled him to every consideration, the case must be decided on the evidence itself, and he must tell them that if the prisoner struck the woman intending to injure her seriously, and she had died as a result to that, then murder had been committed.

The jury, after an absence of twenty minutes, brought in a verdict of guilty, and Holden descended to the cells below with the dread words of the death sentence ringing in his ears. Proved murderer though he was, I found considerable sympathy for him among the warders at Winson Green Prison when I went there on the afternoon of August 15 to carry out the execution, which had been fixed for the following morning. Holden was a likeable fellow, and there was not a person in the gaol who was not sorry that such a loyal ex-soldier should have to die the ignominious death of the gallows.

As it happened, two of the warders, whose duty it was to be his companions in the condemned cell, were ex-soldiers, too. The strangeness of the coincidence does not end there, however, for these same ex-soldiers had also fought in South Africa side by side with Holden. They had all braved death together on the battlefield, only to meet it again in such grim circumstances. Both the officers and their doomed friend were at first considerably affected at the strange chance that had again made room-mates of the trio, but Holden showed no feeling against them, while they, on their part, did their best to make his last days comfortable. Holden was a tall, well-built fellow of 34 years of age, standing 5 ft, 8 ⅜ in. in height and weighing exactly 12 st. He was always docile enough, but could have done with perhaps a little more understanding of the spiritual side of his punishment. Billy Billington accompanied me on this occasion, and was, in fact, acting as senior executioner, for at that time I had not gone beyond the 'assistant' stage.

When we entered the condemned man's cell on the morning of August 16, 1904, Samuel Holden immediately recognised us for the hangmen. He at once sat down on a chair and bluntly declared – 'I don't stir a peg till I get a smoke!'

With that he produced a cigarette from one of his pockets, and with the utmost calmness went on – 'Give us a match, somebody!'

We were all amazed at Holden's behaviour. It was so utterly unlike anything we had ever before seen in the condemned cell.

Furthermore, we did not know if we should be breaking prison regulations by assisting him to smoke.

With such thoughts in our minds, you can easily imagine the scene – officers and executioners all pretending to search their pockets for matches, and none of us wishing to be first to produce a light.

The condemned man's sharp eyes noted our hesitation. Fixing them upon 'Billy' Billington, who was busily groping in pockets where he knew he hadn't got any matches, he suddenly fired off the taunt – 'What are you afraid of?'

Stung by the thinly-veiled contempt in the condemned man's voice, one of the warders then 'discovered' a match, struck it, and held it towards Sam Holden. With a gurgle of contentment the latter lighted his cigarette and luxuriously puffed forth the smoke.

Now he was ready for death. Standing up, he allowed us to pinion him and lead him forth to the scaffold. All the way he puffed vigorously. He ignored the chaplain's prayers. On the drop he pulled hard at the cigarette as if keen on finishing it before death came, and went down with it still between his lips. We who saw him die were probably more affected by his death than ever he was in its anticipation. Sam Holden was indeed a man of iron, soldierly nerve, but I am sure that his two old soldier comrades and companions in the condemned cell would have been better pleased had Sam Holden showed less bravery and more penitence.

Five years later I witnessed a very similar scene at Swansea, when William Joseph Foy was executed. The only vital difference was that whereas Sam Holden seemed to care less as to his future state, Foy showed in several ways how penitent he was and how desirous of making his peace with God. Yet Foy was a much lower type of man than Holden. Indeed, he might truly be described as a 'waster', and both he and the woman he murdered were drawn from the 'bottom dregs! of civilisation'. They had both begun life with every advantage in the way of respectable parents, etc., and had drifted downwards instead of upwards.

The end of the descent came when Foy was only 25 years of age; while the woman, Mary Rees, who perhaps cared more for him than he did for her was a few years his senior. Though both were comparatively speaking so youthful, they had reached the lowest strata of life and become hopeless outcasts. Often enough they had not even the means to purchase a night's rest at a lodging-house, and on such occasions they put up with the shelter of the great caverns outside Swansea, which were once great smelting furnaces, but now stand derelict. And it was here that the murder was committed.

Something that Foy had done had aroused Mary Rees' jealousy, and a fierce quarrel awoke the echoes of those deserted pits. Nobody saw the eventual tragedy, but later on Foy walked up to Police Sergeant Hunter and asked to be locked up. 'What for?' asked the puzzled officer. 'Murder!' calmly replied Foy. 'I have thrown "Sloppy" (as Mary Ann Rees was called) down a hole in the old works.'

He actually took the police to the old blast furnaces, and pointed to the spot where the body would be found. 'I caught hold of her and swung her round, and dragged and dropped her in.'

Poor Mary Rees' troubled life had ended by the time she was found. No doubt she died instantly when flung into that yawning pit. So William Joseph Foy went on his trial for murder.

He was condemned, despite his story that she had fallen in and been accidently killed, and his appeal against his conviction availed him nothing. Although he had disgraced his family in every way, his father and other relatives tried hard to save him by petitions, etc., but all to no purpose.

Foy, as I have already hinted, showed many signs of contrition as the days wore on towards the morning of execution. He had a most affecting and highly emotional last interview with his father and sister, and wrote the latter a letter, in which he confessed his guilt and admitted the justice of his punishment. Yet, despite all this, he displayed the most remarkable courage on the fatal morning. He actually chose the items for his last breakfast, and made a really hearty meal of beefsteak and onions, bread, butter and tea! During his condemnation his feelings had been so much played upon that he lost weight – a most unusual thing in such a case. Curious as it may seem, it is, nevertheless, a fact, that men under sentence of death almost invariably gain weight in prison.

Despite this he was as bright as a bridegroom that May morning in 1909, when I and Henry Pierrepont went to his cell to get him ready for the gallows. He was a big-made, tall fellow, of sandy complexion, and he looked perfectly calm and unconcerned. There was some of the same hesitation among us when he asked for a light for the cigarette he suddenly produced as marked the scene in Holden's cell. But he did not view our clumsy fumblings in quite the same contemptuous way as the Birmingham Man. His face was quite expressionless as he waited for matches to be found, but his eyes lit up with pleasure when the first whiffs of smoke began to issue from his mouth.

When he walked forth with pinioned arms towards the scaffold, he looked the least troubled person in the prison. With huge enjoyment he puffed at his cigarette even while the noose was being tightened round his neck, and he smiled as he fell to his death, although everybody around was deeply touched. That he did actually smile at the moment of death is a positive fact, for the smile was still there when his dead body was drawn up an hour afterwards. And the dead fag-end was still in his mouth!

You may judge of the feelings his brave exhibition aroused among the officers when I quote you the following remark of the Under Sheriff (Mr George Isaac) –

'I would not have your job for £20,000!' he declared to me, adding, 'What hard hearts you must have! If it had to depend on me, they would never be hanged!'

I would like to assure all who, like this gentleman, think that an executioner must necessarily be of a cruel nature that I do not look upon myself as having any more, especially 'hard heart' than the jurymen who find men guilty of murder, or the Judges who sentence them to death, or the sheriffs and prison officials who arrange the details of the carrying out of the executions. We are all part of the same system – that system of British justice of which as a nation we are so proud.

A further five years sped by and then came my third experience of a phlegmatic murderer facing doom placidly with a cigarette in his mouth. This time the man was a sailor, James Honeyands by name, whom I hanged in Exeter Gaol on March 12, 1914. He was a naval stoker, but little more than a boy in years. For he was only 21 years of age when death claimed him on the scaffold. The old, old story of jealousy lay at the root of it, although his defending counsel tried hard to prove a different theory in the hope of saving the young blue jacket's life.

That he actually shot Amelia Jones dead at Plymouth was not denied. The point was whether he killed her out of set purpose or whether – as the defence claimed – his hereditary history and the quantity of drink he had taken, unseated his reason and caused him to commit the crime. Circumstantial evidence consisting of a positive act and two statements served to convict him. Of these, the first was that when he came ashore, quite sober, from his ship on the day of the tragedy he brought with him a revolver which gave ground for the assumption that murder was already in his mind. The two statements were his remark, 'I will do for you', uttered before he shot the girl, and his declaration after the crime that he intended to kill her. On these grounds he was justly condemned to death, and, despite his appeal against the sentence and a petition signed by over 13,000 people, the Home Secretary saw no reason for interfering with the course of the law.

A curious point was troubling the Governor's mind when I reached Exeter Gaol on the afternoon of March 11 in readiness to carry out the sentence on the following morning. 'Would it be wise to hang him in his naval clothes?' he said to me in the course of an interview shortly after my arrival.

My answer was a prompt – 'No!' 'Of course', I added, 'if you insist on this being done I suppose I shall have to obey, but I certainly think it would be inflicting indignity and disgrace upon His Majesty's uniform and upon the Royal Navy.'

The Governor had quite an open mind on the subject, and after hearing my views unhesitatingly decided that other clothes must be found for the culprit. So another suit was found for him, it being just as irregular to hang a man in convict's clothes, although this was actually done in the case of Sergeant O'Donnell, the Aldershot murderer.

Honeyands was a smart-looking youngster, and as brave as he was smart. Although so young, he weighed eleven stone, and was only two and a half inches short of six feet tall. He had the typical neck of a sailor – broad and muscular – and I decided to give him a drop of seven feet three inches.

Nevertheless, despite his manly build, he looked pitifully young to be hanged, and when I and my assistant entered his cell a minute before execution time I could not withhold a feeling of compassion for him.

Young Honeyands, however, seemed quite regardless of the pity which his position evoked in others.

The prison governor had entered the cell behind me, and Honeyands turned to him and uttered a few well-chosen words of thanks for the kind treatment that had been meted out to him. He was perfectly collected in manner, and asked permission to smoke as if going to the scaffold were a mere casual part of his ordinary routine. While the grim process of pinioning his arms behind him and loosening his shirt at the neck were being carried through he smoked on with an air of complete detachment.

One would have thought that he would have been depressed by the loneliness of his end, for he had seen not a single relative or friend since condemnation, his father being too ill to visit him, and his brothers away at sea. His only caller had been the Lord Bishop of Exeter, who found him fairly responsive to his spiritual ministration. But the youth stood there calmly smoking as if he did not know what care was.

When all was ready he walked forth nonchalantly to the execution shed – still smoking. Perhaps his sense of discipline, inculcated on board ship, helped him in his ordeal, but really to watch him you would have thought it was no ordeal at all. The last I saw of him as I drew the white cap over his head, his face wore a quiet smile, and he was still contentedly enjoying the weed. Then came the drawing of the belt, and – oblivion.

It is surely a proof of the instantaneous and painless nature of modern execution methods that in this, as in each of the other two cases mentioned in this article, the unsmoked fragment of cigarette was retained between each man's lips even after death. And their dead faces all bore a smile when they came to be uncovered. Still, although I know death on the scaffold to be a mercifully painless one, it is nevertheless – death! And it is because it is given to few men to cross into the Unknown with such remarkable courage as to be able to smoke calmly on the way thereto that I have put these three cases on record here.

Chapter 6

Three Men Executed in Three Days

(William Frederick Edge, Stafford; George Smith, Armley, Leeds; and John Silks, Derby, 1905)

I regard December, 1905, as one of the busiest periods in my career, for in that month my services were called upon five times, three executions being on consecutive days. The first two executions were at Worcester and Newcastle-upon-Tyne. Then came the rush, during which William Frederick Edge was hanged at Stafford on December 27; George Smith at Armley, Leeds, on December 28; and John Silks at Derby on December 29.

Smith's was the most extraordinary case of the lot, but I propose to deal with the three executions in chronological order, and will therefore allude briefly to my experiences at Stafford.

The murder of which Edge was found guilty was an exceptionally cruel and dastardly one. Edge, who was a billiards marker, lodged with a Mr and Mrs Evans in Neilson Street, Newcastle-under-Lyme. He lost his job, with the result that he got into arrears with his landlady, who, acting under instructions from her husband, requested him to find apartments elsewhere, as they could no longer afford to keep him for nothing.

Edge said he would go, but declared that he would have his revenge before he quitted the house. That same afternoon the man was nursing the five-months-old son of Mr and Mrs Evans. He had always been very demonstrative in his affections for the infant, and on this occasion he sang the baby off to sleep, and then placed him on the couch in the kitchen.

Mrs Evans and her daughter went upstairs, leaving the boarder sitting a short distance away from the sleeping babe. When Mrs Evans was about to return to the kitchen she heard the front door open. Then it closed with a bang. It was Edge leaving the house, but he had taken his revenge in a most cowardly and terrible way by inflicting a frightful gash upon the slumbering infant's throat with a razor. The wound must have proved fatal instantly, for the medical evidence showed that but for the backbone the baby would have been decapitated. This awful discovery of Edge's act was made by Mrs Evans, who on descending the stairs heard a gurgling noise from the direction of the couch. She rushed to the baby, and found that it had been murdered. With the blood-stained razor still in his hand, Edge seems to have proceeded to the police station to surrender himself and make a confession of his crime. To the policeman to whom he made his statement he explained that he had done it for spite.

I was engaged along with Henry Pierrepont to carry out this and the other executions on the two following days. When we arrived at Stafford Gaol we found that the man we were to hang on the morrow had lost the callous demeanour which had characterised his conduct during his trial, and when we went to take stock of him he was exhibiting marked traces of penitence of the crime he had committed. He was a man of 23, wearing gold-rimmed eyeglasses, which seemed to accentuate his delicate appearance.

Although he then appeared to be on the verge of a breakdown and was terribly unstrung, the next morning he walked firmly to the scaffold. Tears coursed down his cheeks as the white cap was placed over his head. A drop of 6 ft. 10 in. was allowed and before he disappeared into the abyss of death I heard him mutter a supplication to his Maker, into whose presence his soul was ushered the very next moment.

We were called upon to hang a very different type of murderer in George Smith at Armley Gaol, Leeds, the next day. When we arrived at the prison we were told a very startling story concerning Smith's behaviour while lying under sentence of death, and from what we saw of the man in the condemned cell we were prepared for trouble. When the execution morning came we did indeed get a surprise, but it was of a character different from that which we expected.

The account of Smith's conduct in gaol showed that he was threatening violence, and if the character of a man's crime affords any index to his behaviour in prison, then you can readily understand that Smith was likely to give trouble. When Smith killed his wife Martha at Ilkley in September 12 he committed a most cold-blooded crime. Owing to the man's indolent and irregular habits, the couple had been separated for some time before the tragedy. They had no settled house, with the result that the wife was driven into domestic service to support herself and her two little children. Out of her meagre reserve of cash she even contributed to her worthless husband's maintenance whilst he was out of work.

Such splendid behaviour by the poor woman met with no return of gratitude on her husband's part. Indeed, the man frequently expressed feelings of vindictiveness towards her, and he even went to the house where she was employed and assaulted her. Smith followed up the assault by insisting that she should leave her place of employment, which extraordinary demand she deemed it prudent to comply with. Mrs Smith went to her parents' home at Wakefield, but subsequently obtained a situation with an Ilkley lady, into whose service she entered on 9 September. Three days later Smith traced his wife's whereabouts, and robbed her of her life.

On the morning of the tragedy, the daughter of the house where Mrs Smith was employed had occasion to visit Leeds. Her parents were away at the time, with the result that the house was left in the charge of Mrs Smith. The last time the unfortunate woman was seen alive was at four o'clock in the afternoon, when a servant at a neighbour's house noticed her standing at the back door.

About this time Smith was in lodgings in Leeds. He was out of work, but told his landlady, a Mrs Storey, that his wife would be paying the money for his lodgings. On the morning of September 12 he left the house saying that he was going to Halifax on a job, but about 2 o'clock in the afternoon he was seen in the neighbourhood of Ilkley. Half an hour later Smith was seen to enter by the back door of the house where his wife worked. At 6.30 the daughter of the house returned, entering by the front door. An eerie atmosphere seemed to pervade the house. Where was Smith, the new servant? The answer to that question provided a startling and horrifying discovery for the young lady, who found Mrs Smith lying dead on the kitchen floor. There were no fewer than 49 wounds on her body. The character of these injuries showed that the poor woman had put up a grim fight for her life.

The police were immediately informed of the affair, and two days later Smith was arrested. The case against him was not over difficult to prove. In the first instance the clothes which he was wearing were bloodstained, whilst a silk handkerchief of a distinctive colour, which was found in his possession, and which had belonged to the husband of Mrs Smith's employer, provided another clue. Also, a butcher's knife which had belonged to his landlady, Mrs Storey, was missing. In the accused man's possession were found a number of letters from his wife, some couched in most affectionate terms.

Smith did not enter into any very powerful defence when he was arraigned on the capital charge at West Riding Assizes on December 7. He went into the witness-box and gave a most dramatic description of the scenes which were enacted in the kitchen where his wife's lifeless body was found. After telling the jury that his wife had been a very affectionate woman, of whom he had been very fond during their eleven years of married life, he later admitted that there was some truth in the allegation that he was going with another woman. Then he alleged that he went to Ilkley at his wife's request.

If that was the case it is unbelievable that Mrs Smith should tell her husband on his arrival, as he swore she did, that she did not want him any more, explaining, 'I have somebody else to look after me now'. The accused man attempted to make out that his wife was the aggressor and that her conduct led to the terrible violence in which he indulged, adding, possibly by way of extenuation, that he was a very short-tempered man, and thought that was how he did what he did. Otherwise he reiterated he and his wife had been the best of friends. Describing the tragedy, Smith said that his wife pushed him away and struck him with a piece of board. 'I had a penknife in my hand', he went on, 'and in the struggle which followed I dug at her, and cut my hands in trying to draw it away from her grasp.' After the struggle with his wife he stayed with her 'until the finish'.

Smith related a moving story of his wife's last moments. He told how he lifted her in his arms, and they kissed each other before she died. 'How did you give her the 49 wounds?' he was asked. 'I kept going like that', he replied, and demonstrated his answer by putting his arm in a striking position and making imaginary stabs with a knife. 'She was struggling with me', he added. Smith's counsel was from the first faced with a fairly hopeless task in attempting to save his client from a verdict of guilty. Nevertheless, he delivered a powerful and eloquent address, in which he submitted that there were circumstances to constrain the jury in their clemency to find for manslaughter.

Having regard to the fact that the accused by his admissions in the witness-box had practically made a full confession of the crime, it was not surprising that the jury after a short retirement returned a verdict of 'Wilful murder'. Mr Justice Jelf, in passing sentence of death, characterised the murder as one of the most brutal crimes it had ever been his lot to try or even hear of. Smith received his sentence unmoved; but he adopted a different attitude when he was lying in the condemned cell awaiting his execution.

Shortly before our arrival at Armley Gaol the Governor had paid a visit to the condemned cell to see if Smith had any particular wishes which he desired to be carried out, and also to see that everything was going well. After his departure the culprit began to talk in a threatening way to one of the attendant warders. He swore, I was told, that he would tear out the Governor's heart if he entered the condemned cell again in connection with the execution, and also threatened to wreak dire vengeance upon the hangmen if they dared to lay hands upon him.

As far as build went, Smith was an average man of 50 years, turning the beam at 10 st. 9 lb for his 5 ft 4 ½ in. of stature. He had followed the trade of a bricklayer and was a powerful-looking man. He had not resorted to personal violence whilst in gaol, but the warder deemed it prudent to report his remarks to his superiors. Thus it came about that when we reached the prison the Governor sent for us and spoke with a grave face. 'I have sent for you to inform you that this man has threatened to cause trouble to me and you', said the Governor, who then asked, 'Is there anything that can be done to prevent it?'

After we had heard full particulars and had considered the situation, Pierrepont said, 'We can simply get the guide ropes and some planks down on the scaffold for the officers to stand beside and hold him while he is on the drop.' 'You know the business best', said the Governor, 'and I rely on you to do everything to prevent trouble!'

Before dismissing us the Governor said, 'It has been my custom with a condemned man to wish him good-bye and to ask if he has anything to say, but this man has used such threatening language that it will not be wise for me to go in in the circumstances'.

We considered his decision to be a wise one. All the same, the outlook for us was not a very pleasing one, though I felt that we would be able quickly to devise some method if Smith became obstreperous or violent.

We lost no time in taking stock of our man. When we went to the inspection-hole Smith was having his tea. Altogether we kept him under surveillance for half an hour, and what we witnessed during that period was not very reassuring.

Having disposed of his meal, Smith suddenly jumped up, and, seizing two pillows from his bed, he swung them round his head as though they were Indian clubs. At length Smith grew tired of this form of physical culture, and he began to pace up and down his cell like a caged animal. 'He is going to be a tough customer', I thought to myself. However, it was no use worrying over the matter then. We had seen sufficient to satisfy our professional curiosity, and believed that the drop of 6 ft. 9 in. which we resolved upon would be sufficient to produce an instantaneous death.

Both Pierrepont and I managed to preserve an outward calm when we entered the condemned cell a few seconds in advance of the fatal hour the next morning. Assistance was near at hand in case Smith put up a fight for his life.

As soon as we entered the cell Smith rose to his feet. Pierrepont stood in front of him, prepared for any move he might make, while I slipped to the rear. To my great surprise the condemned man placed his hands behind his back, just as though he knew what was required of him, on his wrists. His opportunities for resorting to violence were thus considerably restricted but, to our intense satisfaction, he preserved an unexpected docility and quietness. He suffered us to lead him from the cell to the scaffold without a murmur, and he went to instant doom without uttering a word.

After the execution was over the Governor sought us out and complimented us upon the satisfactory manner in which we had carried out sentence of death. 'I am pleased', he said, 'that everything has gone off as well as it did, for, truth to tell, I was expecting some unpleasant scenes.'

We thanked the Governor for his expressions of opinion. And soon after set out for Derby, there to perform the same grim duties on the morrow.

Our third victim within three consecutive days was John Silks, a man of thirty, who lived at Chesterfield, and had been found guilty of matricide. For about eight years Silks had been in the Army, and after his discharge in 1903 he went to live in Spa Lane with his crippled mother, whom he supported. At times he indulged in drunken orgies, during which his conduct was very vicious and brutal. Several times he savagely attacked his mother, against whom he seemed to harbour some resentment when his brain was besodden with alcohol. On the Saturday of the murder, when he was partially intoxicated, he foreshadowed to two men what was going to happen. 'A murder will be done in Spa Lane to-night', he declared. 'It will be our old girl.'

The men, not realising the full seriousness of the threats, advised him to be sensible and not to talk ridiculously.

'I will put someone out of the mess to-night', he persisted, and he fulfilled his awful threats in a terrible manner.

When he reached home he quarrelled with his mother in the presence of a lodger. Overthrowing the lamp, he plunged the room into darkness.

Out of the blackness came cries of 'Oh don't!' and 'Murder!'

Allowing his nerves to get beyond his control, the lodger ran from the house.

It was not until the next morning that the tragedy was discovered. A newsboy who then called at the house found the woman's dead body, terribly battered, lying in the living-room. A broken chair and a broken crutch bore further testimony to the scene of violence which had taken place. The police found Silks in another room fast asleep. When they arrested him he declared that he knew nothing about the murder. Those who were charged with the duty of defending him tried to save his neck by advancing that plea of insanity and drunkenness, but without avail. It was decided that Silks should expiate his revolting crime on the scaffold, and Pierrepont and I became the instruments of the law in carrying out the extreme penalty.

When our victim was handed over to us he was a complete nervous wreck – a miserable, cringing, and cowardly creature, whose demeanour contrasted strongly with that of the Ilkley murderer. Silks walked with a painful slowness to the scaffold. We had measured off a drop of 6 ft. 3 in., based upon his height of 5 ft. 9 ½ in. and his weight of 11 st. 3 lb.

When we got him on the trapdoors he fainted. The noose was already about his neck, and the next instant, before total collapse could take place, the drawing of the lever sent him to a more merciful death than that which he had vouchsafed to his poor crippled mother.

Chapter 7

My First Job As Senior Executioner

(John Davis, Warwick, 1907)

The New Year's Day of 1907 ranks as a red-letter day in my career. For five years I had acted as assistant executioner, and as such had witnessed the deaths of thirty-two murderers. And now came the time when I was for the first time to pull that fatal lever and accept senior responsibility for hanging a condemned criminal. It has occurred to me that my readers might like to know how I felt on that occasion.

There is a huge difference between the duties of an assistant executioner and the senior. It is upon the latter that all the major work falls, and it is he who has to shoulder full responsibility. He it is who must calculate the length of drop required, make certain that the scaffold is in order and all its fixings complete, pinion the condemned man, blindfold him with the white cap, place the noose round his neck, and – pull the lever which, after all, is the most important part of an execution.

The assistant merely – assists! The only task he carries through alone is to strap the doomed man's legs together on the scaffold, while the executioner sees to the noose and the white cap; and even this has on occasion been dispensed with. I in no way mean to infer that an assistant is unnecessary. Indeed, I have always strongly advocated the appointment of an assistant, even when others in authority were inclined to dispense with one. What I wish to emphasise is the difference in the work of the two, in order that you may appreciate how I felt when called upon for the first time to take senior responsibility at an execution.

Almost exactly five years to the day from the occasion of my first attendance at an execution I had been called upon to accept an offer to act as senior at Manchester. Lest there be some who consider that a rather long period of probation, let me point out that very few assistants rise to be senior executioners. Indeed, during all the years of my professional career, only one other man achieved that distinction, and the man who assisted me at my first execution as senior is still an assistant. This reflects no discredit whatever on those who remain assistants. It merely means that there is rarely any necessity for more than one senior, so long as that man gives satisfaction. An opening as senior, in fact, is very rare.

The first offer of a post as senior executioner did not, however, lead to anything material. Two men had been tried for the murder of a Preston warehouseman, and, while one was condemned, the jury disagreed about the other. At the latter's second trial he was found not guilty, and in the excitement that prevailed in Lancashire the condemned man's execution had to be postponed. A week later it was decided to commute his sentence to imprisonment for life, and an intimation that my services would not be required was accordingly sent to me. In the circumstances I considered this was a just decision, and as it happened I had only to wait a few days before I was again given my chance to act as senior executioner.

This time the call came from Warwickshire, where a man well known along the Liverpool dockside had ruined himself by an illicit love affair. He was a silverer by trade and John Davis by name. For years he lived at Aston, Birmingham, and then suddenly decided that his wife no longer filled his heart. A passionate longing to possess another man's wife had no doubt originated this disdain for Mrs Davis. The woman he now wanted was a Mrs Joan Harrison, whose husband had fallen under mental affliction. She had two grown-up sons, who did their utmost to freeze out the interloper, John Davis, but with Mrs Harrison herself encouraging her lover, the young fellows were practically powerless.

Mrs Davis was not ignorant of what was going on. On one occasion she even called upon Mrs Harrison, presumably to beseech her not to lure her husband away from her, but her arguments in no way affected the infatuated couple. Then Davis left her and went to Garston and here Mrs Davis drops out of the story. Davis evidently made many friends in Liverpool and district, and certainly, from my own observations of him, I can honestly say that he seemed a very respectable man. Perhaps it was extraordinary that a married man of 53 years of age should throw up all the ordinary conventions of life out of a passion for another man's wife, but he appeared to see no sin in it. Indeed, he actually interested himself in mission work at the docks, a fact curious of itself, which had a sequel when he lay under sentence of death later on.

Whenever he could manage it, this middle-aged lover of a religious turn of mind would go to Birmingham to visit the woman he ought not to have loved, and never abated one jot of his attentions for all the active opposition of Mrs Harrison's sons. The rift in the affair, which neither quarrels nor threats could produce, came at last through jealousy. Some time in October he began to doubt Mrs Harrison's constancy, and from that time matters went quickly towards the tragic crisis.

On the morning of 17th of that month Mrs Harrison's sons departed for their work, leaving her alone. It is probable that Davis was lurking about watching, for very shortly afterwards a neighbour saw him steal into the house. Two voices raised high in angry talk told of a quarrel in progress. No doubt Davis was reproaching the woman, while she both denied his allegations and challenged his right to control her movements. A woman's scream rings out. The neighbour runs affrightened into her garden, and glancing over the partition wall, sees Mrs Harrison stagger forth with her head hanging horribly on one side, and moaning – 'What shall I do? What shall I do?'

The neighbour seeing blood jumps at once to a dreadful conclusion. Without waiting for proof she cries as Davis appears and makes for the street – 'Murder! Stop him! He has cut a woman's throat!'

The woman's instinctive cries saved the police the trouble of hunting for John Davis. A crowd gathered in the usual miraculous fashion and prevented Davis from escaping. He was soon in the hands of the police, and Mrs Harrison died an hour after being removed to the hospital.

Davis took the line of denying the murder. He declared Mrs Harrison's wounds were self-inflicted. She had complained, so he said, of a very bad headache. And had then suddenly taken out of his hand the razor which he was going to shave with, and had cut her own throat. This explanation was easily rebutted. The doctors admitted that it was not physically impossible for the woman's wounds to have been self-inflicted, but the prosecution had a very neat fact to aid them. Mrs Harrison had evidently been cleaning the firegrate that morning for her hands were covered with blacklead. Yet there were no marks of blacklead on the razor handle or the blade. It was obvious that the razor must have been marked even ever so slightly if the woman had grasped it to commit suicide.

The Judge (Mr Justice Ridley) also pointed out that the accused man had himself furnished a feasible motive for murder as against suicide, for Davis, when first in custody, had remarked, 'It's all through jealousy'. In face of all this the jury's duty was only too clear, and they found him guilty without much hesitation. A few days after he was sentenced to death the postman handed me a letter which I could tell at a glance at the envelope was in reference to Davis' execution. I assumed it would be a request to act once more as assistant, but to my delight it was an offer to carry out the capital sentence in the senior capacity with another man as my assistant.

Naturally, I accepted with alacrity. I do not think my wife ever fully approved of my adopted profession, but when I told her I had received this appointment to carry out an execution on my own she really for the first time manifested an open anxiety that I should succeed and give satisfaction. I went to Warwick filled with a due sense of the importance of the occasion. Never in my previous five years as an assistant had I so fully realised the weight of responsibility that falls upon an executioner's shoulders. If the doomed man Davis had been a phlegmatic fellow, as are so many occupants of the condemned cell, perhaps I would not have felt my position so keenly. His behaviour from the moment he was sentenced to the hour of his execution was very different from the average man in his position, and this naturally affected me considerably.

Davis never seemed to completely recover from the shock of the passing of the death sentence. I don't know if he really expected to get off, but unquestionably he was awfully upset when he came out of the dock with the Judge's solemn condemnation still echoing in his brain. He was almost prostrated with terror, and remained like that for several days. His outbursts were most trying to witness. It was only very, very gradually that he regained anything like possession of himself, and he never obtained that complete calmness of demeanour that, strange to say, is the more usual characteristic of condemned criminals.

Christmas Day intervened about a fortnight after his trial, and then came a remarkable manifestation of charity. The wife he had scorned and left for another actually forgave him so far as to journey to the prison to see and comfort the man who had broken his promises to 'love and cherish! her'. She was accompanied by their son, and the interview, I believe, was one of the most painful that ever occurred within those prison walls. Miles away on the Mersey dockside other remarkably touching scenes connected with this execution were taking place that Christmas Day.

When I reached the prison on the last day of the dying year news of these outside events had got back to Warwick, and the warders told me about them in voices that showed that even they were not untouched. It seems that Davis had opened correspondence with a Mr Cochrane, the missioner at the Garston Docks, where Davis himself had been a religious worker. That Christmas morning Mr Cochrane received a letter from the man lying in the condemned cell, in which Davis made the request that 'two beautiful hymns that I love should be sung at your services'.

He went on to say: 'Sing "Nearer my God to Thee" in the morning, and "Lead, Kindly Light" in the evening. Remember me in your prayers, and remember me especially to the children of the choir. Ask them in your mission room to kneel down and pray to their God to forgive their sins. Say to them "Are you ready?" I can look up to God, now my time has come, and say good-bye to you, and hope to meet you in Heaven.'

The condemned man's pathetic requests were acceded to. The services were held just as he asked, and, I understand, were most impressive. Davis was informed of all that went on there, and on the very eve of his execution he wrote again to Mr Cochrane conveying an affectionate farewell and his thanks for the interest shown in him.

Proved murderer though he was, he obviously had many likeable traits in his character, and I really felt very sorry that he should have to go to such an end.

He looked extremely upset when I obtained my first glimpse of him by peeping through the spyhole in his cell door. His was not the attitude of a craven, but rather that of a man who realised what a mess he had made of his life. There he sat with his head in his hands pondering on his lost chances. A minute or two like this and then he would get up and stride the lengths of his cell as if wishing to fling off the thoughts that were oppressing him. Failing in this, he would again sit down, drop his head in his hands, and remain staring into vacancy, thinking – thinking.

When I had watched as long as I thought necessary I went away to calculate the length of the drop I should allow him, and the Under-Sheriff tackled me on this point. I told him in answer to his question that I proposed giving 7 ft. 9 in., and then for the first, but by no means the last, time in my career became involved in an argument as to whether this was the correct length to give. 'That's too much', asserted the Under-Sheriff. 'I have seen more execution than you have, and I consider that a most unsuitable drop.' 'Very possibly', I returned. 'But seeing an execution is one thing and performing one is distinctly different.'

The Under-Sheriff was clearly nettled, and my own temper was beginning to rise. 'I consider four to five feet quite a sufficient drop', he remarked.

This estimate amazed me, for it would have been much too short for anybody but a tremendously heavy man, whereas Davis was under ten stone in weight. Knowing that if such a drop were given it would certainly only produce a lingering death from strangulation, I delivered my reply. 'All right', said I. 'If you will take full responsibility for whatever happens I will adopt your suggestion.'

To that the Under-Sheriff replied that I had better please myself. 'Then I will give 7 ft. 9 in.', I said, and later, on seeing the doctor, the latter agreed that that would be quite suitable. Indeed, the medico took the other extreme from the Under-Sheriff. 'I don't care what happens so long as he is dead when he drops', he declared.

That night the novelty of my position once more came home to me. I felt desperately anxious that this, my first execution 'on my own', should pass off well, and was so keen about making all things certain that I decided to practise upon my assistant. He offered no objection, so there in the shelter of our room I experimented on my assistant as if he were the condemned man. Several times I went through the process of fastening on the pinioning straps, until I felt confident in my ability to do the deed in the morning without a hitch.

The hour of Davis' ordeal – and mine! – came round at last. Just before eight o'clock I and my assistant joined the silent group that stood in the corridor outside the condemned cell. I now had myself well in hand, and after my previous anxious excitement I was surprised at my own coolness. It was just as if this were my hundredth instead of my first execution as senior. A grave nod from the Governor told me the time for action had come. Followed by my assistant, I pushed open the cell door and entered. Poor Davis's face wore a pitiful expression, and his eyes shone with unwept tears. It wasn't cowardice that lay reflected therein. Rather was it the look of a man who feels all the world is against him and seeks in vain for a glance of human sympathy.

I simply could not resist his mute appeal. My previous night's rehearsal helped me to do the pinioning quite easily, and when that was done and I turned to open his shirt neck I patted Davis on the shoulder and muttered a few encouraging words. The right thing to do and say did not come too easily, for you must bear in mind that I had never before been in such a position. Anyhow, Davis seemed to appreciate what I was trying to do, and made a brave attempt to straighten back his shoulders as we all stepped forward to leave the cell.

The walk from the cell to the scaffold was not arranged as judiciously as it might have been. Davis had been incarcerated in a cell on an upper landing, and as a rule in such cases the doomed man is moved much nearer the scaffold before he has to take his final walk so as to lessen the distance and obviate any risk of an accident when called upon to descend a flight of stairs with hands pinioned behind. Davis, however, had to go all the way, and in his condition this might easily have led to a scene. As it was, when he reached the head of the flight of stairs he paused before attempting the descent, and again looked in that pitiful way of his as if seeking desperately for a kind glance from somebody.

Honestly, the expression of his face wrung my heart, and I am by no means addicted to emotionalism. The scaffold came in sight at length and then I darted in front and received the condemned man, steadying him once more with an enheartening touch on the shoulder. He needed all the encouragement I could give him, and yet I cannot say his attitude contained any cowardice. I am convinced that it was not fear of death itself, but the sting of its disgrace, that troubled him so much. I gave him very little time for mournful reflections. With the best speed I could muster I slipped the noose over his head, and tightened it round his throat. Then on went the white cap. Meantime my assistant had done that which had hitherto been my only contribution to an execution – i.e., strapped the condemned man's ankles together.

One quick glance round. All seemed in order. For the moment I had lost the feeling of novelty in my situation. All my faculties were concentrated on no other end but to despatch poor Davis as quickly as possible and rid him of the agony of mind he was undergoing. My assistant sprang clear of the trapdoors. The chaplain's chanting, which I had hitherto failed to notice, suddenly took a hold on my hearing. Then my hand darted to the lever and I pulled. Davis died at once. There was not the slightest quiver of the rope, so I knew he had had a mercifully instantaneous and painless death.

All my anxieties and fears had come to naught, and judging by the remarks of those present I had every reason to be satisfied with myself. It is a strange feeling to realise for the first time that at the bidding of the law, you have deliberately held chief responsibility in taking away another man's life. Even my wife who, as I have already said, never displayed any particular liking or interest in my work, must have felt something of this, for she questioned me closely about it all when I returned – a thing she had never done before nor ever repeated. I felt glad, not only for my own sake, but also on behalf of those who had to mourn for Davis, that I could honestly say all had gone off decorously and well.

Chapter 8

The Last Request of John Dickman

(John Alexander Dickman, Newcastle, 1910)

Was John Dickman an innocent victim of the scaffold? Was the right man found guilty of the famous Newcastle train murder? Many times I have heard and read discussions on the topic and must confess I have been inclined to smile at the heat with which some debaters claimed that Dickman was only found guilty on flimsy circumstantial evidence and because of that he should never have been hanged. Let me begin this article by declaring my belief that John Alexander Dickman whom I hanged was guilty of the murder of Mr John Innes Nisbet and I speak with knowledge.

Dickman was a man who earned nothing but the dislike of the warders and others whose duty it was to look after him during his last days. They, as always, did their duty in this respect in the kindest possible manner but there was something about Dickman that alienated sympathy. Folk may take it from me that never did a rogue deserve less credence for his protestation of innocence than this man.

The victim of the train murder was a clerk and book keeper in the employ of Stobswood Colliery Company and it was part of his duties to go every alternate Friday to a Newcastle bank and draw a sum of money for the payment of wages to the men who worked in the mine near Widdrington. Sometimes he carried as much as a thousand pounds, and he almost invariably travelled from Newcastle to Widdrington by slow train that left Central Station at 10.27 every morning.

He went by this train as usual on the morning of Friday 18 March 1910 but owing to a coal strike was not carrying quite so much money as he generally did. He had £370 9s 6d on this occasion, the coin being in canvas bags, which were all put into a small, locked leather bag. Two cashiers – Hall and Spink – were also travelling on the same errand as Nisbet but to their respective collieries. Hall, on looking out of the window just before the train started, saw Nisbet coming along the platform with another man wearing a light overcoat, and noticed Nisbet open the door and his companion in the coat boarded the train. Mr Nisbet was a married man, 44 years of age, of slight build and of inoffensive disposition. He was the last man in the world to be likely to have enemies hating him sufficiently to murder him. His domestic happiness was such that it was his wife's custom to go to Heaton Station every time her husband was travelling through, the station being close to the Nisbet's home and she did so for the last time on the morning of 18 March. It had far-reaching consequences.

Nisbet usually travelled in the rear of the train but on this occasion his wife found he was near the engine and he put his head out of the window to attract her notice. The compartment was quite close to the tunnel and a shadow fell on the seat of the carriage but Mrs Nisbet still noticed a man with his coat collar turned up who never moved. On the train's arrival at Alnmouth the foreman porter, William Charlton, on opening the door of the third compartment in the first carriage made a gruesome discovery. From under the seat came three streams of blood and in his bending down he discovered the body of a man lying face downwards and pushed as far back as possible. Murder had been committed. That was plainly evident, for the unfortunate man had been shot in the head no fewer than five times and a pair of broken spectacles showed that life had not been surrendered without a struggle.

Two bullets were embedded in the head and it was found that one of these was nickel-capped and the other lead, and that they were of different calibres led to the conclusion that two revolvers had been used. But no traces of the weapons themselves were found, and I may add that they have never been found to this day. A soft felt hat on the door of the carriage led to the identification of the dead man. It was Mr Nisbet and the money he had carried was gone. Like the weapons that caused his death, this money, except for a few pounds, has also never been traced. The murdered man was a trusted servant of the colliery company, which promptly offered a reward of £100 for the discovery of the murderer.

Then came a valuable clue. A local artist named Mr Wilson Hepple came forward and told how, while on the Central Station on the morning of 18 March he saw a man whom he did not know was Nisbet go with a man who he did know – Dickman. Mr Hepple saw them at the door of the third class compartment close to the engine. Detective Inspector Tait at once went to the house of John Alexander Dickman in Jesmond to question him. He held no warrant for his arrest nor did the police really suspect him at that time. They just wanted to know if Dickman had been in Mr Nisbet's company and whether, if so, he could throw any light in his mysterious fate.

After some conversation Dickman told the inspector he had seen Nisbet on the morning of the murder, had booked his ticket at the same time, had travelled by the same train but had not seen him after the train had started, as he did not travel in the same compartment. The detective suggested that Dickman should go with him to see Superintendent Weddell and Dickman agreed willingly. 'I shan't be long. I shall be back for tea' he said to his wife as she left. But he never returned again.

When he saw Superintendent Weddell at the County Police headquarters at Gosforth just outside Newcastle he made a statement that helped to hang him. Dickman stated that he took a return ticket for Stannington and that Nisbet who he knew, was in the booking hall at the same time. Dickman bought a sporting newspaper at the bookstall then went to the refreshment room, and afterward took a seat in a third class compartment near the end of the train. He passed Stannington Station without noticing it and got out at Morpeth. After starting to walk back to Stannington he was taken ill and returned to Morpeth to catch the 1.12pm train back to Newcastle. This he missed but caught the 1.40pm train instead. He claimed the object of his journey was to see Mr Hogg at Dovecote Colliery.

This statement being in contradiction to evidence already in the possession of the police, they now began to entertain serious suspicions about him and he was placed under arrest. Dickman protested 'I don't understand the proceedings' he said calmly, 'It's absurd to make it. I can only say I absolutely deny it. It was first of all Mr Hepple's statement that raised the doubt in the minds of the police about Dickman's truthfulness. Mr Hepple declared most positively that he had seen Dickman talking to Nisbet at the door of a compartment, and yet Dickman said he spoke to nobody. Strenuous efforts were made by the accused man and his counsel to damage Mr Hepple's testimony, but as the latter had known Dickman for many years and was only standing 18 feet away when he saw Dickman at the station, the point went dead against the accused.

Now that the first move had been made by the arrest of Dickman, other links in the chain began to be quickly joined up. In his possession was found £17 9s 11d, a discovery which bore double significance. In the first place, Dickman was known to be very hard up; in the second place, some of the money was in a bag, stamped as belonging to Lambton & Co and Mr Nisbet had been given just such a bag at the bank that morning when he fetched the wages money.

The leather bag in which Mr Nisbet was carrying the smaller bags of coin was subsequently found in the bottom of a disused pitshaft between Stannington and Morpeth, and it will be remembered that Dickman had himself said he walked between those two places on the morning the crime was committed. A large hole had been cut in, leaving the lock still secure. The colliery manager was able to say that Dickman knew of the existence of the Isabella Pit and of the collection of water in it and that he knew Dickman personally, they had been fellow workmen.

All this was not direct proof that Dickman had thrown the bag down the pit, but it was strong presumptive evidence. Item by item came other small discoveries and the net closed around Dickman. Amongst the clothing seized by the police at Dickman's house were a pair of trousers and a pair of suede gloves, which were found to have blood stains on them. These gloves were the subject of cross examination at the trial during which Dickman stated that the gloves had fitted badly and had been discarded some three months previously. Why or how the bloodstains had been found on them he could give no explanation. Blood stains were also found on the inside of a trouser pocket he suggested may have come from a nose bleed or after cutting his corns.

Many other points of circumstantial evidence kept cropping up. The appointment Dickman claimed he had with Mr Hogg at Dovecoat Colliery was a falsehood. Mr Hogg knew of no appointment. The most unassailable part of the case for the prosecution lay in those who identified Dickman as the man in the light overcoat, last seen in the murdered man's company. Not only did Mr Hepple recognise Dickman, Mr Hall the cashier identified Dickman without hesitation from a line up of nine men. More damning still was Mrs Nisbet's own identification of Dickman in the Magistrate's Court when after she had given her evidence, and was turning to leave the box when she suddenly fainted after she caught a profile view of the face of the man in the dock – the same profile she had seen in the dark corner of the train carriage compartment at Heaton.

The small things made up a terrible list. They convicted him in the eyes of the jury. There were so many small incriminating things that the newspapers were unable to describe them all in their reports of the trial and as a consequence the impression got abroad that the evidence was not complete enough to justify conviction on the capital charge. Dickman fostered this belief stating that he had been unjustly convicted claiming 'I am entirely innocent of this cruel deed'. He appealed against his conviction but failed and the machinery of the law was set in motion to carry out the death sentence. The Under Sheriff of Northumberland Mr E G Harvey wrote to me offering me the choice of two days for Dickman's execution, I accepted Tuesday 9 August.

On Monday 8 August I set off for Newcastle Upon Tyne and as I stepped out at the Central Station – that place that had played such a conspicuous part in the story – I could almost feel the city's excitement over the event that was fixed to take place inside its confines the following morning. There were thousands of people congregated outside the grim Newcastle gaol as I and my assistant arrived, and they were all greatly excited after only a few minutes earlier a cab had arrived at the prison entrance and Mrs Dickman, the condemned man's wife, stepped out. At the sight of her those in the crowd who were convinced of Dickman's guilt gave evidence of their hatred of her husband until she disappeared through the big black gates. They were still so moved over this incident that my assistant and I entered unrecognised.

When I got inside I was informed that Mrs Dickman was having her last interview with her husband. At the end, so I learned, Mrs Dickman wanted to kiss the condemned man but this was contrary to prison regulations. When she had gone I went to have my customary peep at the condemned man, taking my assistant with me. Dickman was living his last few hours in the hospital, which is a big room capable of holding twenty-six convicts, though of course Dickman was the only one kept there at the time. The door was purposely left ajar so that I could peer in without attracting the doomed man's attention, and my first glance was directed with professional purpose at his neck. It was an extraordinary strong one – a thick, muscular 'bull' neck – and consequently I had to decide on a rather longer drop than his weight (160 lbs) and height (5 ft. 5in.) would otherwise have permitted. I mentally resolved to give him a 7ft 1in. drop.

He was quite a decent looking broad-shouldered man, and his smart moustache and well brushed hair gave him the appearance of a respectable businessman. Hs true character, though peeped out in his expression and demeanour. They were typical of a man who lacked humane feelings and he impressed me as looking the very sort of man who would do any mortal thing to gain his own ends. I had soon seen enough of him and gave way to my assistant. Unfortunately, he gave the door a push while he was glancing through and to my consternation the door banged wide open. Plucking my assistant by the arm I pulled him round the corner out of sight of Dickman, who had been startled by the sudden opening of the door. He jumped to his feet and rushed almost out upon us shouting 'Does anyone want to see me?' The officers inside, realising what had happened calmed the suddenly excited man and led him back into the room assuring him 'It was nothing'.

Next morning I was early to rise. My assistant and I visited the scaffold about 6.30 and put things in order there. We pulled up the sack of sand which had been suspended all night at the end of the rope to test its strength and remove any stretch or twists that might be in it. Then I measured off the rope for a 7ft 1inch drop, pulled the lever once or twice to release the trapdoors and see they were working smoothly. Other minor details were attended to and at last we left the grim shed standing all in readiness to receive its victim. I made a startling discovery as I crossed the prison yard on my way back. I could see a man perched on a house roof overlooking the prison and he was gazing in our direction with evident intention of watching the execution. I immediately pointed him out to an officer standing by, and he raced off to inform the Governor. 'You must fetch him off" exclaimed the Governor, an order that was easier to make than carry out.

An officer was sent to the house in question but the man on the roof, who proved to be an enterprising journalist, absolutely declined to budge. He said the prison officers had no jurisdiction over that house as it was private property, which was true enough. After much heated parleying the warders retired defeated and the triumphant pressman seated himself more firmly still on his dangerous perch. But his ingenuity availed him nothing. Executions are no longer things to pander to the morbid taste with. They are private now in every sense of the word, and the Governor was prepared to go to any length to prevent that journalist from gaining an unlicensed peep at Dickman's execution. A large sheet of canvas was hung by hooks from a wall to completely block out the view of the execution shed. This done we all breathed freely again. I had to admire the journalist's daring cleverness, but I was not sorry that there was now no danger of a lurid 'eye witness' version of the execution.

While all this was going on Dickman, who knew nothing about the incident, was under the ministrations of the chaplain. Alas, the poor cleric was making little impression on the hardened heart of the condemned man. A few minutes before the final moment when we were to enter to take Dickman forth to the scaffold, the chaplain put a despairing question to him. 'Dickman' he said solemnly, 'Will you die with a lie on your lips?' 'I will say nothing' he replied firmly.

Then came the moment when the door was pushed open and I approached the doomed man to pinion him. As soon as he saw me he buttoned up his coat in such a strange, venomous fashion that I wondered if it was his purpose to resist. 'We are ready' I said gently and getting behind him I quickly strapped his wrists together at the back. I was glad this had been accomplished so quickly and with so little trouble, for frankly, I was expecting resistance but as I was opening his shirt at the neck he suddenly stretched himself up and exclaimed 'I am not going to die with my coat on. I am going to pull it off'. My mind acted swiftly. Should I accede or refuse? It was unprecedent to take the pinioning straps off once they were on; but this was a situation that was of itself unprecedented. There was a nasty gleam in the man's eyes, and I foresaw dire trouble with him unless he had his own way. Above all things I meant to avoid an unseemly scene and so without a word I stepped round behind him and took off the straps, leaving him free to remove his coat. Why he would not die in it I cannot say. Who can account for a man's actions in such an extremity.

The coat was removed with calm deliberation and on went the straps again. He made not a murmur after that. The scaffold was quite a long way from his cell, but he never spoke a word as he covered the ground with a firm step. I was waiting on the scaffold for him when he arrived and within a few seconds he was dead. His execution on evidence of an admitted purely circumstantial character led to quite a revival of the agitation for the abolition of capital punishment but I wish I was as sure as of many things as I am sure of Dickman's guilt.

Chapter 9

Dr Crippen

(Hawley Harvey Crippen, Pentonville, 1910)

Now that the Crippen affair is a thing of the past I can afford to smile at my own agitation over it but it is a positive fact that it was about the only time in my life that I almost regretted the office I held. It was purely a personal question. To doubt as to Dr Crippen's guilt ever entered my mind. My troubles centred in the extremely unpleasant notoriety that I was endowed with because it was I who was to hang the man who had caused the sensation of the day.

Crippen! What thrills the name recalls. Even now its owner needs no introduction. Everybody knows something about him – his cold blooded dissection of his wife's body in the cellar of his house in Hilldrop Crescent, his flight with Ethel le Neve dressed in boy's clothes, and his dramatic arrest through the intervention of wireless telegraphy after an exciting race across the Atlantic by Chief Inspector Dew. These things in broad outline are familiar fact but it is my part to tell how this man faced doom on the scaffold.

Some folk found Crippen guilty in their own minds long before he was captured, and during all the excitement of those days when it seemed possible that he might yet escape the sleuthhounds of the law, there was never any question as to whether he was guilty or not. It was merely, will he be captured?

But when he did at last come before the Bar of Justice the cocksure ones got nervous. For it is one thing to believe a man guilty and a different thing to prove it. Then when these doubts disappeared and the man was sentenced to death the reaction in public excitement sent unwelcome attention in my direction. For once in a way the hangman was one of the most conspicuous personages in the kingdom. It was a popularity I did not relish in the slightest. I hardly dared to stir out of the house, not because there was the slightest danger but for the opposite reason that I was too popular. Whenever I went out people would point at men and tell their friends in awestruck accents – 'That's him! That's the man who is going to hang Crippen!'

It was the reverse of pleasant. The worst of it was that I was particularly open to being approached by the morbidly curious for I kept a barber's shop at that time and my saloon was always crowded with men who came for no other reason than to see me and talk to me. Even when the execution was over and done with, it by no means put a stop to this influx of curious questioners. In fact, for a time it got worse. They wanted to know all Crippen had said and done. 'How did he go?' 'Did he confess?' 'Was he nervous?' etc. These and a hundred other questions were put to me by people in all conditions of life and even the newspapers have articles that purported to be character sketches of my personality.

All this was extremely odious to me. I have always seen that it was my duty to keep silent over things that happened during the carrying out of my duties and so I had no compunction about snubbing those who pestered me with questions about Crippen. I was also averse to notoriety on the streets and the newspapers because I never wished the impression to be gained that I unduly gloried in my work. I was never ashamed of it, but still I took no personal merit in executing a murderer. I was merely the humble instrument of the law.

Dr Hawley Harvey Crippen was an American and his medical degree was granted by an American college so he was hardly on the same high footing as our own doctors and lent himself to all kinds of patent medicine institutions which our own medical men would not be allowed to be associated with. While still in America – in 1892 to be precise – he married his second wife – Cora Turner, who was known on the stage as Belle Elmore.

The couple came to live at Hilldrop Crescent, in North London in 1905. At the time when the main incidents in the story occurred Crippen would have been 47 years of age. He was quite a short man, less than 5 ft. 4 inches in height, and by no means good looking. His hair was scant and inclined to be sandy and there was a bald patch on the top of his head. He had a straggling sort of moustache and eyes when behind his spectacles had a rather bulbous look. His nose had a flat bridge and taken altogether he was a slovenly and by no means a captivating man.

Be that as it may, he was known among his friends as a kindly, human man, and he managed to secure the affections of his young typist Ethel le Neve. Herein lay the seat of the trouble. Outwardly he maintained and air of affection for Belle Elmore, but inwardly he raged against being tied to her when his heart called him elsewhere. Ethel knew he was married but believed his tales that Belle Elmore was entirely out of sympathy with him, and when one day in 1910, he told her that Belle had gone away to California she willingly agreed to act as his housekeeper at Hilldrop Crescent.

Belle's friends however were very surprised to hear of her sudden departure without a word of farewell to any of them, and were still surprised when there appeared an announcement in a theatrical paper to the effect that Mrs Crippen had died in California on March 23. So it happened that some of these friends met in New York in May, and being very uneasy, they wrote to California to verify Belle's death. The reply from the Chief of Police in Los Angeles stated emphatically:

In reply to yours, no person named Crippen or Belle Elmore has died here.

Where then, was she? What had become of her since the night of 31 January, when she helped to entertain some friends at a card party at Hilldrop Crescent? She was then her usual vivacious self, but had said nothing of an impending journey. From that night nobody had seen her and her death which her husband said had occurred at Los Angeles, was proven a myth. Suspicious, one of the friends called on Dr Crippen as soon as he got back from the states and received such contradictory explanations of the mystery from the agitated doctor that he went straight to Scotland Yard and reported the matter, and he and a police sergeant went to see Dr Crippen at the latter's place of business. No doubt he had shook when he learned his callers profession, but probably he felt that, having kept his guilty secret intact for six months, he could safely continue to do so. So he adopted a tone of false frankness: 'I will tell you the truth', he said 'So far as I know, she is not dead at all!' This was an admission that he had been telling lies all along, but he had a fine story ready to explain this away:

'For a long time my wife had threatened that she would leave me for a man who, she said, could keep her in a better style. On 31 January, the day before I wrote to the Guild, [Cora was secretary of the Ladies' Music Hall Guild] Mr and Mrs Martinetti came to our house for dinner, and after they had left my wife began to abuse me and said she was tired of me, and that she meant to leave me next day and that I should never hear from her again. Next day, on returning from my surgery, I found she had carried out her threat. I sat down to think how to cover up the scandal and wrote a letter to the Guild saying that she had gone away. I afterwards said she was ill, and later that she had died of pneumonia in California. All these statements were untrue, but I made them to spare the feelings of her friends.'

The detective suggested that in order to be fully satisfied it would be better for him to search the house at Hilldrop Crescent and Dr Crippen readily agreed. So they went through the house and found nothing! At one moment they were possibly on the verge of discovering something in the cellar but Crippen got them out of it before they suspected anything. 'Well', said Inspector Dew, 'we must try to find your wife. I suggest the insertion of an advertisement in the papers asking for her whereabouts.' 'Certainly' replied Crippen with alacrity and accordingly the following advertisement appeared in the press:

Will Belle Elmore communicate with HHC, or authorities at once. Serious trouble through your absence.

But poor Belle Elmore could never communicate with anybody again, as the wily doctor knew well enough and the police found too – when it was almost too late. For when Inspector Dew went round to the house again several days later Crippen had disappeared, and it was not long before that grim cellar delivered up its dreadful secret. For remains which were afterwards proved to be those of Belle Elmore were dug up from under the flagstones that day.

At once the hue and cry was raised. The newspapers were taken into Scotland Yard's confidence and the public were immediately informed of the discovery of the crime and the necessity for information about the missing doctor. A reward of £250 was offered, and the wanted man's description was circulated all over the world. For a fortnight the only topic everywhere was 'Where is Crippen?' Detectives, both professional and amateur, took up the hunt, the newspapers spurred them on and every kind of rumour, theory and possibility was exhaustively investigated. Yet Crippen remained at large.

Then came a staggering happening. From the centre of the Atlantic Ocean a message winged its way to land to declare that Crippen was on board the SS *Montrose*! Wireless telegraphy had for the first time in the world's history led to a murderer's capture. The message came from Captain Kendall of the SS *Montrose*, whose ship had been boarded at Antwerp by a man and his 'son' travelling under the name of Robinson. At that time the papers were full of the Crippen affair, and Captain Kendall suspected these Robinsons. The 'boys' figure was curiously girl like.

Communicating his suspicions to a few of his trustworthy officers, they all set to work to watch the suspected couple. Captain Kendall found that the man would often forget that his name was Robinson and both he and his 'son' seemed unaccountably nervous at first. At last the captain was convinced that the man, despite his lack of moustache, was Dr Crippen and the 'boy' Ethel le Neve. Captain Kendall waited for one final clue before being absolutely convinced. The police description of the wanted doctor stated that he possessed false teeth. Had Mr Robinson false teeth? A ruse was hit upon to settle this point. The captain laid himself to get Robinson to open his mouth in a hearty laugh and one day he told an especially funny tale which achieved that object. Sure enough, false teeth glinted in Mr Robinson's mouth. The chain was complete and Captain Kendall sent the telegram.

Scotland Yard moved at once. Within a remarkably short space of time Inspector Dew was steaming out of the Mersey on board the SS *Laurentic*, a White Star Liner, whose mission it was to race the SS *Montrose* across the Atlantic to arrest Crippen before he landed in Canada. The whole world held its breath during that dramatic race and the only unconcerned persons were the passengers on the Montrose who were ignorant of what was happening. SS *Laurentic* reached Canada first and it only remained for Dew to devise a scheme of securing Crippen's arrest before he suspected his disguise to be penetrated. It was customary for ships like the *Montrose* that were bound up the St Lawrence river for Quebec to take on board a pilot at Father Point. When the SS *Montrose* hove into sight on 31 July – eight days after Captain Kendall's first wireless message to Liverpool – Dew went off to her with two other officers, all dressed at ship's pilots, the real pilot making the boat's fourth passenger.

Crippen watched the arrival of the skiff without anticipating the real nature of the men aboard but when they boarded the SS *Montrose* and one of them turned towards him Crippen recognised Inspector Dew and knew the game was up. He had the wisdom to say nothing when the nature of the charge was read out to him, but the poor girl at his side fainted at the horror of the discovery of her lovers' real nature. The SS *Magantic* took the principals in this life drama back to England, where they had their parts to play in subsequent proceedings. Then a new obsession crossed the public mind. It was doubted if the evidence would be strong enough legally to convict Crippen of the crime which everybody was morally convinced he had committed.

It had to be proved that the remains were really those of Belle Elmore, and some stronger connection between them and Dr Crippen than had hitherto been recorded had to be produced. Both things were forthcoming. Science stepped in and figuratively speaking, put the rope round Crippen's neck. Dr Augustus Pepper the Home Office pathologist, after an exhaustive examination of the few fragments of flesh found buried in the cellar produced a description of a woman in the prime of life, somewhat stout, who wore hair that had been bleached. This fitted Belle Elmore but it could also fit many other women. The clinching point in his description was that the woman had undergone an operation, for he found a scar on a piece of the flesh which he believed to be the lower part of the abdomen. Belle Elmore had just such a scar from an operation.

Her identity proved, it now remained to connect the accused man with the remains. Here again science gave the connecting link. A chemist declared that Dr Crippen had purchased a deadly poison from him called hyoscine and made a declaration in the poisons book that was afterward found to be false.

Dr William Willcox was also sent sample of the remains and palpable traces of hyoscine were detected. Crippen made one other fatal slip. He had buried with the remains a bit of the arm piece of a suit of pyjamas and the trouser portion of this self same suit was found upstairs in Crippen's boxes. The case for the prosecution was indeed a masterpiece but the defence created quite a sensation by the bold move of placing the accused man himself in the witness box. If anything, however, Crippen still prejudiced the case against himself, for his behaviour there was such as to call forth rebuke from the Lord Chief Justice.

Crippen went on the plan of boldly admitting that he had told lies about his wife's death, but said he did it to 'save her good name'. When cross-examined on his hypocrisy in pretending to mourn her death when he said he knew she was alive was merely laughed at in Court. He declared that he still believed her to be alive and put forward the theory that the remains in the cellar had been put there by somebody else during his occasional absences from home. 'I know it doesn't sound probable' he said, 'but nevertheless it is possible'. The jury however believed this story to be neither probable nor possible and that it was Belle Elmore and that Crippen had foully murdered her and passed their verdict accordingly.

Crippen went deadly pale and sank back into his chair in the dock as the fateful words were spoken. His mouth twitched and his eyes bulged further out and all together he was a piteous figure of collapse. 'I still protest my innocence' he said abjectly before sentence was passed and one of the warders in attendance upon him told me that when that dread ordeal was over and he went below out of sight of the spectators in court he completely collapsed. A few days later Ethel le Neve was placed on trial for being an accessory after the fact, but after five hours hearing, during which she was brilliantly defended by Frederick Smith [created Earl of Birkenhead in 1922], she was acquitted. She was obviously an inexperienced young girl who had been completely deluded by her unscrupulous lover.

Arrangements for the execution were at once made. On the Monday following the Saturday on which Crippen was sentenced to death Mr Metcalfe, the Under Sheriff wrote to me asking if I would undertake the execution, which was provisionally fixed to take place at Pentonville on Tuesday 8 November. I wired acceptance, but Crippen appealed against his sentence and the execution was cancelled. It was about this time that I began to be pestered by questioners and I was so worried about it all I almost felt tempted to throw up the job. Rumours also went around that Belle Elmore was actually alive and had been seen in New York. Quite a number of folk were ready to believe this might be true but Judges in the Appeal Court were evidently certain that Crippen had murdered her, for they dismissed his appeal and it was decided that he must hang on 23 November.

There was a fortnight between receiving notification of this date and the fatal day and it was a fortnight of sheer mental agony. To a man of my mental temperament the amount of pestering to which I was subjected meant so much real torture. Quite a number of men lay under sentence of death at that period. In Pentonville Prison itself there were actually three other condemned men. They were still under the shadow of death after Crippen paid the penalty, but two of them were subsequently reprieved. The remaining man, Noah Woolf was duly hanged by me on the morning of 21 December.

I arrived in London from Lancashire in good time before the prescribed arrival time of 4.00pm on the afternoon preceding Crippen's execution and entered Pentonville unobserved. I went through the usual formalities of interviewing the governor and the doctor and viewing the scaffold. From them and other officers I learned that the condemned murderer had been deeply disappointed when he found that all hope of a reprieve must be dismissed from his mind. He seemed to have convinced himself that he would never be hanged and when the truth came home he was on the verge of total nervous collapse.

Terrible though the shock was, he soon controlled his feelings once more and became his old cool, calculating self, a fact of which we were to have startling evidence that very night. The peephole in his cell door provided me with means of observing him and as I gazed in at the man I marvelled at his calmness. He sat there writing and would occasionally break off to chat pleasantly and in a most affable fashion with the warders whose duty it was to watch him night and day until the scaffold claimed him. Even though he was garbed in the hideous clothes of a convict, Crippen possessed a dignity that Smith of the 'Brides in the Bath' case never equalled, though he tried hard to ape the gentleman. Smith was one whose mannerisms annoyed me, but I will say this for Crippen, he had a natural amiability and innate gentlemanliness that even seized the affections of his warders.

I daresay this impression of the man will be absolutely new to most readers who will have been accustomed to look upon Crippen as a monster in human guise but I speak of men as I find them. Crippen undoubtedly committed a hideous crime which admits no excuse but he had two sides to his nature, and it was the pleasant only that was uppermost during my contact with him. Yet, that very night he showed that behind his suave graciousness lay power to make firm life and death decisions. Just before midnight one of the warders in that silent cell had an awful discovery. Crippen was in bed and the men watching his progress through his last night on earth felt uneasy at Crippen's restless motions. The strain on warders in such a position is a most intense one and these men would have been superhuman if they had not felt overweighted with the responsibility that was resting upon their shoulders.

At last one of them went to Crippen's bedside to satisfy himself that his charge's movements were nothing more than the usual restless thrashings of a condemned man on his last night, but to his amazement he found he was just in time to deny the scaffold its victim. For some reason never explained Crippen had been allowed to retain his glasses and the determined man had deliberately broken one of the lenses with the intention of using the jagged edge to cut his throat. This was discovered when the warder, seeing that Crippen's glasses were not in their usual place had asked him where they were. 'They are here' he replied, pointing under the bedclothes. He was at once ordered to get out of bed and the frame with one of the lenses broken out of it was then found. This act was about the only one Crippen ever did that caused his custodians any trouble, for he was a most considerate prisoner, never making unnecessary trouble and always doing exactly what he was told. His attempt to commit suicide threw the prison officers into further throes of anxiety, but the execution hour arrived without any other untoward incidents.

That morning I arose about 6.30 and got everything in readiness on the scaffold. When I was engaged by Mr Metcalfe he told me that Crippen's height was 5 ft. 4 inches and his weight 136 lb and he suggested a drop of 7 ft. 6 inches. After my observations of the condemned man in his cell we decided to allow a drop of 7 ft. 9 inches. I accordingly measured off the rope and put everything in the death chamber in readiness for administering the supreme punishment. It was a dark, cold and foggy morning but notwithstanding a large crowd gathered outside the prison. As a matter of fact they were not even to have the doubtful satisfaction of hearing the death toll on the prison bell. This usually begins to ring as the procession leaves the condemned cell for the scaffold but out of kindly consideration for the feelings of the other three men there under sentence of death it was decided to drop the custom on this occasion. This decision was typical of the way in which the prison authorities everywhere try to spare condemned men anything that will cause them undue mental suffering.

Dr Crippen was up early and was given his own clothes to dress in. For the last time he donned his famous grey frock coat and was taken forth to the Roman Catholic chapel to attend a special service at which apart from the priest and three warders he was the only participant. His face throughout wore a set, calm expression. His warders looked more distressed than he was and nobody glancing at him would have realised that this was the man who had committed such a fearful murder, had attempted to commit suicide a few hours earlier and in an hour and a half would have to walk to the gallows from which he would not return alive.

Inscrutable though his face was, his thoughts were evidently busy. Whatever may have been their nature they prevented him from doing any sort of justice to the breakfast that awaited him at 8.00am. He knew he had but an hour to live and being a man or more than ordinary intelligence he preferred to spend the time communing with his thoughts. Did he confess? I've been asked that question many a hundred times and my answer is always the same. So far as I know he did not confess.

The fatal hour of 9.00am was almost upon us when the usual knot of officials gathered in silence outside the condemned cell door. A grave nod of the head from Mr Metcalfe and I knew what was expected of me. The door was thrown open and I and my assistant entered. Crippen was sitting down in a corner of the cell with officers on each side of him. The first was speaking in low tones, but stopped when he heard us come in.

The condemned man's position was rather awkward from my point of view. He was shielded by the table and a chair and I had to shift both out of the way before I could get to him. This naturally wasted a few seconds, and seconds seem like hours at such a time. The doomed man rose without a word when he saw my purpose and placed not the slightest hindrance in my way as I began to pinion him. He wore no lined collar, of course, but even so he looked very smart and dapper. Neither had he been shaved and yet he looked much than men in his situation usually do. You may be sure I wasted no time in observing him. The things I've mentioned merely flash across my mind as I swiftly strapped his wrists behind his back and saw his neck was fully bared. Then I initiated a new feature at executions – I left the condemned cell at once and proceeded to the scaffold alone. I mentioned having done this at various executions but it was when Crippen went to the gallows this further humane procedure was first put to use.

I had got the idea the previous evening from the chief warder. Hitherto the executioner always walked behind the condemned man but this time I left Crippen to come to the scaffold in charge of my assistant and the Under Sheriff etc while I having sped on in front was ready on the scaffold waiting for Crippen to arrive. The saving in time and the avoidance of confusion when the scaffold was reached were so noticeable that ever afterwards I used the same system at every execution I officiated at. As I stood on the scaffold I could see the procession come into view twelve yards distant. Behind the praying priest came the notorious Dr Crippen, no longer a murderer to fear but rather a man to be pitied. Yet his attitude was not that of one who asks for sympathy. If he had ever shown cowardice or collapse he displayed none now.

I could see him smiling as he approached and the smile never left his face up to the moment when I threw the white cap over it and blotted out God's light from his eyes forever. On a trice he was on the trap-doors with his legs strapped together and a rope round his neck. One swift glance round to be assured that all was right and my hand shot to push the lever. Thud! The fatal doors had fallen. The slack rope tightened and in an instant was still. Dr Crippen was dead. He had never spoken in my hearing. There was no second appeal for mercy from his Maker – no last minute admission of guilt. He crossed the threshold without a word or a sign.

The prison doctor was afterwards inclined to argue with me, his contention being that I had given too long a drop. He based this argument on the fact that his post mortem examination showed every bone in Crippen's neck had been broken. On my part I held that this was rather a good sign as it showed that the man had died absolutely instantaneously.

Chapter 10

The Most Trying Week In My Career

(Thomas Rawcliffe, Lancaster Castle; Henry Thompson, Liverpool; and William Broome, Reading, 1910)

The 'Crippen period!' – the latter part of 1920 – was notoriously productive in the criminal sense. There was hardly an Assize in any part of the country where a death sentence had not to be delivered.

Strangely enough, quite an abnormal number of these condemned men narrowly escaped the scaffold through the medium of eleventh-hour reprieves. Nevertheless, I carried out the death sentence on no fewer than four men in nine days in that hectic November when Crippen paid the penalty, and three of those executions occurred on successive days.

When I add that these executions were carried out in places as far apart as Liverpool, London and Reading you will realise that I had no sinecure on those three days.

The first case in the series of four need not take long in describing, though it contained one or two unusual features. The man who suffered was Thomas Rawcliffe, and his chief claim to distinction lies in the fact that his execution at Lancaster Castle on 15 November 1910, was the first time for 25 years that a man had died on the scaffold in that ancient prison.

Rawcliffe had gone up to a policeman one morning, and told him he had strangled his wife the night before. A pathetic sight greeted the eyes of the officers who investigated this confession, for the dead woman's body lay in bed, with her living baby lying innocently by her side. Rawcliffe supplemented his admission by declaring that he and his wife had agreed to die together, and that he had tried to take his own life by swallowing rat poison. Some support for this story was forthcoming in the discovery of a bottle of rat poison in the house.

The plea for the defence that Rawcliffe was not responsible for his actions owing to a serious injury he had once received to his head failed to save the accused man, though it procured him the jury's recommendation to mercy. This was backed by a petition containing 1600 signatures, but a reprieve was denied, and at 8 am on November 15 Rawcliffe stood upon the scaffold. The execution was not as smoothly conducted as were the generality of such ceremonies owing probably to the morning being so eerily dark that it was difficult to see anything clearly. Unhappily, the doomed man's nerves were not equal to the strain of the slight delay which was thus caused, and he fainted, and almost fell into my arms. I had to keep him up with the aid of the rope around his neck, and then, signalling to my assistant to get out of the way, I jumped to the lever and delivered Rawcliffe out of his mental agony.

When Rawcliffe paid the extreme penalty there were quite a number of murderers lying under sentence of death all over the country, but those who were to expiate their crimes on the scaffold were weeded down by reprieve to three. These three went to the scaffold on successive days, one of them being the famous Dr Crippen.

I have already fully described the last named famous affair, so there is no need to recapitulate it. But the influence of this notorious criminal could be strongly discerned in the case of Henry Thompson whom I hanged at Liverpool on the day before Crippen was executed at Pentonville. The third case, that of Broome, 'The Slough Murderer', had characteristics all its own, for it retains an element of doubt even to this day.

For the sake of clearness let me, before describing them in detail, set out the dates of these important executions which followed so quickly upon each other. They took place as follows:

Nov. 15 – Thos. Rawcliffe, executed at Lancaster.
Nov. 22 – Hy. Thompson, executed at Liverpool.
Nov. 23 – Crippen, executed at Pentonville.
Nov. 24 – William Broome, executed at Reading.

Leaving the Crippen murder out, the other three affairs – those of Rawcliffe, Thompson, and Broome – were all strangely alike in one detail. Each of their victims died by strangulation. This method of committing murder is a rare one in criminal history, and it is really remarkable that three almost contemporary cases should be alike in this respect.

Henry Thompson's victim was his wife and he himself was as callous a man as ever went to a well-deserved death on the scaffold.

This may be judged from the way in which he echoed 'Amen!' in mockery at the end of the pronouncement of the awful death sentence. He and his wife lived in York Street, Liverpool, where their life was a sordid round of drink and quarrels. Thompson undoubtedly behaved like a brute to his wife, and had indeed made an attempt on her life some five or six years prior to the ultimate tragedy.

One Saturday night she flies terror-stricken into the room of a woman who lodged in their house and ejaculated, 'For God's sake, let me hide!'

The lodger advised her to get down on her hands and knees and hide between the bed and the wall, but presently Thompson came raging in, and, despite the lodger's declaration that his wife was not in the room, he found the hiding woman and carried her off to their own room.

This was indeed to be a night of horror for the lodger, for presently she heard Mrs Thompson cry out – 'Harry, don't choke me!'

'Mr Thompson, leave the woman alone!' exclaimed the lodger, to which she got the blunt reply – 'Mind your own business!'

Later on in that night of terror the lodger heard mysterious noises in the Thompson's room. There was a sound as if someone was being dragged along the bedroom floor. Then came a silence that terrified her more than anything else.

The secret of that awful Saturday nights' doings was not revealed till the Monday morning. In the meantime nobody saw Mrs Thompson, and Henry Thompson saw to it that nobody but himself entered their room.

The lodger got her opportunity to go in on Monday morning, and, stealing in, she discovered Thompson lying asleep on the bed. Beside him lay the still form of his wife with a red handkerchief over her face. Another neighbour was called in, and in fear and trembling the two women drew away the handkerchief. Murder stood revealed. Mrs Thompson's troubles were over – and her husband still lay sound asleep beside her!

When Henry Thompson awoke a policeman was standing in the room. With a phlegmatic remark he allowed himself to be arrested. At the inquest he offered the theory that his wife died in a fit, explaining that he found her dead in the morning. Doctors, however, attributed death to strangulation, and Thompson was accordingly committed for trial.

The defence was then slightly varied, and an attempt was made to prove the accused irresponsible for his actions, but this failed to influence the jury, who, after only a quarter of an hour's absence, returned with a verdict of guilty.

Then came an extraordinary exhibition of callousness on the part of the prisoner when the Clerk of Assize (Sir Herbert Stephen) asked Thompson whether he had anything to say as to why sentence should not be passed.

'No; let 'em go ahead with it. I don't care. I never was frightened of death', was the prisoner's startling reply. His Lordship, having assumed the black cap, proceeded to address the prisoner.

'Henry Thompson', he began in tones of deep solemnity.

'Yes, my Lord', broke in the prisoner.

'I'm not guilty'.

One of the police ushers here cried 'Silence!'

'I'll not silence', retorted the man in the dock, glaring savagely in the direction of the officer. Then, before the Judge was able to resume, Thompson's voice rang out again – 'I'm not guilty. You can sentence away now!'

John Ellis, 'The Rochdale Hangman' (1874–1932); executioner 1901–1924.

230 OLDHAM ROAD, ROCHDALE.

Oldham Road, Rochdale, where both John Ellis and his father Joe had their barber shops.

The rattling looms of the Lancashire cotton industry. Originally, John Ellis did not want to follow in his father's footsteps and become a barber, so he first found employment at the Eagle Cotton Mill in Balderstone.

John Ellis's Hairdresser, Stationer and Newsagent shop at 413, Oldham Road, Rochdale, with the man himself and one of his daughters in the doorway.

A typical entrance to a condemned cell with adjacent execution chamber in a British prison during the early twentieth century.

Henry Pierrepoint (left) and John Ellis leaving Swansea Prison after the execution of William Foy on 8 May 1909.

Newgate Prison, London as John Ellis would have known it when he trained there to become an executioner in 1901. Demolished in 1904, the site is now occupied by the Central Criminal Court 'The Old Bailey'.

The wood-fronted structure with the glazed panels in the roof to let sunlight in on the right of this photograph is the Newgate Prison execution shed c.1900. The hinged door on the frontage of the shed would be opened to allow officials and invited reporters to watch the execution.

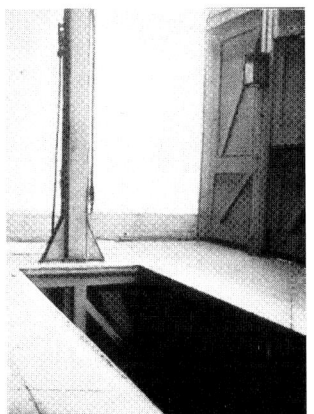

Inside the execution shed were the infamous Newgate gallows where so many infamous criminals were hanged over the years. It was here that Ellis acted as assistant to William Billington at the last execution to be carried out at Newgate — that of George Woolfe on 6 May 1902.

Pentonville Prison, North London c.1905. After the closure of Newgate Prison the gallows were removed and installed at Pentonville where Ellis would hang some of the most infamous murderers of the early twentieth century.

Samuel Dougal 'The Moat Farm Murderer' being removed under arrest from the farmhouse near Clavering, Essex, in 1903.

The crowd outside the Moot Hall, Newcastle upon Tyne, after hearing that sentence of death had been passed on John Dickman 'The Railway Murderer'. 10 July 1910.

The Governor, senior staff and warders at HM Prison Newcastle upon Tyne, c.1910.

Dr Hawley Harvey Crippen, executed by John Ellis at Pentonville Prison at 9.00am on 23 November 1910.

Dr Crippen and Miss Ethel le Neve in the dock at Bow Street Police Court where they were charged with the murder of Crippen's wife, Cora. 1910.

An imaginative artist's impression of Dr Crippen on the cover of *Le Petit Parisien* of 11 December 1910. The Crippen story made international headlines and brought Ellis a great deal of unwanted attention.

Poisoner Frederick Henry Seddon, executed by John Ellis at HM Prison Pentonville on 18 April 1912.

The 'Hooded Man' case. The funeral procession of Parade Inspector Arthur Walls makes its way through streets lined by mourners at Eastbourne on 16 October 1912.

The *Illustrated Police News* feature on the execution of George Ball (alias George Sumner) 'The Liverpool Sack Murderer' by John Ellis at Walton Gaol, Liverpool, on 26 February 1914.

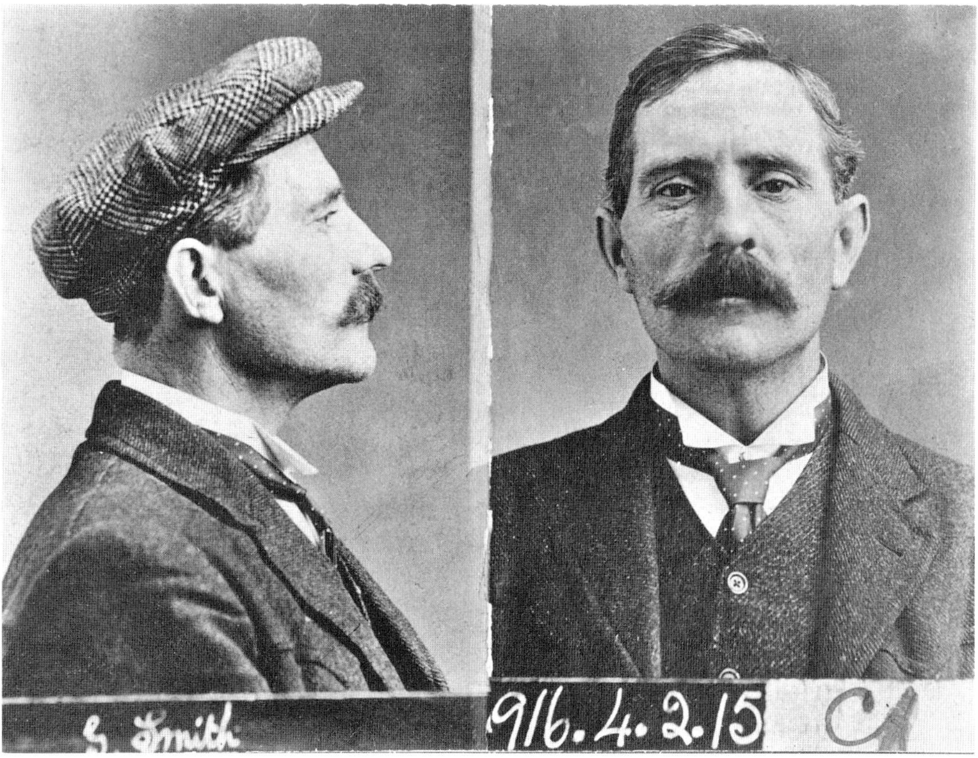

George Joseph Smith, 'The Brides in the Bath Murderer' was executed by John Ellis at HM Prison Maidstone on 13 August 1915.

An artist's impression of murderer George Joseph Smith calling for help after discovering one of his wives 'accidentally drowned' in the bath.

Sir Roger David Casement, who was found guilty of treachery and was hanged by John Ellis at Pentonville on 3 August 1916. Ellis would describe him as '... the bravest man it fell to my unhappy lot to execute'.

Solicitor, Major Herbert Rowse Armstrong, 'The Hay Poisoner' was executed at HMP Gloucester by John Ellis on 31 May 1922.

Henry Jacoby (18) was hanged by Ellis at HMP Pentonville on 7 June 1922. Jacoby's youth in age and his immaturity of mind made Ellis feel 'it was wrong to hang the child'.

Edith Thompson (29) was hanged by John Ellis on 9 January 1923 for her complicity in the murder of her husband by her lover, Freddie Bywaters. Her traumatic execution haunted Ellis for the rest of his life.

Crowds gather outside Holloway Prison on the morning of Edith Thompson's execution on 9 January 1923.

Armley Prison, Leeds, where John Ellis carried out his last execution when he hanged Sheffield murderer, John Eastwood, on 28 December 1923.

John Ellis with his assistant, Leo Scott, ready to demonstrate the hangman's craft at one of Ellis's fairground side show performances.

TRAGIC FATE OF JOHN ELLIS, EX-HANGMAN

The *Illustrated Police News* feature on John Ellis after he tragically took his own life by cutting his throat with one of his razors on Tuesday, 20 September 1932.

In calm but impressive tones his Lordship continued the discharge of his final task —

'The jury have done their part', he said; 'it remains only for me to do mine. The law knows only one sentence for the crime of which you have been convicted.' The customary formula of the capital sentence was then pronounced.

Whilst this was being done the prisoner leaned over the bars of the dock and glared, half in wonderment and half defiantly, at the Judge, and when the latter had closed with the invocation, 'May the Lord have mercy on your soul', Thompson thrust his hands in his pockets, and with mock solemnity ejaculated, 'Amen'. Then as the warders closed around him the condemned man turned flippantly to some of his companions in court, 'So long, Jack!' 'Good-bye', he cried, and with a cheery wave of the hand he disappeared below.

You may well imagine that a man of this type would be a warm handful in prison, and so he proved. He was not violent but he was utterly callous, and played some strange pranks. I learned some extraordinary tales about him when I went to Walton Gaol on the afternoon of November 21, his execution being fixed for the following morning. He declared himself a Buddhist, and as a follower of his cult he often assured the warders that he would return to the prison in the form of a bird.

'I'll come back and have a look at you all!' he assured them.

To me Thompson appeared exactly the type of man I had mentally pictured from all I had read and heard about him. He was rather tall, standing 5 ft. 10 ½ in., but was proportionately well built, scaling at something over 12 stones. He was, in fact, a typical dock labourer in appearance.

As I gazed at him through the cell door spy-hole on the last evening of his life he seemed not a whit perturbed. This was characteristic of the nonchalant behaviour he had displayed all through. He actually cracked grim jests about tomorrow's proceedings. For instance, he knew that Crippen was to be hanged on the day after his own execution, and this provoked him to a most sardonic utterance. 'I shall be senior to Crippen at the other shop!' he remarked, with a grin, to the utter discomfiture of the warder sitting in the condemned cell with him.

At no time did the doomed man worry about his impending fate. One day the doctor, understanding the man's strange humour, asked him why he hadn't committed suicide when he had so much time between the commission of the murder and its discovery.

'Not me!' returned Thompson. 'I am not such a fool as to do somebody out of a job when he is paid to put me out!'

I presume I ought to be grateful to him for his great consideration for me and my profession.

Even as his last hours ebbed out on the night before the execution he lost none of his scorn of the scaffold. He even ventured to give a sort of rehearsal of the final scene.

'I expect it will soon be over, Mr Warder', he exclaimed, adding, 'It will only be something like this.'

With that he leapt on to his chair and then jumped to the floor.

'I suppose it will be just as quick as that!' he said with a smile, while the warder looked on aghast at this display of callous indifference.

Neither his soul nor his conscience – if he possessed either – were at all troubled right to the end. He walked to the scaffold next morning with an air of utter unconcern, and I can safely say I never hanged a cooler man in my life.

I left Liverpool at noon that day for London, where, at Pentonville next morning, I sent the notorious Dr Crippen to his last account. I have described this execution earlier, and I will pass on to the third of the remarkable series of executions. The Crippen affair had evoked so much sensation that a crowd of newspaper men were waiting outside Pentonville to waylay me for information. Being apprised of this, I left the prison by an unaccustomed door, and made a detour to avoid them. One journalist, more enterprising than the others, spotted my ruse, and followed me, even getting on to the omnibus I mounted. He could not get near me on the bus, though, so he accosted me when I got off, and tried to get me to make a statement. It took me some minutes to convince him that I should decline to speak on the topic of the day, and it was only with extreme difficulty that I at length shook him off.

Then I caught a train about 10.30 a.m., and was soon inside Reading Prison making arrangements for the execution of William Broome, whose murder of an old woman at Slough would have received more attention had it not been overshadowed by the Hilldrop Crescent crime. The Slough murder was, indeed, one of those cases where the evidence for and against the accused balanced so evenly that one would have thought it better to give the man the benefit of the doubt. Add to that the man's own declaration of innocence on the scaffold and you have a mystery worthy of close attention.

A lady going to call on an aged relative in Slough who kept a second-hand store noticed a bicycle standing outside the shop door. She entered the shop and made a tragic discovery, but when she came outside again the cycle had disappeared. Was its owner the real culprit and not Broome in the mystery then unfolding itself? The 'tragic discovery' already referred to was no less a one than that of murder. In the little room behind the shop the old lady whom the young woman was calling upon lay dead on the floor. It required very little investigation to show that old Mrs Isabella Wilson, who was 70 years of age, had been stunned, bound, suffocated, and robbed. By whom? That was a question which obtained no answer for several days.

At first the theory was that the crime had been committed by a tramp, for Mrs Wilson's shop was situated on the great Bath Road, which was much frequented by gentry on the highway. One can, therefore, imagine the sensation that was caused when the Scotland Yard experts who had been called in to solve the mystery arrested William Broome, a young fellow whose family was well known and highly respected in Slough. William Broome was 25 years of age, and had been in both the Regular Army and the Berks Yeomanry. He had served two years in the South African Wars, and afterwards in India. He had an excellent character, and was shortly to be married. Mrs Wilson, the murderer's victim, was a pleasant old lady, much liked in the neighbourhood, and up to the previous mid-summer Broome had lived with his parents in the house next door to her.

This was fact number one in the circumstantial chain of evidence against Broome, for obviously he would know the old lady's habits, and the man who murdered her must have possessed that knowledge. It was the old lady's custom to take a rest every day in her inner room about 1 p.m., and it was then that the marauder, whoever he was, entered, overcame her resistance, suffocated her with the aid of her own silk shawl and a cushion, and then ransacked the house.

The proceeds of the robbery of themselves formed a strong point against Broome. Mrs Wilson most certainly had a fair sum of money in her possession just before her death, yet only three halfpence could be found in the shop when the police searched it. They, however, found a piece of paper in which the old woman had had some gold pieces wrapped, and when this was submitted to Dr Willcox, the Home Office expert, he declared that the markings on the paper showed that it had probably contained nineteen sovereigns and two half-sovereigns.

When Broome's boxes were searched, precisely that number of coins were found in it. Broome himself maintained that this was a mere coincidence. The prosecution looked upon it as something considerably more sinister. He said the money was what was left of £40 which he had had for three months, but the prosecution alleged that he had been extremely hard up just before the murder. If the latter was true, it was surely a grave fact that he should so suddenly be found in possession of £20, and that this sum should be made up of exactly the same number of coins believed to have been part of the proceeds of the robbery at the murdered woman's shop.

Here a strange fact obtrudes itself. The question of the accused man's means was obviously a material one, yet practically no effort was made at his trial to disprove the statement by the prosecution that Broome was hard pressed for money at the time of the murder. Those who conducted his defence tried to remedy this omission at the subsequent appeal by calling his mother to give evidence to this effect, but this was not allowed by the Lord Chief Justice, as she had not been a witness at the trial.

One of the most vital links in the chain of evidence was the condition of Broome's face, which, though without any marks when he was seen in Slough just before the murder was committed, was proved to bear two large parallel scratches very shortly after the murder. More important still, Broome was so anxious to obliterate these scratches – which might easily have been made by a woman struggling vainly with her murderer – that he visited two chemist shops and asked to have his face dressed so that the scratches should not show.

Broome betrayed himself over these scratches more than anything else in the case. He seemed extraordinarily nervous about them in the interval between the murder and his arrest. What, for instance, could be more capable of a certain interpretation than the following remarks which he made to his landlady:

'It is rather awkward having these scratches on my face. If people see these they may think I have been robbing someone for their money.'

Surely that was a strange thing to say seeing that nobody had yet accused him of doing anything of the kind. If you or I had scratches like that on our face, obtained, as he said were in an innocent way, should we at once assume that people would think we had been committing a robbery?

Broome gave three explanations about these scratches. Speaking to his sweet-heart, he declared they had been 'done with the back of a boxing glove'; to one of the chemists when he asked to conceal the scratches he explained that 'coming from Paddington Station he had brushed against the wing or splashboard of a motorcar'; and to Chief Inspector Bower, of Scotland Yard, who arrested him, he said 'they were done by a man I had a few words with outside a public-house in Camden Town'.

These varying stories introduced the first element of real weakness in his defence. He also told untruths as to his movements on the afternoon of the murder in order to prove an alibi. At first he declared he was not in Slough that day, but remained in London all the time. This was easily disproved by those who had seen him in Slough between 12.30 and 1 p.m. that tragic Saturday afternoon, which was also approximately the time when old Mrs Wilson met her cruel end.

Falsehoods on important points spoken by a man accused of murder simply add suspicion to the other circumstances against him. Yet his counsel's explanation was plausible enough. He declared that the untrue statements were made simply because he was frightened. He knew from the newspapers, said his counsel, that the murder had been committed, and that the money was missing. He knew, too, that he had exactly the same amount of money in his possession, and had been in Slough during the hours when the murder must have been committed. He knew these facts, together with those awkward scratches, would form strong circumstantial evidence against him, and in his terror he made the mistake of telling lies. This was clever special pleading, for it accentuated the fact that the prosecution had nothing but purely circumstantial evidence to go upon. Other parts of the case were attacked by the defence, such as the question of that piece of paper in Mrs Wilson's room which Dr Willcox had declared to contain nineteen sovereigns and two half-sovereigns. The defence admitted that the paper no doubt may have contained those coins at some time, but there was no proof that they were in the paper on the day the woman was murdered.

Finally counsel for the defence returned to a fact which I mentioned at the opening of this particular case, viz, that mysterious bicycle seen outside Mrs Wilson's shop just before the murder was discovered, and which disappeared a few moments later. Could it have belonged to the real murderer? I am afraid this theory was looked upon as a mere red herring drawn across the path. It was far too weak to gain much support, and was more or less ignored by the Judge and the jury. But the counsel stuck to it that the cycle probably belonged to the man who committed the crime, and when the verdict of guilty was at length brought in against Broome at the Assizes trial, the theory was again brought forward at the Appeal Court. It gained no more credence there. The Lord Chief Justice, in confirming the death sentence, admitted that the case contained no evidence of premeditation, but held that the jury were justified in coming to the conclusion at which they had arrived, and had no doubt of the correctness of the verdict.

And so Broome was doomed. And a few hours after I had hanged Crippen I was peeping in on this other man who was to be the third murderer I had to execute within 48 hours. He was a spruce, youthful looking fellow, and by no means of the criminal type. In the ordinary way one would have been prepared to swear that a fellow of his stamp could not possibly be so villainous as to deliberately strangle a harmless old lady merely for £20. His was a stocky kind of build, being less than 5 ft. 5 in. in height, and turning the beam at 11 st., and his neck was the usual powerful one of a soldier. He was calm enough when I saw him, but it appeared from conversations I had with the warders that the condemned youth feared his coming ordeal.

On the morning of the execution, after I had arranged the rope for a drop of 7 ft. 9 in., one of the warders who had been in attendance on Broome came to me and told me something the condemned youth had said the previous night.

'You have heard them talk of men walking firmly to the scaffold', he had said, 'but I will not be like that. You will have to carry me!'

Knowing of the kind of man I had to deal with, I did not construe Broome's remarks as threats to cause trouble. My interpretation of them was that he doubted if his nerves would sustain him sufficiently and that he feared a breakdown. I therefore advised that he should be given a stiff dose of brandy, and this was done at once. Its effect was, as usual, remarkable. Almost instantly he threw off the feelings of depression and fright that were beginning to lay hold of him. He pulled himself smartly together, and when the time came for him to go to the scaffold after I had pinioned his arms behind his back, he stepped out as bravely as possible. Only one incident of note marked the final moments on the drop. Broome, with the rope round his neck, suddenly interrupted the chaplain's praying. 'I am innocent!' he exclaimed. Next moment he was dead, but his words left behind them an eternal doubt to cloud the issues in this extraordinary case. He was not the kind of man who lies habitually and it is more easily possible to believe that he told the untruths that were a feature of the case against him out of sheer fright that that he would face death uttering a lie of such enormity as the denial of his guilt.

Altogether, this was a case that frankly puzzled me. I did my duty as I was bidden to do, but I feel that justice would have been equally well served if Broome had been reprieved until some stronger backing to the circumstantial evidence against him could have been secured. I have known men with far less doubt in their cases escape the death penalty.

Chapter 11

A Fight in the Condemned Cell

(William Henry Palmer, Leicester, July 1911)

I believe it is a common impression among some people that an executioner has fierce struggles with most condemned men before he can get them pinioned and removed to the scaffold. That is a long, long way from what happens, but I can certainly recall one affair of this kind. Indeed, it is one of the few really terrifying experiences of my career.

Whenever I think of William Henry Palmer, 'The Walcote Murderer', I see again that writhing mass of men in fierce conflict within the narrow limits of the condemned cell at Leicester Gaol. Before Palmer could be overpowered and pinioned, he fought against ten men – fought with fury and despair, his natural strength trebled by the knowledge that death waited for him just around the corner. The crime that brought him low was a brutal one, and his attitude was truculent and callously indifferent throughout his trial, but at the end the mask of bravado was torn away, and the man's cowardliness stood revealed.

Palmer was evidently born for the gallows, for, if his own condemned cell confession is to be believed, he was in the remarkable position of having twice been sentenced to death. Not only that, but I was told on a good authority that still a third murder charge could have been brought against him. It was on 24 January 1911 that William Palmer committed the murder for which he ultimately paid the penalty with his life. His victim was an aged widow named Ann Harris, who lived alone in a cottage at Walcote in Leicestershire. On that morning Miss Harris was found lying dead on the floor of her kitchen, clad only in her nightdress. A piece of webbing tied tightly around her neck. One end of it being fastened to a chair, disclosed the cause of her death.

Robbery was the motive of the crime, the disorderly condition of the house making this obvious at once to the police. The door downstairs had been burst open, and the bedrooms ransacked. Two empty purses lay on the floor, while a third containing two half-sovereigns, a lion shilling, and five farthings, was on top of a chest of drawers, having escaped the attention of the murderer. The connecting of Palmer with the crime was due to smart detective work. Palmer was a painter by trade though for some time previous to the murder he ben engaged in fish hawking at Manchester. Being out of work in January, he decided to go 'on tram' and a few days later reached the Lutterworth district. To get his living he rested on his ability to 'tell the tale' and as a side line he carried some bootlaces, which he offered for sale. He wore tattered clothes to give the impression he was extremely hard up, but he was not so badly off as he pretended.

One of the parties he accosted was Reverend C E Ward, vicar of Bitteswell, who, in presenting him with some money remarked, 'A fine strapping fellow like you has no business on the road'. And indeed, I may as well state right here that Palmer was one of the most powerful men I have ever hanged. He weighed fourteen stone and his arms and body rippled with muscular development. That same night Palmer was refused admittance to a lodging house at Lutterworth because he put in an appearance after the regulation closing hour. He turned away dejectedly, and shortly afterwards asked a constable the way to Northampton. On the road being pointed to him he set out in that direction.

Little is known regarding Palmer's movements during the hours of that dark, wintry night but Mrs Elizabeth Gibson, a widow residing in Voss's Yard at Walcote, near to the house occupied by the murdered women, emphatically declared that by the light of matches which he had struck she saw Palmer crouching in front of the door of a house in the yard. On the following morning he was seen in the waiting room at Lutterworth Railway Station. He purchased a ticket for London and thence journeyed to Folkstone to visit his sister-in-law.

At several places he bought food and drink, indeed after his arrival in the town he stopped at an inn and imbibed freely, showing liberality in paying for drinks for several fishermen. During his presence in this establishment he got rid of about twelve shillings and when he left its portals he was in that mood which may be described as hail-fellow-well-met to all the world. In striking contrast to his poverty of the previous day, he now seemed plentifully endowed with money. A significant fact in this connection was his possession of a large number of three penny pieces – coins which the deceased woman had been in the habit of collecting.

Palmer also got rid of his tattered overcoat while in Folkestone, and at an expenditure of 3s 6d procured from a second hand dealer a garment more in keeping with the apparent condition of his finances. Four days elapsed, during which he tried to drown the memory of that little kitchen wherein he had strangled to death a frail old woman. Then liberty for him ceased to exist. The police had followed up all the clues and Detective Inspector Taylor arrested Palmer in the midst of his celebrations. Palmer strenuously denied his identity and declared that his name was William Thompson. He knew nothing about a party called William Henry Palmer, and was as innocent of the murder of Ann

Harris as the man in the moon. When questioned about how he had obtained his newly acquired wealth he declared he had found it in a field Northamptonshire, but stumbled over exactly where he had found it.

When he came before Mr Justice Pickford at the Assizes it transpired that in the cistern of a lavatory which Palmer had entered at Rugby there had been discovered a watch and chain, a reading glass and a purse, all of which had belonged to Ann Harris, and were missing from her house at the time of its being searched by the authorities.

Despite the grave and weighty character of the evidence, Palmer displayed an air of unconcern in the dock, and there were times when he even laughed at the stories told by the witnesses. There was little room for doubt as to the ultimate verdict of the jury, and it did not take the twelve men long to announce the accused guilty. Then a sudden change took place in Palmer's demeanour. Showing signs of emotion for the first time, he declared in a voice that trembled – 'I am as innocent as a new-born babe. I know nothing at all about it, and I hope you will have mercy upon me'. Mr Justice Pickford, in passing sentence of death, stated that he did not see how the jury could have come to any other conclusion. The crime was one of a particularly brutal character and all the evidence presented clearly pointed to the guilt of the man.

I was engaged for Palmer's execution which was fixed for 19 July, and two days prior to that date I received a letter from Mr George Roylatt, Under Sheriff of Leicestershire asking me to please remember that I was due at the prison on the following afternoon for the purpose of carrying out the death sentence. I reached Leicester Gaol in good time on the afternoon of 18 July and there met the man who had been appointed to act as my assistant. The quarters in the gaol to which the Governor assigned us were comfortable, and the officials did their utmost to make our stay as pleasant as possible.

After tea I paid a visit to the shed containing the scaffold, which was distant about forty yards from the cell occupied by the doomed man. I carefully tested all the apparatus to ensure it being in perfect order, and found everything to my satisfaction. I then fixed a heavy sandbag on the end of the rope which was to hang like that until the following morning in order to take out any twists or stretch in the rope. That same evening I had a peep at the murderer who was to meet his fate on the morrow. He was seated on a chair with his arms folded and his head bent forward. Palmer seemed buried in gloomy thought and was quite unconscious of my scrutiny.

I was impressed with the muscular build of the man and his appearance fully bore out the physical measurement supplied to me by the prison doctor. His height was given as 5 ft. 6 inches and his weight 206 lb. He was fifty years of age. I have indicated that Palmer was a powerful man and before I had done with him he was to provide me with a most convincing demonstration of the fact. Nevertheless I noted during my brief survey that his neck was flabby, and this led me to that conclusion that it would be inadvisable to give him a long drop. In view of his weight and the manifest weakness of his neck I made up my mind to give the culprit one of the shortest drops I ever gave in my professional career, namely 5 ft. 8 inches. Newspapers announcing the execution added that it 'passed off without a hitch', the execution took place all right, but it was not the smooth affair suggested by the press.

My assistant and I spent a very quiet evening in gaol that night. At intervals we were joined by various prison officials and naturally the subject of Palmer and his crime cropped up. I was informed that Palmer had given no trouble since the passing of the death sentence upon him. He had been moody and morose and the only matter that he cared to discuss was that of his innocence of which he had been convicted. No hint was given that Palmer might be inclined to offer resistance and the thought never occurred to me. I had seen so many men go to their deaths calmly and unprotestingly that I took it for granted Palmer would conform to the rule.

Come the morning of the execution I was early astir, and along with my assistant pulled up the sandbag, and subjected the scaffold to a final and minute inspection. Everything was in perfect order, the trap doors answering to the pull of the lever instantaneously. The execution had been fixed for 8.00am, and when I finished my examination of the scaffold it waited fully an hour to that time. While waiting for the summons to perform my duty, I learned that Palmer had scarcely closed his eyes during the night. He had conversed freely with the two warders who were in his cell, but had chiefly confirmed his remarks to his innocence.

'I'm going to be murdered in the morning' he cried out on several occasions and then he would add 'Yes, I am going to be murdered, for I never killed Ann Harris'. At such moments tears would then fill his eyes – not tears of remorse for the victim or his past life, but tears of self pity. Palmer left his last breakfast practically untouched and also paid but little heed to the ministrations of the Wesleyan chaplain, who strove to prepare the doomed man to meet his fate calmly, strong in the knowledge of mercy for the penitent in the Great Beyond.

A few minutes before 8.00 I received instructions to proceed to the condemned cell and accompanied by my assistant, I at once obeyed. Palmer was standing in the middle of the cell when we entered. He looked a formidable figure as he stood there and glared at me but I advanced without hesitation. Swiftly I stepped behind the murderer and seized hold of his left arm by the wrist, my object being to twist it into position behind his back. I was surprised to discover that the arm did not yield to the gentle pressure to which I subjected it, and I expected some more force, but this also proved insufficient. Palmer was deliberately resisting, and in the second that this truth came home to me the silence was suddenly broken by the man whose minutes on earth were numbered.

'Warders' he shouted at the top of his voice 'are you going to let those fellows murder me?' On hearing the uproar the Governor of the gaol appeared and tried to pacify Palmer, but without success. 'I'm innocent, I'm innocent' cried the prisoner 'and I'm not going to allow myself to be murdered without putting up a fight.' Meanwhile my assistant was doing his utmost to get Palmer's right arm behind his back. My assistant ought to have been standing behind Palmer, but in the excitement he stepped up in front of him.

Yelling 'I'll get you' Palmer let drive a vicious kick. He was wearing heavy hobnailed boots – they weighed seven pounds – and but for the fact that my assistant sprang nimbly aside he would undoubtedly have suffered grave injury. Pandemonium now broke loose in that cell. The four warders in attendance rushed to our assistance but even the six of us could not overpower the murderer. He fought savagely with feet and hands and even tried to bite us. We pulled him down to the floor, where he showered blows upon one and all promiscuously and cursed and raved like a maniac.

Other four warders joined in the conflict and for a minute or two no fewer than ten men were struggling against Palmer. There were too many of us and this circumstance benefited Palmer who, buried beneath the bodies of the prison officials still managed to wriggle and twist and kick. During the scuffle I had on several occasions felt the strength of Palmer's blows, but eventually my suggestion to turn the murderer over with his face to the floor was carried out. In this position I succeed in pinioning his arms and he was raised to his feet.

Breathing heavily and still defiant, Palmer uttered terrible oaths and until he somewhat regained his composure it was necessary for the warders to keep a grip of his legs. It was a scene I shall always remember – the rebellious, straining figure of the man about to die, and the white faces of the warders who clung to him. I have never yet been able to analyse the feelings that surged upon me at that moment. I only know that I heartily wished it was all over. The fear clutched me that Palmer would fight every inch of the way to the gallows and even on the trapdoors he would continue his struggles.

The Governor, like everybody else was deeply affected by the horror of the thing and an interval elapsed before he found voice to address Palmer and point out the futility of his conduct. 'You are only making it all the harder for yourself Palmer' he said. 'Pull yourself together and act like a man, not a coward.' To which Palmer growled 'I am innocent, and I'm not going to let you murder me!' This had got to stop. I tapped Palmer on the shoulder and said 'Now, we are ready'. He turned towards the door of the cell, and was hurried along the corridor and out into the yard.

In that short walk to the place of execution I resolved to dispense with the pinioning of Palmer's legs when we got him on the trapdoor. Nor did I wait until he stood on the scaffold before placing on him the white cap. He was ten yards distant from the spot when I pulled the cap from my pocket and slipped it over his head. I was determined that Palmer should have no opportunity of creating further trouble. 'Don't pinion his legs' I whispered to my assistant. 'As soon as you get him on the trapdoor jump back, and I'll pull the lever.'

Palmer's feet did not touch the floor of the gallows for more than a few seconds. He hurried to the chalk mark on the trapdoor, and I fixed the noose about his neck in the twinkling of an eye. My assistant and the warders sprang away from his side and I instantly pulled the lever. That was the end of William Henry Palmer, and also the most exciting execution of my long career.

Chapter 12

The End of Seddon the Poisoner

(Frederick Henry Seddon, Pentonville, 1912)

When I admit that I made a special point of going to the Old Bailey to hear part of the trial of Frederick Seddon, the poisoner, and his wife, I trust I shall not give the impression of being a flinty-hearted hangman gloating in advance over a possible future victim. I should despise myself if such a thought ever entered my head. Certainly I was interested already in this amazing poisoning mystery just as thousands of others were all over the kingdom. But my main object was to see and hear the famous barristers engaged in the case. Among them were three men who then bore the names, Sir Rufus Isaacs, Mr R. D. Muir, and Mr E Marshall Hall – men who even then were celebrities, and who since have risen still higher – and I was anxious to see what sort of men they were.

As it happened, I arrived in London on the opening day of the Seddon trial, as I was summoned to Pentonville to hang the man Abromovitch, who committed the notorious double murder in a Spitalfields gambling den. So I was fortunate enough to hear Sir Rufus Isaacs (now Lord Reading) make his opening speech against the Seddons in his role of Attorney-General. I could not help admiring the silvery tones of this great barrister's voice. From him, as he poured forth his view of the case, my gaze shifted to the dock, where the accused couple sat drinking in every syllable that fell from his lips. The man appeared very calm indeed, and I was told by an old court officer, who had seen many a murder trial, that he had never seen a man so self-possessed when faced with the capital charge.

Now and again Seddon would finger the waxed ends of his fair moustache, or pass his hand over his head – so thin and fair that it almost made him look bald. But he never gave the least sign of nervousness. The woman by his side wore a perpetual smile. She herself explained that this smile was more of less an involuntary contraction of the face over which she had no control whatever. She, too, did not appear in the slightest degree nervous about the issue, and husband and wife often whispered and joked quietly, while around them the grim forces of the law contended over whether or not their lives were to be forfeited. I was to see other strange evidence later on of this man's peculiar detachment from the vital facts of life – a man, who could so far forget that he was to be hanged in a precious few hours as to display anger over a matter of shillings in relation to the sale of his household furniture. Despite the man's religious pretences, he did not seem to have a soul that could rise above money. Nevertheless, all who heard Mr Marshall Hall speak on his behalf would agree that the famous barrister made an extremely gallant fight for Seddon all through the ten days' trial and the subsequent appeal.

I have often met people in later life who have been doubtful whether Seddon was really guilty of the murders, for which he was hanged, but I have no doubts in my own mind. The man's behaviour when he actually came under my personal notice on the eve of his execution showed him to be an abnormal type, and only cool, deliberate, far-seeing individuals of this kind can successfully use poison to secure the death of the person whose 'removal' is desired. It is the most difficult of all 'instruments' and unhappily it is also the most difficult to prove against the suspected person. Consequently, criminal history is full of poisoning cases in which the perpetrators evaded the death on the scaffold which they had obviously deserved and yet cleared themselves of; and other poisoning cases where the accused persons although convicted descended to the condemned cell with a halo of doubt around them.

In this latter category comes the Seddon arsenic drama – a case I consider to be the strangest of its class. It is a bold statement perhaps, but when you consider that all the great poisoners who preceded Seddon to the scaffold were possessed of expert knowledge by reason of their membership of the medical profession one wonders still more that an insurance superintendent should have known sufficient to make his conviction a matter for grave doubt. Look at the list of great poisoners – Dr Palmer, Dr Neill Cream, Dr Pritchard, Dr Lamson, Dr Cross, of Shandy Hall, and Dr Crippen. They were all geniuses in their own particular line, but when I hanged Seddon I handled a man who was far more difficult to prove guilty than any single one of those others.

It took ten days to try this man, and at the end, when the jury had given the verdict which settled his fate, he made a remarkable statement, in the course of which he said:

'My position in this case is this. I am surrounded by a set of circumstances from which there seems no way of extricating myself.'

He was right. There was no direct evidence against him. He could stand accused only upon the surrounding incidents of the crime, or if you prefer it that way – upon 'circumstantial evidence'. Seddon's friends bitterly complained that he was the victim of a wave of prejudice which they said crept in on the case right at the beginning, but, having heard some part of the trial at the Old Bailey, I must honestly say I could not imagine how a case against an accused man could be handled more fairly than the way in which the then Sir Rufus Isaacs conducted this prosecution. Even Mr Marshall Hall (for the defence) admitted this.

Before I describe how Seddon behaved at his execution let me give a survey of the facts that led up to it. An eccentric, and somewhat cantankerous spinster of 49 named Eliza Mary Barrow, who had been living for some time in the house of Mr and Mrs Seddon at Tollington Park, North London, died on September 14, 1911, and was duly buried. On the face of it, such a happening presents nothing out of the unusual. Yet, behind, lay concealed what I have already characterised as the strangest of poisoning cases. Miss Barrow had quarrelled with all her relatives, and it was not until a week after her death that any of them knew she was gone. When they called on Mr Seddon for some particulars of her end, he expressed surprise that they had not responded to his letter inviting them to come to the funeral. 'We never received any letter', said one of the relatives, whereupon Seddon assured them he had written, and in proof produced a copy of the letter he had sent. It then came out that Miss Barrow had been buried in the meanest possible way. She had been buried in a 'public' grave.

Shocked and suspicious, the relatives wanted to know why this had been necessary seeing that Miss Barrow was known to be a woman of some means. She had £1600 invested in India stock, owned leasehold property that brought her in £120 a year, and, being an eccentric, usually kept several hundreds of pounds in gold in her cash box. Altogether she must have possessed something like £4000. Why should such a comparatively well-to-do woman be buried in a 'public' grave? Seddon's reply was that after he death he searched her room but could only find £4 10s in her cash box. Consequently there was only just enough to pay the doctor's fee and bury her in a common grave – that is, a grave in which five or six persons would be buried. Mystified by the disappearance of all the money, the Home Secretary was petitioned to allow the woman's body to be exhumed. The result was startling. Dr Wilcox, the senior analyst to the Home Office, found Miss Barrow's body simply saturated with arsenic.

Before any information as to this discovery could leak out, the Seddon family had a huge surprise. The police swooped down and arrested not only Mr Seddon but his wife too. In fact Mrs Seddon was already in custody when the husband was placed under arrest. 'Absurd!' was Frederick Seddon's characteristic remark when told he was charged with the murder of Miss Barrow, and his tone of indignant but contemptuous tolerance was maintained by him to the very day of his execution. He well knew that all his tracks were marvellously well covered and that it would be difficult if not impossible to convict him. As things turned out it did prove extremely difficult – but not impossible.

Both Mrs and Mrs Seddon were arraigned before Mr Justice Bucknill and a jury of the Old Bailey, and thus one of the most sensational trials of modern times began on March 5, 1912. Listening to the Attorney-General, I could see that the prosecution were not going to be able to produce any direct evidence that Mr and Mrs Seddon or either of them actually murdered Miss Barrow. The fight was to be waged over purely circumstantial evidence – the interest of the parties in Miss Barrow's death, their opportunities for poisoning her, and their conduct afterwards. And I was deeply interested in seeing the skilful way in which Sir Rufus Isaacs and Mr R. D. Muir brought out all the facts relating to these three points. With regard to motive, it came out quite early in the trial that Miss Barrow, being bothered about her investments and her property, had given them all to Mr Seddon on condition that he gave her an annuity amounting to £72 a year.

Three days before her death Seddon had drawn up a will for Miss Barrow, in which she appointed him her sole executor and trustee. She left her furniture, jewellery, and personal belongings to two adopted children when they came of age, but made no disposition respecting her loose cash or other property. Here, then, were the necessary motives. If Miss Barrow were dead the annuity would stop, and her invested money and house property and cash would all go into the pockets of the Seddons. They were the only persons who could gain her trust. Nobody else but the Seddons waited on Miss Barrow. She became ill of what the doctor said was epidemic diarrhoea, and died in the presence of Mr and Mrs Seddon on 1 September.

The theory of the prosecution was that the Seddons had purchased arsenic fly papers, secured the poison from them by soaking them in water, and administered this to the helpless woman in her food and medicine. They produced a chemist who positively declared he had sold some of these arsenical fly papers to a person connected with the Seddon household. I say at once that the defence threw doubt upon the chemist's identification of the person who bought the fly papers. Their suggestion was that Miss Barrow had accidentally or purposefully poisoned herself, but Dr Wilcox's evidence showed that the quantity of arsenic in the body proved that the poison must have been administered for some time. This ruled out the explanation of an accidental or intentional dose by Miss Barrow herself.

The question of the conduct of Mr and Mrs Seddon after the death was one that produced many strange disclosures during the trial. Both of the accused admitted that Miss Barrow's death was very unexpected, yet the natural act of sending for the doctor was not performed. Instead, there was an immediate search for her money, of which Seddon declared he only found £4 10s. The manner of her hurried burial was also a curious feature. Seddon had even haggled with the undertaker, who wanted £4 for interment in a public grave and reduced his price to £3 7s 6d!

In justice to Mrs Seddon it may be admitted that her conduct after Miss Barrow's death was not at all out of place. She seemed genuinely upset, and bought a wreath for her departed friend. There was also a dramatic story told of how she kissed the dead woman as she lay in her coffin.

In brief, that was the case against the Seddons. It was purely circumstantial evidence, and for the defence Mr Marshall Hall naturally attacked this point. He admitted that Seddon had shown himself possessed of 'monstrous meanness and covetousness', especially in the matter of Miss Barrow's funeral, but he submitted that the evidence of motive were not strong enough to allow one to say he had positively murdered her. Mr Marshall Hall's main contention was, however, that there was no proof that Seddon ever handled the fly papers or administered the arsenic.

Even the prosecution had to admit the truth of this, but the weight of the other evidence was reckoned sufficiently strong to convict.

After ten days of evidence and arguments of this kind the trial reached its close. It had produced many remarkable scenes, the chief of which were produced during the two long and dramatic cross-examinations of Mr and Mrs Seddon, neither of whom, I was told, looked in the least degree shaken after their separate ordeals in the witness-box. But, of course, I was not there then. In the final speeches it was evident that the prosecution, while firm in demanding a verdict against Seddon himself, were quite willing to receive an acquittal verdict on Mrs Seddon's behalf, and the Judge's summing-up was in the same direction. This was reflected in the jury's findings, for after an hour's deliberation they declared Seddon 'Guilty' and his wife 'Not guilty'.

The sensations in this extraordinary trial were, however, by no means at an end. Before Mrs Seddon could be removed, husband and wife threw their arms round each other, and in the eyes of all in court kissed and took an affectionate farewell. Then Seddon once more assumed his air of calm detachment, and delivered himself of a great speech in his own defence. With the utmost self-possession he dealt point by point with the evidence against him, and said in conclusion – 'The prosecution have not traced anything to me in the shape of money, which is the great motive suggested by the prosecution for me to commit this diabolical crime, of which I declare before the Grand Architect of the Universe I am not guilty. If I say more I do not suppose it will be of any account, but if it is the last word I have to speak, I say I am not guilty of the crime for which I stand judged'. As he made his appeal to the Great Architect he raised his hand pointed aloft, and gave the Masonic sign. Every Freemason in the court saw this, and naturally it did not escape Mr Justice Bucknill, who was Provincial Grand Master of Surrey. It evidently intensified his emotion. He could scarcely speak. He had to choke back the tears to cough out the ends of his sentences. He could only just be heard.

With the square of thick cloth which is called the black cap upon his wig, the Judge brokenly declared that he agreed with the jury in both their verdicts. The motive for the crime was greed of gold. 'I don't know', he said, 'exactly when or how you poisoned this woman, but I think I do know that you wanted to make great pecuniary profit by felonious means.'

Seddon stood with his hands clasped and his thumbs together on the front of the dock. He listened with polite attention, exactly as if he were listening to a speech about somebody else.

'I have no wish to harrow your feelings', the Judge continued —

'It doesn't affect me, sir', Seddon's voice rang out clear and strong. 'I've a clear conscience.'

The Judge paid no attention, but continued his address. 'Try in the short time left you to make peace with your Maker', he urged.

'I am already in peace', again interrupted Seddon.

'I appeal to you', went on his Lordship with emotion. 'Both you and I belong to the same brotherhood, and that makes it doubly painful for me, though it makes no difference to my duty. It may be some consolation to you to know that I agree with the verdict in regard to your wife. Whatever she has done that was blameworthy without criminal intentions she did it to help you. I am satisfied that the jury have decided wisely, and that they have done justice to you both.'

Seddon heard the dread sentence without a sign of emotion, and then turned at once and made for the stairs without waiting to be told. The case had to go to the Appeal Court before Seddon would believe there was not a chance of escape left open to him. Mr Marshall Hall again made a great effort for his client, but failed to influence the Judges to overturn the verdict already given.

During the period that elapsed between the time when I received the Under-Sheriff's instructions to hold myself in readiness to execute Seddon and the actual day itself (April 18, 1912) the country was deeply touched by the extraordinarily energetic measures taken by Mrs Seddon to try to secure her husband's reprieve. She wrote touching letters to the papers, published her husband's still more touching letters from the condemned cell, entreated people to sign a petition to the Home Secretary on Seddon's behalf, and got her five children all to help her in securing signatures. News of the refusal of the demand for a reprieve had already been conveyed to Seddon when I reached Pentonville on the afternoon of April 17. It did not seem to affect him in the least. No man ever showed less emotion over his own doom.

That same afternoon he sent for his solicitor, and we all wondered what his purpose was. Will it be believed that this man, standing on the edge of certain death, sent for his solicitor with no other object than to learn what certain articles of his furniture had fetched at auction! What a clue to his sordid, money-grasping nature that was! He created quite a scene in the condemned cell over this business. He was roused to a fury of indignation because the amount realised was smaller than he had hoped for. Striking the table at which he sat, he declared in tones of scorn and resignation, 'That's done it!' he said that as if the mere matter of those few extra shillings were of more moment to him than the imminent prospect of an appearance before the Great Judge with murder on his soul.

He was still greatly agitated over this affair when I saw him at exercise. In order that I might have the necessary glimpse of the condemned man the Rev. Mr Swanston (the chaplain) got Seddon to go into the prison yard for a walk. The Governor took me to the reception room, from the window of which I could look out on to the lawn at Seddon. I put on a warder's uniform cap so that the condemned man should not know it was the hangman who was looking at him if he should happen to catch sight of me.

Precautions of this kind are always taken so that men under sentence of death should not be unduly harassed. Seddon soon came into sight with the chaplain by his side. Whether he was telling all about that disappointing loss of a few shillings at the auction I cannot say but he was certainly talking in an extremely animated fashion. It was obvious that the chaplain could not get in a word of the ministrations of his office. Seddon insisted on doing all the talking. I have seen men in all stages of behaviour on the day before execution, but Seddon set up a new record that has never since been beaten. He walked and talked and gesticulated and argued as if death were the remotest contingency which did not concern him in any way.

That evening, after I had been to the scaffold and examined the apparatus, I chatted with the warders who had been in attendance upon him in the condemned cell. They informed me that Seddon had been a most voluminous writer. He was always at it. Letter after letter he wrote to his wife, and all of them were so long that it would take up several columns of my space if I were to attempt to reproduce them all. Remarkable to relate, they were full of religious quotations and Biblical references. In his last letter to his family he sent his children a father's blessing from the condemned cell, referred to Mrs Seddon as 'a good wife to me and an ideal mother to you all', and enjoined his daughter Maggie to bear in mind his advice and warnings. To beware of pitfalls, and to 'remember that this is a dangerous world for young and inexperienced girls'. He told his wife to get a miniature white marble monument and keep it under a glass shade, 'sacred to the memory of your loving and devoted husband, who departed this life. 18 April 1912. Asleep in Jesus'.

To his father he wrote in similar strain. This letter, too, was packed with religious talk. One might have imagined him as one of the great Christian martyrs, judged by the tone in which he wrote. Never for a single moment did he allow anybody to think he meant to confess his guilt. To the attendant warders he maintained the same air as he did to the chaplain and everybody else. This attitude is best summed up in his own words. He said to them one day:

'It is my destiny, and I trust to meet my fate bravely as a Christian. I shall die resting on the true finished word of Christ. No mercy in human law has been extended to me. I am a victim of a gross miscarriage of justice. My execution will be a judicial murder, for I did not murder Miss Barrow. If a prisoner is deprived of the benefit of the doubt to which he is justly entitled then there is no excuse for the law when it makes the error of condemning and executing an innocent man.'

As if his voluminous letters were not enough to occupy his energy, he set to work in his condemned cell to compile an account of his own career. Here again I have to regret that space is not elastic enough to allow me to give his own story in full, but I append a short summary of it.

'I am charitably and religiously disposed' he wrote and added that he had been a Sunday School teacher and a preacher; was a prominent Freemason; was a member of the Order of Buffaloes and had been one of the first to organise charity concerts in aid of wives and families of Boer War heroes.

True though all this probably was, I feel that Seddon omitted to do justice to himself in the one most important respect of all – his passion for money. I have already told you how he behaved on his last afternoon in life over a few trumpery bits of furniture. Yet this man, on his own admission, had an income of something like £600 a year. He himself often spoke of this as if it proved his innocence.

'Do you think that a man of my position would kill a woman for the mere sake of not paying an annuity of £723' he would exclaim. Well, I know what my answer would have been if he had put that to me. His behaviour in squeezing a paltry 12/6 out of the undertaker by making him reduce his estimate for burying Miss Barrow from £4 to £3 7s 6d was a sufficient index to his miserly character.

However, the morning of April 18th was to see the last of him, and even the most cruel of murderers has to receive sympathy on the last morning of his life. All the same, Seddon in no way looked for it. When the chaplain went to him soon after Seddon had risen from bed he was received in the same detached way as usual. The condemned man was now wearing his own clothes. For a man sentenced to death always leaves off his prison garb on his last morning. He made rather a poor breakfast of tea, bread and butter but although he was evidently in a more dejected state of mind than ever before he still declined to bow his proud head. He was still 'innocent' when the chaplain went in to prepare him for the coming ordeal and no prayers or persuasion could get him to drop this pose.

On my way to have a final look at the scaffold to see that all was in order, I heard that Mrs Seddon had been seen haunting the precincts of the prison already that morning. According to one story she had been there all night. She had taken a room facing the prison gates, and there she kept her vigil, waiting in agony for the hour of 9 o'clock to strike – the hour when her husband was to go to what he had told her was an undeserved death.

The last moments approached swiftly. While the crowds gathered silently outside and the woman who had shared the prison dock with Seddon waited to know that he had met his death which she herself had so narrowly escaped, there was a silent bustle inside the prison. I had everything in readiness for the execution. The grim chamber stood ready and the rope lay coiled against the beam just over where the doomed man would stand. I had measured off for a drop of 7ft 1 inch. The signal to enter the condemned cell came at a moment or so to 9 o'clock. Stepping briskly up to Seddon I pinioned his arms behind his back. He took not the slightest notice of me.

He was only a medium sized man. Officially he stood 5 ft. three and one quarter inches in height and 136 lb weight, but he had a way of proudly holding himself that made you think him a much bigger man. From the cell to the scaffold was about 20 yards. As Seddon left his cell he had to turn to the right into a short corridor and then to the right again. This led him across the yard and straight on to the scaffold.

The procession was just forming up to leave the condemned cell when I slipped out and went on towards the scaffold so that I might be there to receive Seddon. The Chaplain began to recite the solemn service specially set for such occasions but Seddon took no audible part in it. When I from my position on the scaffold, saw him entering upon the straight position of the path leading to where I stood I saw that Seddon was looking extremely pale, although he still held his head high. Suddenly he caught sight of the noose dangling from the beam, and it unnerved him.

He immediately closed his eyes to shut out the vision and walked the remaining part of the way with his eyelids down. Two of the officers ranged by his side, noticing what he had done, caught hold of his arms. I expect they fancied he might be about to faint. Seddon, however, was still quite firm and all that was necessary was to lead him towards the spot he had so emphatically refused to look at. I put the cap over his head as soon as he got within my reach and had the rope round his neck in a trice. My assistant (T W Pierrepoint) had been equally smart in strapping Seddon's legs and without waiting for anything further I pulled the lever and precipitated the most impudently calm murderer of my career to his death.

The execution was something of a record in the matter of speed. The chief warder timed me from the moment I entered the condemned cell until the drawing of the bolt on the scaffold after Seddon had walked the twenty yards that separated the two places. The result was rather startling. From start to finish it had all been accomplished inside 25 seconds.

Chapter 13

The Hooded Man

(George McKay alias John Williams, Lewes, 1913)

It would be very unwise for a man holding the office of public executioner to worry himself unduly about the possibilities of the innocence of men he has hanged. To outsiders, however, I am aware this question of the hanging of possibly innocent men is one of intense fascination. Several times in my career I have been the storm centre of agitations on this question. Two of these cases spring to my mind. There was the Dickman affair [Chapter 8] and the other was the 'Hooded Man' mystery at Eastbourne.

Let me state right away that in none of my cases have I felt any compunctions about the man I was to hang. I have supreme faith in the justice of British law. If there is a doubt the condemned man invariably gets the benefit of it, and as a proof of this I may say that quite half the men I have been engaged to execute have been reprieved. Therefore, if John Williams, the 'Hooded Man' of the Eastbourne murder case, had had any really truthful basis to his pleas of innocence he most certainly would not have perished on the gallows. Yet the Assize Court jury thought him guilty; the Judges in the Court of Criminal Appeal thought him guilty; and the Home Secretary, the final arbiter of fate, evidently thought the same.

In face of all this he must surely have been guilty. And yet there are many features in his case that have bothered me. Certain points were dealt with in a way that strikes me as unsatisfactory, although I still firmly believe that it was he who shot Parade Inspector Arthur Walls. From the point of view of the public, one of the most attractive things in the case was the air of mystery that surrounded the accused man. In order that witnesses who would have to swear to identification should not be prejudiced in any way, 'John Willams' face was hooded when he made his police court appearances. It was believed too, that behind the mask of the name 'John Williams' he concealed his true name, and one that showed him to come of high bred stock, and though at the time for family reasons the full truth was concealed from the world it is now possible for me to draw the veil that hid so many facts in the Eastbourne murder.

In its essentials this murder was not a very remarkable affair. It was simply the case of a burglar, surprised by an officer, shooting the latter and escaping. There is surely nothing romantic in that; but there were so many side issues that it rose eventually to a first class mystery. The scene of the murder was at No. 6 South Cliff Avenue, Eastbourne, the residence of Countess Flora Sztaray. The Countess was leaving her home to go out driving with a friend, when the coachman informed her that he had observed a man like a burglar in the porch. Immediately on hearing this the Countess drove back to the house and telephoned the police.

According to the account of the coachman (David Potter), when Inspector Walls arrived the Countess said to him 'There's a man over my door'. The Inspector stepped back and shaded his eyes as he looked up to the balcony. Then he called to the man and said 'Look here, old chap, come down'. The 'old chap' made a movement as though getting into a sitting position, and Inspector Walls stepped to the right hand side of the door, among the shrubs to receive him. There was then a sudden gunshot and a flash was seen from the edge of the balcony. Inspector Walls then dropped into a sitting position then staggered towards the gate. The unfortunate Inspector died and the hue and cry went out for his murderer. I can remember with what close interest I watched the newspapers as they reported developments.

That the culprit was a burglar was self-evident. Eastbourne for months had been the happy hunting ground of a gang of burglars, and as the Countess was well known locally to be the possessor of a number of valuable jewels it was believed that the murderer, aware of the fact, was waiting for her to leave the house so that he might enter by the dressing room window. Chief Inspector Bower of Scotland Yard, who among other well-known cases, was engaged in the Moat Farm murder ten years previously, arrived in Eastbourne the next day with two detectives from the Criminal Investigation Department. They explored the Countess's front garden and the ivy-clad balcony above the front door, where the man was concealed, in search of foot-marks and finger prints. It is understood that they found two or three good footprints. A light fawn trilby hat was also found where the fleeing murderer had apparently dropped it.

Only a vague sort of description of the wanted man was in the hands of the police but nonetheless the countryside was scoured. A vigilant watch was kept at the railway station until all the night trains had departed, while all roads out of the town were kept under close observation. Motor cars were made use of in the search and many constables on cycles were sent to places as far away as Lewes, Brighton and Hastings. When he came on the scene Chief Inspector Bower very quickly made up his mind as to the identity of the man he was searching for and that he had managed to slip through to London, so he and other Scotland Yard men did not stay long in Eastbourne. They returned to the metropolis and not long afterwards the news was that they had made an arrest.

Accompanied by Detective Sergeants Pearce, Cooper and Hayman together with Inspector Parker of Eastbourne, he went to the buffet at Moorgate Street Railway Station, where he saw the man he wanted drinking with someone else. The man's back was turned and the officers were able to go up behind him and secure him before he knew of their presence. He made no attempt to get away, and when informed of the charge made no reply. The arrested man gave his name as John Williams.

So much hung upon the question of identity that extraordinary precautions were taken to prevent unauthorised persons from seeing his face. He was taken to Eastbourne, and on the way from the railway station to the police station his head and shoulders were completely covered by a thin dark blue fabric with white spots. Who was John Williams? Not until he was hanged was his real identity revealed but what was known was that he was an admitted burglar. He was not of the ordinary type, he was as near as possible the 'gentleman cracksman' of a thousand fiction tales.

The prosecution's contention that he was the burglar who shot Inspector Walls relied upon the testimony of his girlfriend Miss Florence Seymour who had been out with Williams on the evening of the murder. Williams had left her sitting on a seat where South Cliff Road joins the sea front, almost 150 yards from the scene of the murder. When departed he had been wearing a trilby hat. He returned about half an hour later bare headed. On the way back to the lodgings he threw away on the beach a parcel containing a rope ladder which was found there the following morning. She also told how on the morning following the crime Williams had busied himself cleaning a revolver. Williams knew he was known to the police, and this led him to rub up the revolver, remarking as he did so 'If they see finger prints on it they will accuse me of murder'. Shortly afterward he went and buried the revolver in the sands on the beach, where it was afterwards found.

When the girl was called to give evidence at the trial, however, she declared that she and the accused man were in a picture house at the time the murder was committed. Williams' counsel held that the case was by no means proved. He pointed out that there was no identification of the accused man, even Potter, the coachman had been unable to identify Williams as the man he saw. The case for the prosecution was one of pure circumstantial evidence but in fifteen minutes the jury made up their minds after a hearing that lasted three days that Williams was guilty.

I had no hesitation in accepting the commission to carry out the execution at Lewes Gaol on 29 January 1913. Three weeks before the day fixed for

Williams' execution I was at Lewes to fulfil the law's decree upon a man called Albert Rumens. This man had committed an incomprehensible murder of a ten year old schoolgirl. There was no visible motive. Rumens was always an inoffensive man, but there was insanity in his family. The jury held that he was responsible for his actions, but I can easily believe what he told the warders, that he 'remembered nothing or the murder'.

However, I had my duty to do, and I did it. He went quietly to his doom. The prison, up to that morning, had held two condemned men, and it must have been agonising for Williams to hear the death knell being tolled for Rumens. No sooner was the execution of Rumens accomplished, the Under Sheriff Mr Bartlett approached me and said, 'I suppose you will be at liberty to execute Williams on the 29th'. I said I would and took the opportunity to go and see him.

At that time he was suffering as he had never suffered in his life before. His sweetheart Florence Seymour was pregnant and he had written to the Home Secretary to request permission to marry her. Such an appeal was unique, and the public were greatly agitated over it. One section held it would be a human thing to save the child from the brand of illegitimacy, while the other side held it would be a worse brand for the child to have as its acknowledged father a man who was hanged for murder. The Home Secretary replied:

'I am in receipt of your letter and am unable to accede to the request therein contained.'

The refusal had arrived a couple of days before I was at the prison and Williams was still obviously bowled over by it.

My visit to Lewes at this time put me in possession of a heap of facts about the true identity of the criminal known to the public as John Williams. Although these facts were pretty generally known inside the prison, they were not allowed to leak outside until after the execution.

The purpose of this secrecy was again an evidence of how deeply human at heart was their condemned murderer and professional cracksman. It appeared that his aged mother was seriously ill and he was so afraid lest she should be killed by shock of knowing what was happening to her ne'er do well son that he chose to go to his death under the assumed name of John Williams and forbade any publication of details of his career in case they might come to her notice.

There can also be no doubt that Williams was engaged in nefarious work when the murder of Inspector Walls occurred. In fact Williams nonchalantly admitted at the trial that he had been making a reconnaissance to see if there was a house in Southcliffe Avenue that could be burgled by means of rope ladder.

I am now quite at liberty to reveal his real name as George McKay, the second son of a highly respected Scottish minister, born in Edinburgh on 23 February 1883. He was thus a month short of his 30th birthday when I hanged him. On 28 January I set off for Lewes in company with my assistant. We were not the only persons connected with the 'Hooded Man' who travelled to Lewes that day, for Miss Seymour and her baby were also on the same train. We had seen her get aboard at London, but did not know who she was. But when we alighted at Lewes others on the platform recognised her. 'She is going to have her last look at him' we heard people say not unsympathetically as they gave way respectfully for that touching figure carrying her child.

Miss Seymour and her lover had one last tearful parting at the prison. I had the chance to observe her as she left from the bedroom window of the gatekeeper's house. She was dressed entirely in black, and looked very nice. Her face bore a calm expression, but she looked a very frail little woman, and it was impossible not to feel very sorry for her. It would be an hour or two later when I went to have another peep at her doomed lover. My first impression was that he was the finest specimen of a man, physically, I had ever clapped eyes on. There was not an ounce of superfluous flesh on his body. He had the appearance of a regular athlete, and I could see that the ordinary scale would not provide sufficient drop for him. The Governor told me that the most recent examination had shown him to be 5 ft. 8 in. in height and 148 lb . I gave him 7 ft. 6 in.

When they told me in the morning of the bad night he had I suggested that a glass of brandy should be given to him but the officers assured me he would decline it. He was the kind of man who would scorn even the appearance of weakness. As it happened he pulled himself together of his own accord, and from the time he arose until the moment he disappeared into that fatal pit he never showed the slightest sign of a falter.

The weather was miserable that morning when McKay paid the extreme penalty. A heavy mist covered everything and a drizzling rain was falling. This, however, did not prevent several knots of people from gathering outside the gaol to await the sounding of the death bell. He looked very smart and very composed when I entered the condemned cell to pinion him. He stood there dressed in the frock coat suit he had worn at his trial, the only difference being that he now wore no collar and tie, and his face did not present quite the clean shaven look I had seen before.

He stood firmly while I fastened his wrists behind, and he stepped out of the cell and along the path to the scaffold with the demeanour of a man well prepared to see it through. He took absolutely no notice of the crowd of officials and the pressmen gathered to see the execution. He took his place on the drop without a word, and within 68 seconds of my entry into the condemned cell –

the doctor took the precise time – McKay, once more hooded but in the white cap this time, had gone down to his death.

He never confessed. Steadfastly, from the hour of his arrest, he maintained his innocence, but in the condemned cell he never referred to the subject of his crime except in his numerous letters, wherein he again and again declared that he had not murdered Inspector Walls. Nevertheless, he did not trouble to aver his innocence on the execution morning – neither did he express any contrition for the crime he undoubtedly committed.

Chapter 14

A Mistake and an Innovation

(Josiah Davis, Stafford, 1914 and Robert Upton, Durham, 1914)

It is no small gratification to me – not in a personal, boasting sense, but from the standpoint of pride in the proper accomplishment of duty – that only once in my long career was I the subject of an adverse report to the Home Office. My error had been to give too long a drop at a Stafford execution, and the doctor wrote to the Home Office in complaint. As a consequence special instructions were issued from London when I went two weeks later to hang a man at Durham, but the details of the whole affair were such that I in no way suffered for what happened at Stafford.

Personally, I have always felt that it was serving the cause of humanity better to make sure of causing instantaneous death than by giving too short a drop, to run the risk of inflicting lingering agonies upon the poor doomed wretches. I think I can safely leave the public to give a verdict on this question of principle. The facts in the episodes referred to are, however, sufficiently novel to justify narration, and in regard to one of the cases involved showed how well advised criminals would be if they adopted 'is golden' as their watchword.

Certainly, in my opinion, Josiah Davies would never have hanged had it not been for his unwise tongue. He was an ironworker, aged 58, and he lodged in Wolverhampton, with a Mrs Martha Hodgkins, a highly respected person. On the morning of 4 November 1913 a neighbour was startled by a cry of 'Murder!' issuing from Martha Hodgkins' house but hearing nothing further all suspicions were lulled for the time being.

Several hours passed off uneventfully and then the neighbour who had heard the cry began to wonder why she had seen nothing of Mrs Hodgkins that morning. She decided to investigate. The door was open, so she walked in. All was silent. The neighbour ventured fearfully into the bedroom and there made a dreadful discovery. Martha Hodgkins lay dead on her bed. She had been strangled, as was testified by the bandage tied tightly around her neck and fastened to the bedhead.

The police came with a doctor and theories to explain how the woman came by her death were quickly formulated. Murder had been committed. They held that it was proved in more or less positive degree by the cry 'Murder!' by the fact that the portion of the bandage between the woman's neck and the bed rail was loose in a way that could not have come about if she had committed suicide and from the presence of a number of scratches and abrasions, showing that great violence had been used in the commission of the deed.

The murderer had carried out their plans very neatly. He had failed to convince the police that Mrs Hodgkins had committed suicide but had left behind absolutely no clue to their identity. The contents of the woman's purse were missing but as nobody knew what it contained, that did not help matters very much. That same day Josiah Davies was arrested and charged with the murder. The evidence against him was of thinnest possible description but they sent him to stand trial at the Assizes before Mr Justice Lush. The prosecution was as weak as ever. The only evidence against Davies was that he had a number of scratches and abrasions on his hands and a few minor ones on his face. This and the fact that he was hard up, constituted the bulk of the case against him.

While lying in the cells awaiting trial, the counsel for the defence said he was in solitary confinement for two months —he suddenly lost his self-possession and broke down, he told the prison doctor what amounted to almost a complete confession. He admitted he had struggled with Mrs Hodgkins and added – 'I must have been worried because I was out of work'. Those few words settled his fate. Had he never spoken them I am sure the case would have been far too thin to justify even a conviction. But in face of his own admissions it was impossible for his counsel to do very much.

Nevertheless, a praiseworthy fight was put up on his behalf. It was argued that the house had been left open for many hours and it was quite conceivable for anybody to walk in and commit the murder. It was denied that Davies was so much without resources to kill Mrs Hodgkins to replenish them, for he had sons, who willingly gave him assistance whenever he required it. It was pointed out also that no part of Mrs Hodgkin's property had been traced to him. Accused's counsel took the matter of Davies' scratches under review and argued that these could easily have been caused by gathering blackberries, which were exceedingly plentiful around there just then. Surely it was remarkable, he urged, that all the scratches were on Davies' hands and very few on his face?

All this was quite plausible and would have been sufficient had the case rested there to have established a very strong doubt but his statement to the doctor proved his undoing. The jury returned to consider their verdict and they returned in barely eight minutes with a finding of 'Guilty'. Mr Justice Lush had two death sentences to pronounce at the Assize, for on the day before Davies' case came on, a Walsall man had been condemned for the murder of his wife by cutting her throat. In this case, however, the jury's recommendation for mercy was followed by a reprieve.

I was engaged for the double execution but the commutation of the Walsall man's sentence left Davies to go alone to the scaffold. The date for this final scene in the tragedy was fixed for 10 March 1914, and when I reached Stafford Prison on the previous afternoon I put everything in order in the usual way. Davis was taking his condemnation with calm philosophy, and I anticipated no trouble so far as he was concerned. He was rather short and stocky in stature, standing just 5 ft. 2 inches and weighing 147 lb.

I decided on a drop of 7 ft. 6 inches and I have no doubt that would have been just about right. The Home Office list of drops would have given 6 ft. 10 inches for a man of this build, but I gave him a bit more than the list. In this instance, however, accident intervened to increase the length several inches beyond my own intended drop. And I got into hot water as a consequence.

The execution morning was very dark, and when I went to the scaffold a short time before the grim ceremony was timed to begin in order to take off the sand bag that had hung there overnight, I had trouble awaiting me. Try as I would it was impossible to see the pencil mark I had placed on the rope to fix the drop. There was not time to measure it all off again, for that is a complicated and technical manoeuvre far more difficult than it sounds so I made a very careful guess. Perhaps I was over anxious not to give too short a drop, but I would always rather err at the other extreme than risk letting a poor wretch die slowly from strangulation.

When the death hour arrived Davies faced it with quiet courage. He stood calmly even while I pinioned him; he walked steadily from the condemned cell to the scaffold and he never flinched during the few seconds delay entailed by the fixing of the rope around his neck and the strapping together of his ankles. I moved the lever over and the white capped figure disappeared. The rope stood still almost as soon as Davis' dead weight was transferred to it, and I congratulated myself that, despite the missing mark on the rope, I had given him a painless, instantaneous death.

As things turned out, I was premature in my self-satisfaction. When the body was drawn up it was found that the rope had slightly grazed his skin. There was no effusion of blood and altogether nothing to make any bother about but when the doctor discovered it he was very upset. 'You have given this man too much drop' he asserted. As a matter of fact that was quite true, for I found on measuring up afterwards that I had given him 7 ft. 10 inches. But the circumstances were so exceptional and the results so trivial that I could see nothing to make a fuss about. He thought differently and entertained such strong views on the matter that he took the extreme course of reporting the matter to the Home Office.

I knew nothing of this at the time, but a fortnight later, when I was at Durham for the execution of Robert Upton, I was faced with the intimation that the Home Office had sent a special instruction that I must not be allowed to exceed the official table of drops. As I hardly ever took the table into account and nearly always made a practice of giving longer falls than the regulation ones, this order might have caused me considerable anxiety but I was able to satisfy everybody, myself included.

Upton's crime revealed some extraordinary details of life in the underworld. It all centred round a woman who, by a tacit understanding, it was said, would live half of each week with Upton and the other half with another Jarrow man named Charles Gribbin. Jealousy hung around between the two men and became accentuated, it was stated, when the women showed inclination for still a third man. When this was announced Upton boldly declared he would murder Gribbin and the other man rather than she should go to them, and one day when drink got the better of him, he tried to carry out the threat.

On that occasion his fourteen year old son saved Gribbin's life, but the second attack was so successful that Gribbin died two minutes after Upton attacked him with his razor. The murderer turned the fatal blade on to his own throat, but failed to kill himself. Naturally he never had the slightest chance of escaping the death sentence when he came to trial at the Assizes. The jury failed to see that the undoubted insanity in his family in any way absolved him from responsibility for the deed that he had committed, They found him guilty and Mr Justice Ridley sentenced him to be hanged. Consequently his name was added to the already long list of men whom I was instructed to hang in that extraordinary month of March 1914. I was engaged to execute no fewer than seven men in the fortnight beginning 10 March and ending 25 March, and only two of them were reprieved.

Between the execution of Davies at Stafford and that of Upton at Durham, I had been to carry out similar duties at Exeter [James Honeyands, see Chapter 5] and the day fixed for the carrying out of the sentence at Durham, I was due at Cardiff to perform the law's extreme punishment upon young Bindon, the footballer. [Author's note: Edgar Bindon (19) shot and killed his girlfriend, Maud Mulholland, after she broke off their relationship.]

One of the first things I learnt of when I reached Durham was the Home Office direction to the prison that the official table of drops mush have observed, and on no account be exceeded. This was the first time any order of such a kind had ever been issued regarding the way in which I carried out my duties, but the doctor at Durham was a real sport and he let me understand that I need not disturb myself about it.

As a matter of fact, even if there had been no instructions from the Home Office, I should have given him only a short drop in this case because of the fact that Upton had cut his throat in the attempt to commit suicide. A long drop in such circumstances would have been dangerous, so I was able to observe the Home Office instruction without in any way violating my own opinions on the subject. Between us the doctor and I decided to give a drop of 5 ft. 5 inches, but I also instituted a new feature at this execution which made it possible to give longer drops in cases where condemned men had cut their throats.

Such cases always put the executioner in a quandary, for with a long drop the weakened neck might give way, while with a short drop there could be no guarantee of a quick, painless death. To achieve the latter was my constant endeavour, and posterity might well feel that, murderer though he was, Robert Upton contributed a valuable addition to the cause of more humane methods in the performance of the death penalty.

He was a model prisoner, so the warders informed me. He was turned 50 years of age and somehow despite the proved immorality of his life prior to the murder, he awakened considerable sympathy in all with whom he came in contact. Perhaps it was his sincere penitence for a badly spent life; or perhaps it was his touching gratefulness for anything that was done for him. Whatever it was, there could be no doubt that all the prison felt a real regret that the man had to go to the scaffold.

I suppose the history of crime is full of such cases – men with plenty of good in them who have drifted carelessly down the sloping path of loose living until they tumbled over the precipice into grave crime. Such men are not incorrigible criminals but, unhappily, when they fall into doing murder they get no chance for reform. So it was with Upton. On the whole not a bad fellow, one could well believe his frequent declarations, 'I didn't know what I was doing at the time, not one bit'. He often told his cell attendants that drink had been his ruin, but also, his eyes were opened too late. Nothing now remained but to make his peace with his Maker. No amount of penitence could do him any good on this earth.

The chaplain found him very patient and attentive under his ministrations and had taught him to hold his hot passions and emotions so firmly in check that when the time came for me to go in and pinion him, he received me with utmost calmness. I strapped his wrists together while he listened with reverence to the words of comfort and consolation that the chaplain was uttering. Then we moved off towards the scaffold. I had gone on ahead, as was my usual custom, in order to save delay, and I was struck by the absence of reporters. Up till then – and that was the thirty fifth man to be hanged at Durham since the days of public executions – representatives of the press had always been admitted at that prison. Now, however, change had apparently been made and Durham had fallen into line with other prisons, where newspaper men are excluded. Much could be written of the pros and cons of admitting reporters on such occasions but personally I have always advocated their exclusion. Their presence serves no good purpose that I can see, and they are only an added distraction such as might lead to trouble of some kind.

I had hardly reached the scaffold when the grim procession came in sight. The chaplain walked in front chanting the prayers for the dead on behalf of the still living man who walked erect just behind him. Upton was a short, sturdy man and he strode along with the utmost fortitude.

It was a bright morning – too fine to think of death. There had been a shower of rain earlier on, but the sun now shone out, dispelling the clouds. The birds round about were persuaded to break forth into song and even a cock in the vicinity ventured into a belted crow. Robert Upton strode along with fixed gaze, apparently seeing and hearing nothing. Presently he took his stand on the trapdoors and I whipped the white cap over his head.

When it came to the fixing of the noose I put into operation the new method that I had thought of. In the ordinary way the position of the knot (almost under the left ear) throws the man's chin upwards when he falls. My idea was to put the knot further back in cases where he had tried to cut his throat, so that the man's head was thrown forward on to his chest. In this way I hoped to obviate opening the old wound, but it remained to be seen whether it would afford such a sure and speedy death as the ordinary way. Robert Upton formed my first experiment with the new idea. I put the knot behind his ear, my theory being that when he fell it would work round quite to the back of his neck and throw his chin downwards instead of upwards.

Immediately I had completed this adjustment I leapt to the lever and pulled. Down went Upton, and to my intense satisfaction I saw my theory become a practicable fact. He died at once and yet despite his cut throat, the wound never opened in the slightest degree. All this may seem rather cold hearted in the telling, but I am sincere in saying that my sole intention was then, as always, to so standardise the methods of an execution as to do away entirely with the seeming indifference to a condemned man's feelings that used to characterise such affairs. I always felt that no man could pay a bigger price for his crime than to sacrifice his life and it seemed a work of humanity to spare the wretches as much needless pain as possible.

Thus the discovery of this new principle at the Upton execution provided me with the utmost satisfaction, and whenever possible I used that new method at all subsequent executions of men who had inflicted wounds on their necks after committing murder.

Chapter 15

The Liverpool Sack Murderer

(George Ball (alias Sumner), Walton Gaol, Liverpool, 1914)

One afternoon I stood outside the gates of Walton Gaol, Liverpool, on the point of ringing for admission, when a man stepped up to me out of the crowd of folk standing about.

'Has Ellis, the hangman, arrived yet?' he asked, looking quizzically at me.

I saw he had not recognised me, so offhanded replied —

'I really don't know whether he had or not!'

He moved off satisfied, and I was safely inside a few minutes later. Evidently the people standing about must have been awaiting my arrival, for they knew that a man whose deeds had rung through the whole kingdom was doomed to be hanged behind those grim walls the following morning. The occasion, in fact, was the execution of George Ball (alias Sumner), the perpetrator of the crime known everywhere as 'The Liverpool Sack Murder'.

It had been a sensational affair from beginning to end. The murder itself was of an unusual type, as also were the means adopted to hide its traces, but the greatest feature of it all was the wonderful way in which the suspected man evaded capture for nine days, although he was living right under the noses of the police the whole of the time. The first hint of mystery in the affair was when the disappearance was reported of Miss Christina Bradfield, who looked after one of the offices of her brother, a well-known manufacturer of tarpaulins. Every likely corner was searched for her, and the police were beginning to be absolutely baffled, when, as the result of an accident, this mystery was solved – and another brought to light.

A bargee called Francis Robinson was coming up the Leeds and Liverpool Canal, but at a lock near Lightbody Street his progress was barred. He tried to open the conclusion that a 'fender' was causing the trouble. So he got a boat hook, and commenced to grope for it under the water.

'I was unable to see anything', he said afterwards, 'but after a while the hook struck something soft, and I pulled. Immediately I saw a bulky sack come up dripping with water.'

When the sack was hauled to the bank he was horrified to discover that it contained a human body.

'It was clear that there had been foul play', he continued. 'The sack seemed to be quite new, and round the neck was a piece of strong, tightly-drawn cord. To add to the mystery it seemed as if the sack was sewn up both sides!'

The police were informed, and thereupon the mystery of Miss Bradfield's disappearance was solved. For this was her body. There now awaited a solution to the mystery of her death. For it was obvious she had been murdered. Suspicion fell at once on two youths who worked in her office. Miss Bradfield's staff consisted of a lady typist, a packer named George Sumner, aged 22, and a handcart boy named Samuel Eltoft, aged 18. It was upon these two youths that the police fastened their suspicions, and within an hour or two of the definite identification of Miss Bradfield's mutilated body, Eltoft was in custody.

Then a third mystery developed. Sumner could not be found. He had vanished as if the ground has opened and swallowed him up! His very disappearance was a significant admission of some connection with the crime, and Eltoft himself very quickly furnished more definite grounds for the issue of a warrant against the missing man. Eltoft, indeed, admitted that he had helped Sumner to wheel the dead body in its enveloping sack on a barrow to the canal, but he declared he knew nothing of the murder nor even knew what the sack contained.

I have, so far, called the missing man Sumner for the sake of clearness, but his real name was Ball. He was one of eleven children of a respectable public-house manager, but had quarrelled with his people, and for two years had lived in lodgings under the name of Sumner. He left these lodgings on the day after the discovery of the murdered woman's body, his disappearance dating almost from the hour when the late special editions of the Liverpool evening papers announced the tragic find in the canal.

The days that followed were full of excitement. All over the kingdom police, amateur detectives, and the general public were following up all sorts of clues in the hope of tracing George Ball, whom I will now refer to under his real name. Even the authorities at Scotland Yard did not disdain to search London as if it were a Metropolitan crime. While the hunt is on, let us glance for a moment at the personality of Miss Bradfield and the details of the murder.

Miss Bradfield was 40 years of age and lived across the Mersey at Birkenhead. She was of quiet, amiable temper, but was, all the same, a cool-headed person, well able to take care of herself. A reconstruction of the crime showed that the attack upon her must have been made in Messrs Bradfield's warehouse on the Wednesday evening just after she had put on her hat and furs in preparation for going home. That the lady had made a gallant fight for her life was evident from the fact that her clothing was disarranged, her hands badly bruised, and her eyes discoloured, and that she had wounds on the head and face. One of the fingers was found at the post-mortem to have been almost split open. She had apparently raised her hand to cover or protect her head from the blows raining down upon her.

Eltoft told the police he knew nothing of this, but confessed to a share – he put it as an unwitting one – in that later proceeding. This was what he said:

'Miss Bradfield told us to go home on Wednesday night, and when we got to the door George said to me, "Wait outside until I come back; I won't be long." I waited half an hour, when he came out with a handcart, with something in a sack covered with a cart sheet. He told me to push it along Great Howard Street, and walked alongside me to show me the way. We took the handcart across a field until we came to some stones, when we were not able to push it any further. We took the sack out, dragged it down to the canal and threw it in.'

The details of this confession should be remembered, for Ball later on told a story that varied from it in several essential features. However, it was perfectly clear that the body had been wheeled away in the barrow, for several persons came forward who had seen the two youths pushing it away from the warehouse in the direction of the canal, which was three-quarters of a mile away, although, of course, these witnesses at the time never even guessed what the barrow contained.

And now let us once more take up the hue and cry after George Ball. Minute descriptions of him were published everywhere, and the papers were full of photographs of him. Yet he could not be found. A reward of £50 was offered; ship captains were warned to keep a lookout on board their vessels and to send a wireless if he was recognised among the crew of passengers. Specimens of his handwriting were circulated and bands of people worked together as amateur detectives to scour their own particular districts for the man 'with the glittering eyes', as one person acquainted with Ball described him. Even astrologers volunteered their services.

It was all very reminiscent of the hunt for Dr Crippen about four years previously. All sorts of innocent men were suspected and police officers were scurrying all over the kingdom to look at men detained owing to the too enthusiastic machinations of amateur detectives. Nine days of this sort of thing went on – almost precisely the same period as the Crippen hunt lasted.

Just when people were really beginning to believe the theory put forward that Ball, knowing the game was up, had committed suicide in some out-of-the-way spot, he was found. The discovery was the most dramatic and in one sense the most farcical incident in this remarkable tragedy.

He was run to earth in a Liverpool lodging-house within a stone's-throw of a police station. He had never been out of the city. Neither had he made any attempt to hide himself. He had moved freely about the streets, rode on public vehicles, read his own descriptions posted outside police stations and visited picture palaces, where his photograph was thrown on the screen. His very daring was his finest protection, while all around him were hundreds of people whose one aim was to lay hands on him.

Naturally he had his very clever but also quite simple disguise to thank for his immunity. He had merely shaved off his dark eyebrows, covered one eye with a shade and donned a pair of green spectacles. With this ridiculously simple alteration to his appearance he adopted the daring course of never evading observation and thus for nine days he walked about in absolute safety.

At last however, he was recognised by a former school-fellow, who followed him back to the lodging-house, and then set the police on his track. At first he tried to bluff the sergeant who came to interview him, but when the point-blank question was put to him – 'Are you Sumner?' he answered after a little hesitation – 'Yes. I am the man'. By a coincidence he had been arrested on his twenty-third birthday, and possibly the weary youth was speaking genuinely when he remarked – 'I am glad it's all over'.

Ball, however, still intended to fight for his life. He had a cut-and-dried story all ready to tell, and at his trial he went into the witness-box and narrated such a marvellous concoction that it deserves to be given in his own words. He told how when Eltoft had left that evening Miss Bradfield, who was getting ready to go, sent him upstairs to turn out the lights.

'When I came down', he said, 'I saw a man come from behind a bundle of sacking. He had a marlinspike in his hand – I don't know where he got it from – and he hit Miss Bradfield on the head. As she fell the man dropped the marlinspike. The first smack he gave Miss Bradfield he pointed a revolver at me and threatened me, and said – "Stand back! Do as I ask you to do!" I was then in a state, that I did not know where I was standing. I heard Miss Bradfield fall. The man had his arm on the body, and pointed the revolver at me. I could not see what the man was doing owing to the partition. He was in a kneeling posture, still pointing the revolver at me. The next thing I saw was he had turned the body round. The chap then got up and snatched at her satchel, and the watch fell on the floor. I cannot say whether it came from the satchel or fell out of her hand. As he snatched the satchel the man said – "I'll clear out of this here, and leave you to it". He then rushed out of the shop, pulling the vestibule door behind him.'

At this point his counsel (Mr Tobin) asked Ball – 'Why didn't you attempt to do something to stop this?'

Ball – 'I was on the stairs all the time. If I had been down the stairs I could have moved, but where I was the way he threatened me would have frightened anybody. I could neither move down or up the stairs. Eltoft then came in and asked me what I was looking so white for. I explained to him how the man had come from behind the sacks. I told him he had struck Miss Bradfield on the head, and I showed him the bloodstains on the trousers where I had had the head on my knee. Eltoft said, "It looks rather black against you". I said, "If anybody comes in now I will get blamed for it right away".'

Ball then told how he and Eltoft had put the body in a sack and wheeled it off to the canal.

For two hours after telling the Court this story Ball had to withstand the heavy fire of searching cross-examination, and his version of the affair suffered severely at the hands of the prosecution. It was an amazing defence, far too full of improbabilities to merit any measure of belief. There was also more definite evidence at hand. For instance, he had said that the man who committed the murder had gone off with Miss Bradfield's satchel. Now that bag had contained about £7, and on the morning of the crime Ball had been so hard up that his landlady had advanced him 3d to cover his tram fares and cigarettes. Yet while he was in 'hiding' at the lodging-house he had spent money very freely, and one of the men there swore he had spent at least £3 10s while in his company. Where had he got this money from unless it were the money he had taken from Miss Bradfield's bag. This bag, by the way, was never found.

Altogether there was very little room for doubt. Ball was only too obviously the murderer, and his cock-and-bull story only made his guilt more manifest. In the matter of Eltoft, who was tried at the same time, one could not be so certain. It will be noticed that his own explanation that he helped to remove the wheelbarrow without knowing what it contained was contradicted by Ball, who spoke of Eltoft coming in and assisting in getting the body into the sack. But Ball's story was so clearly an invention in most of its essentials that it was open to question whether he had not lied also in this respect.

In any case, the jury decided to give him the benefit of the doubt. They found him guilty of being an accessory after the fact and Mr Justice Atkin, influenced no doubt by the jury's recommendation to show mercy on account of his youth and on the ground that he was influenced by Ball, sent him to penal servitude for four years. The sentence gave rise to a painful scene, for Eltoft's mother, who was in court, sent out piercing screams, and then fell into a torrent of hysterical weeping.

As for Ball, the sentence of 'Guilty of murder' was no surprise.

'It was a cruel and heartless murder', characterised the Judge. 'Your victim was a good woman; she had been kind to you, and yet you murdered her and did away with her body in circumstances which are revolting.' Quite unmoved, Ball stood erect and received the dread sentence of death. Then he turned at once, gave a swift glance round the court, and descended nonchalantly to the cells. It was a pitiful exhibition of youthful flint heartedness.

There was never the slightest effort made towards presenting a petition for his reprieve. Ball's youthfulness awakened a little sympathy, but this was estranged by his own callous behaviour in court after telling a lying story, which, even if it had been true, only showed him up as a coward, who dared not go to the assistance of an attacked woman. Nobody for a single second believed him to be otherwise than guilty, and consequently it was only too tragically certain that he must expiate this sin on the scaffold. The execution day was fixed for Thursday, February 26, 1914, and when I reached Walton Gaol in accordance with instructions to carry out the death sentence I heard a remarkable story of Ball's behaviour and of how he had passed from his careless nonchalance at the trial through varying stages of passionate outbursts and restless dolefulness, until he at length reached the ultimate point – and confessed!

This is how one of the warders there described them to me during a chat we had after I had been to see the scaffold was in good working order.

'At first', he said, 'Ball spent a great deal of his time in sleep. He would waken sometimes after slumbering two or three hours, pull himself together as he sat upon the edge of the prison settee, or bed, and his eyes were generally then fixed in one particular direction, and he would remain for a period apparently in a condition of stupor. Then he would suddenly bound from his bed and pace the room, as if trying to get rid of some terrifying thoughts. Resuming his former gaiety, real or pretended, he conversed in animated tones with his warders, exhibiting all his former callousness and indifference. He always spoke well, and to some extent he was an interesting conversationalist. He is by no means without intelligence or general knowledge of such things of the world as sport, especially football.'

'When seized with these passionate fits he would stamp his foot on the floor and cry bitterly, "Humbug! Hang the law", or some such words, rapidly uttered. He would throw himself on the settee, rolling about restlessly, but he could not rest or get the repose he sought to choke off the horrid spectres of his mind. He would bound up again and call out fiercely, "Eltoft!" his eyes blazing, especially the peculiar one, which all through the course of the tragedy was in such strong evidence. It was with difficulty he could be tranquillised, and when he eventually became calm he would throw himself back on the settee and fall asleep. On this account he was a convict difficult to manage and we were always glad these paroxysms were over.'

'The nights were, as a rule, long and weary, for Ball slept so much, or lolled so often on his settee during the day that he did not enjoy sustained sleep like a person who had no trouble on his mind.' It then appeared as if Ball was passing into a new stage. He grew quieter, his looks got serious, and his playfulness less marked. He began to show terror of the end which was so near, and too long for religious consolation. At times he showed positive cowardice. This phase developed until the Tuesday – the day before my arrival at the prison – and then came his sensational breakdown. Flinging aside all his previous tales and inventions, he opened his conscience to the chaplain and confessed his guilt.

The Bishop of Liverpool (Dr Chavasse) was immediately sent for, and to him the miserable culprit, welcoming the relief his confession had brought him, made an appeal for confirmation. All his bravado was gone. He was in the throes of a repentant spirit, and, giving him his fullest sympathy, the Bishop agreed to the condemned man's request. The sacred rites were accordingly carried out. On the afternoon of my arrival another pathetic scene had transpired within the prison walls.

Ball's father, sister, brother and brother-in-law went for a last interview with the doomed youth, and had it not been for the fact that I arrived rather late at the gaol, I should have seen them. I had alighted at the wrong station, and everybody I asked seemed to have a different idea in which direction Walton Gaol lay. For three-quarters of an hour I wandered around lost, and it would be quite 4.20pm before I found the prison. Ball's relatives had gone by that time.

My explanation for being so late was accepted by the Governor for, strictly speaking, the executioner is always under orders to be in prison before four o'clock on the afternoon preceding an execution. But, although I had missed seeing the relatives, I nevertheless was given a faithful account of their talk with the condemned youth. One of the officers told me that when Ball's father approached the grating he greeted his doomed son with the words —

'Well George, how are you keeping up?'

'All right', replied young Ball in a low tone. He was evidently labouring under considerable distress, as indeed were all members of that sad family party.

Then came a shock for the relatives. All the prison officers, of course, knew what had transpired at the Bishop's visit, but news like that is kept very close in a prison. So the relatives knew nothing of it, and possibly still hoped that George was innocent of the foul crime alleged against him.

George Ball disillusioned them at the interview, and the officers could see how unexpected it was to the relatives by the emotion and shock they displayed.

'Father', said Ball slowly and quietly, 'I have confessed to the Bishop I did it.'

The poor father reeled as if struck, and as he was led away almost overcome, Ball cried out miserably – 'I hope you'll forgive me father.'

That melancholy scene left a deep impression on Ball and he still appeared under its disturbing influence when I looked through the inspection glass at him a few hours later. He was then calmly writing a letter, but his face showed the ravages of recent emotion. He was, of course, dressed in convict clothes, which ordinarily hides mush of a man's physical build. Nevertheless, he appeared to be a strong-looking sort of fellow for his age.

My room that night was on one side of the hospital, while on the other side were a number of prisoners. Among these was young Eltoft, the youth who stood his trial along with Ball, and got off with four years penal servitude.

The officer-in-charge pointed Eltoft out to me, and I was amazed to find him ever more upset than Ball. He was sitting there gloomily with his head buried in his hands, and, hearing us at the door, lifted his face and turned it towards us. He looked fearfully white and troubled. No doubt his imagination was picturing to him his former companion, Ball, in the condemned cell below, and one can imagine the terror with which Eltoft (who was only a lad of 18) waited for the morning light which was to usher his friend across the portals of death. Who shall say that this hour of itself was not almost enough punishment for whatever degree of guiltiness the youth possessed.

I sat up very late that night chatting with the warders who came to my room for a pleasant hour or two. It would be quite 2.30am before I went to bed. In the morning an unpleasant little thing happened. My watch suddenly fell off the swivel and fell to the floor, breaking the glass. In the ordinary way I am not the slightest degree superstitious, but for some unnameable reason that incident made me feel very uncomfortable. I wondered if it portended that the morning's grim task was not to go off all right.

Putting all thought of omens out of my mind, I went downstairs and out to the scaffold. Here I measured off the drop I had already decided upon – 7 ft. 6 in. – which I had based upon my view of Ball, coupled with a knowledge of his height 5 ft. 5 in. and his weight 149 lb. Ball, I was told, was bearing up extremely well. Ridding his soul of his guilty secret had eased him mightily, and he was now a different fellow altogether from the boastful young murderer who had entered the condemned cell three weeks previously.

The pinioning, I was informed, would not take place in the condemned cell, but in a storeroom much nearer the scaffold. Usually this room was almost entirely an unfurnished chamber, but when I went in to prepare Ball at a moment or so to nine o'clock I was astonished at the transformation in the place. An altar had been erected surmounted by a crucifix, carpets laid down, and some beautiful flowers put up. Ball was on his knees there praying, with the chaplain by his side. The solemnity of the occasion seemed intensified by all this, and I almost felt like an intruder. Duty, however, had to be done, so quietly stepping up to Ball, I gently tapped him on the shoulder. He arose at once, and after I had fastened his arms behind him he moved off at once without a word.

I had gone on in front immediately the pinioning was completed, and as I stood on the scaffold I could see young Ball walking as firm as if it were an ordinary constitutional he was taking. In front of him went the surpliced clergyman praying and reading the special form of service used on such occasions. Ball never wavered when I placed the white cap over his head and the rope round his neck. Cowardly though he had showed himself in his previous life, he was brave enough now. I did not keep him standing there many seconds. While I was tightening the noose my assistant fastened the strap round the condemned man's legs. All preliminaries were now accomplished. My hand darted to the lever. Briskly I moved it, releasing the trapdoors on which Ball stood. And in a quicker space of time than it takes to tell it, Ball was dead.

Chapter 16

The Brides in the Bath Murderer

(George Joseph Smith, Maidstone, 1915)

This will be the first time George Joseph Smith's statement on the scaffold has ever seen the light of print, though it has always seemed an extraordinary thing to me that the secret should have been preserved all these years, seeing what a tremendous sensation the case caused. I must frankly admit that I was really glad I was given the opportunity to hang this man, who made bigamy and murder his trade. And there were many hundreds of men in Great Britain at that time who would willingly have put away all previous scruples and taken the job from me.

Public detestation such as this man earned was of itself no proof of his guilt, but the revelations made at his trial, and things I heard afterwards, left no room for any question as to the man's guilt. For this reason I shall always remember his dramatic plea of innocence on the scaffold as the crowning piece of lying hypocrisy in a life that was full of deceit.

Before I go into that scene in detail let me show how George Joseph Smith graduated in crime from boyish thieving to triple murder. Smith was fated for the gallows almost from childhood. His parents were respectable folks living in Bow, London, but when George Joseph Smith came into the world on January 11, 1872, something vital must have been lacking in his moral make-up. He was more than ordinarily mischievous – he was positively vicious, and nothing that his parents or his teachers could do ever seemed to make the slightest impression on him.

When at last he overshot all bounds he was packed off to a reformatory school, an occasion which led his mother to make a remarkable prophecy.

'He will die in his boots', she remarked. And he did!

He wasn't long out of the reformatory before he went to prison. A bicycle stealing episode at Lambeth when he was only 18 earned him six months' hard labour, and his punishment, far from curing him, was utilised for thinking out new ways of living without working. He came out with his head full of cut and dried ideas, and these same ideas, modified and developed, served to rule the rest of his career.

The basic idea was to prey on women. In his early days his plan may be described as 'love and larceny'. Later it developed into 'marriage and murder'. In both stages of his plan he relied on his extraordinary influence over women, and it is an undeniable fact that although men invariably detested him and the majority of women disliked him, yet he could always be sure of a certain number of easy victims to his doubtful charms. It was at Leicester that Smith entered into marriage bonds for the first – but by no means the last – time in his life. 'George Oliver Love' was the name he was then living under, and it may be here mentioned that only once in the seven matrimonial adventures of which we have ever been able to learn anything did he use his full real name.

This marriage – to a girl named Caroline Thornhill – was the one that stamped all his subsequent weddings as bigamous, for Miss Thornhill was still living when Smith stood charged with the murder of three of his 'wives'. In fact, she provided one of the dramatic sensations of the case against him, for she was brought all the way from America to testify that this infamous Bluebird was actually the man who married her at a church in Leicester on 17 January 1898.

In 1908 Smith entered upon a new phase of his career, for he then met and married Edith Mabel Pegler, of whom Mr Bodkin, the great Treasury counsel, afterwards coined a phrase that became famous. She was, he said, 'the woman to whom Smith always returned'.

Five times he left her, ostensibly on business journeys. On each of those five occasions he married a new 'wife'. He robbed all of them, and got rid of three by drowning them in their baths.

And after each of these adventures he would always return to Miss Pegler with plenty of money and a picturesque story of how he had made it in a business deal.

Smith had a shop as second-hand dealer in Bristol in the summer of 1908, and among his neighbours was Miss Pegler. He wanted a housekeeper, so advertised for one, and Miss Pegler, without knowing whom the advertiser was, applied for the situation and got it. Within a month he had promoted her from the position of housekeeper to that of 'wife', for they were joined in what Miss Pegler firmly believed to be the 'holy bonds of matrimony' at Bristol Registrar's Office on August 30, 1908. She was a deeply religious woman, and desired a church wedding, but somehow the bigamist never fancied any more marriages in church after he wedded Miss Thornhill, and all his subsequent matrimonial knots were tied in registrars' offices.

The shop at Bristol might have been made into a good business concern, but it didn't suit Smith's restless spirit. He soon closed it, and opened others in succession in Bedford, Luton, and Croydon. He wanted some quicker road to fortune, and at last he found it.

He took unto himself a third 'wife', and took everything she possessed.

The story of this woman has never before been dealt with properly, but I can now with perfect propriety, tell some of the details. She was a Southampton girl named Miss Foulkner, and three weeks after his first meeting with her, Smith put a wedding ring on her finger. This was in October 1909.

Miss Pegler married him in his real name but to Miss Foulkner he was 'George Rose'. He took 'Mrs Rose' to London for her honeymoon, got possession of all her money (£350) and her jewellery (£200) and left her 'for a few moments' in a Kensington art gallery. He never returned. Neither did the girl's money or her jewels. He even robbed her of her boxes of personal clothing which brought his haul up to the value of about £660. He returned to Miss Pegler with the £660, which he said he had made by the sale of a genuine Turner picture at a big profit, and went to live at Southend, where he bought a house.

Three months later their home was again shifted back to Bristol, where Smith opened a shop once more. This was merely his temporary eerie from which this human vulture could conveniently issue forth to find suitable victims. He was not long in finding one. In the early part of August, 1910, he met a Miss Beatrice Munday at Clifton, who straight away was overpowered by the charms of her experienced lover, 'Henry Williams', as he called himself. Of course, it was her money Smith was after, but he had a set-back at first. Miss Munday was the daughter of a bank manager, and when he died she inherited £2500. As, however, she had no business capabilities, she voluntarily gave her uncle and brother the charge of her money as trustees.

Smith had hardly reckoned on this, and when he discovered it after the wedding he decided that he had better retire from the scene until such time as he could discover a safe way of getting at the money. Miss Munday was but a pawn in the game he was playing, and he had no intention of consulting her feelings in the matter. Consequently he had no qualms of conscience when Miss Munday had enjoyed a fortnight of 'married bliss' in unobtrusively disappearing. And with him went £130 of Miss Munday's money too.

We now reach the final stage in the criminal development of this fiend. He wanted Bessie Munday's £2500, but he could only touch it if she were dead. As calmly as he had left her, Smith quite as calmly went back to Miss Munday. His vile plans lay well concealed at the back of his mind when, about a year and a half after he had deserted her, 'Henry Williams' affected delighted surprise at his 'chance' meeting with his most recent wife, whom he met in the streets at Weston-Super-Mare. Knowing the man and his schemes, I've no doubt whatever that that meeting was no chance affair.

In an incredibly short space of time the man whom Miss Pegler thought was in Canada on business was back in the good graces of Miss Munday, and was living in happy reunion with her while he got through the necessary preliminaries to encompassing her death. He took her to Herne Bay, and by delicate campaigning arranged that they should make mutual wills – that is, he would make a will leaving everything to her at his death, and she would make a will leaving all she had to him. She agreed. A solicitor set to work to prepare the draft wills. Meanwhile Smith went out to buy a bath. Events moved rapidly now. On 5 July 1912, the bath was installed in their lodgings. It had no pipes or taps – just a bare bath. And the heartless wretch had even got Miss Munday to go to help choose it.

On July 10 he took her to a doctor and tells him she has had a fit. The doctor found little evidence of fits, but prescribed for her and visited her on the subsequent days. By then all was in readiness for the final coup. The wills were finished and signed, and the doctor knew the woman was subject to fits. It only remained that she should apparently have a fatal seizure, and the deed was done. That 'seizure' came on the morning of Saturday, July 13. At 7.30 Smith went out to buy fish for breakfast. At eight o'clock he was gasping out, in the doctor's surgery. 'Come at once. I am afraid my wife is dead'. Dead she was.

The doctor found her lying in the bath with her head submerged, and acting under the subtle suggestion of his previous examination of the woman, which Smith had so cleverly arranged, he never imagined any other explanation but that she had been seized with another fit in her bath, and under its influence had fallen into the water and been drowned.

The Coroner's jury accepted this theory without much persuasion. Miss Munday's brother, when informed of her sudden death, was inclined to be suspicious, and he wrote to the Coroner, asking him to make the investigation as thorough as possible. Smith was most indignant at this, and acted his part of bereaved husband so well that he gained considerable sympathy. He also gained something still more to his purpose – a verdict of death by misadventure, which left him free to lay hands on her property under his will.

For the time being Smith had thrown dust into everybody's eyes. He had successfully become a murderer, and was yet safe from detection. Having accomplished his task of ridding himself of the obstacle to the money he coveted, he returned to Miss Pegler with a glowing story of having made a great profit in a deal in Chinese images. The 'woman he always returned to' had drawn him back once more.

With Miss Munday's £2500 safely in his custody and her body safely in the grave, he once more began his wanderings in company with Miss Pegler. They opened shop after shop in various parts of the South of England, but Smith was so elated at the success of his scheme at Herne Bay that he wanted to try it again. This method of death in a bath looked so easy to accomplish and so safe from detection that it must be done again.

In September, 1913, he had found a new 'subject' to operate upon. He had met the ill-fated Miss Alice Burnham.

'I'm going to Spain on a business tour', he told Miss Pegler, and she believed him. If he had said – 'I am going to Blackpool to murder a young girl', he would have been nearer the truth.

His scheme for marrying and disposing of his brides was now more or less cut and dried. Within eight weeks of his first meeting at Portsmouth with Alice Burnham, a sweet-faced nurse, he married her. Then he had her insured for £500, and induced her to make a will leaving everything to him. Next he took her to a doctor with same tale of fits as in Miss Munday's case. Finally, with all these things well and smoothly laid, he drowned her in her bath a month after her wedding, and again succeeded in hoodwinking doctors, Coroner, and jury that the death was accidental.

He acted this little drama in the name of George Smith, a significant act of daring, seeing that his full real name was George Joseph Smith. But he made a bad slip at Blackpool. He was too callous. At the time his obvious relief at having got Miss Burnham out of the way and the road clear to her money did little more than occasion the ire of his landlady. But, as I will show presently, it was this same ire that eventually led him to the scaffold.

He made scandalously mean arrangements for the funeral, robbed the dead woman of her wedding ring, and did other things that so upset this woman's ideas of how a man bereaved of his young bride should act that when he had gone she got her daughter to write these prophetic words on a postcard – 'George Smith. Wife died in the bath. I shall see him again some day'. By Christmas Smith was back again with Miss Pegler. Everything had been accomplished in the intervening three months. Another 'bride' had come and gone, and his pockets were the heavier for her £500 insurance money and £104 in ready cash.

For some months after his return to Miss Pegler, Smith continued to search for new victims. Perhaps he found them not so easy to find; at any rate, he descended to small game in the following September (1914). At that time he met a Miss Alice Reavil at Bournemouth, and a fortnight's wooing sufficed before they entered the nuptial state on 17 September at Woolwich. Driving from the registrar's office to their lodgings, he worked the confidence trick on her. He showed her a bundle of notes, which, he said, were to the value of £72, whereupon she entrusted him with the £14 which she had in loose cash. Then he got her to withdraw all she had in the Post Office Savings Bank (£76), and give it to him for the purpose of opening a shop for the sale of antiques. Next day he disappeared with the lot, and took even her luggage with him, this of itself containing clothes, &c., worth £50. The poor girl was left without clothes and without a penny on the day after her wedding. But I guess she had cause in after life to be relieved that Smith had not found it part of his plan to take her life too.

Bigger game soon fell in the path of the murderous bride-hunter. It was destined to be his last hand in this game of human lives that he was playing. Flying from Miss Reavil, he met Margaret Elizabeth Lofty, and immediately saw in her the possibilities for another bath murder, with adequate compensation. It took him about six weeks to move from the stage where he introduced himself to Miss Lofty as 'John Lloyd' to marrying her. Matters proceeded from that point with a speed that was swift even for this lightning Bluebeard.

It all went through with the despatch of a man who 'knew the ropes', but this affair was to bring him greater knowledge of a different kind of rope. There was the usual precautionary visit to the doctor, who was afterwards sent for to see the drowned woman, and there was the same execution of a will leaving all Miss Lofty's money in the bank and her recently made insurance policy for £700 to her sorrowing husband. Smith smiled as he again saw the Coroner's jury once more swallow the story he had so cleverly concocted, but this very inquest was indirectly the cause of his downfall.

The romantic circumstances of the girl's death earned notice not only in the local paper but also in some bigger London journals, and the headline 'Bride's Death in a Bath', attracted some attention. Smith had made a fatal slip on choosing London for this murder, for London papers are read all over the kingdom. Consequently it was not remarkable that the landlady in Blackpool who had been so upset over the death of 'Mrs Smith' (Alice Burnham) in a bath in her house should wonder if there was more than a coincidence in the fact that a 'Mrs Lloyd' had died in similar fashion also but a few hours after being made a bride.

She communicated with the police, and Detective-Inspector Neil, of Scotland Yard, was instructed to investigate. There were to be no more victims for George Joseph Smith. His race was run.

As he went along a London street on his way to draw Miss Lofty's insurance money Detective-Inspector Neil arrested him.

'Are you John Lloyd?' he asked.

'Yes', replied Smith.

'You were married to Margaret Elizabeth Lofty on December 17 last, and she was found dead by you in a bath at Bismarck Road, Highgate, the following evening?'

Again Smith admitted this, wondering when the detective revealed his identity, what was coming next.

'You are also said to be identical', continued Neil, 'with George Smith, whose wife was found dead in a bath under similar circumstances on December 13, 1913, at Blackpool, and whom you married a few weeks before.'

'Smith!' cried the murderer in feigned puzzlement, 'I'm not Smith. I don't know what you are talking about.'

Inwardly, however, he was quaking, for Smith, as I found afterwards, was a coward at heart. He waited in fear for the officer's next words. They were to the following effect:

'I intend taking you to the police station, and if it is found that you are George Smith you will be charged with causing false entries to be made in your marriage certificate.'

False entries! The murderer might have been excused from laughing aloud. He had expected to be charged with murder, and instead here was this Scotland Yard man talking about false entries in marriage certificates! With a chuckle he submitted to being marched to the police station.

The smile faded soon enough. Evidence began to pile up. All the facts that I have recounted already came gradually to light until it became clear that he was not only 'John Lloyd' and 'George Smith', but that he was also 'George Oliver James', 'Henry Williams', 'George Rose', and 'George Oliver Love'; all of them merely aliases whereby different wives knew the man who was born as George Joseph Smith.

The simple-looking 'false entries' charge soon developed into something that sent Smith's miserable soul into a Hades of doubts and anxieties. It was dropped, and a charge of bigamy appeared in its place. And later this too made way for the indictment for murder.

I can well remember the way in which the case, which at first seemed likely to attract but little notice, suddenly jumped into first place in the newspapers, and became everybody's topic. The great war had just broken over Europe, but for the moment even it was dwarfed by public interest in this most extraordinary case. When at length it came to trial at the Old Bailey people would stand for hours in queues in the streets waiting for the doors to open in order to secure a seat at this life and death drama. The case lacked nothing to convict him. Mr Marshall Hall, who defended Smith, could do nothing with the wall of facts against him, and Smith was found guilty.

With a scornful smile Smith saw the Judge don the black cap. He pretended he didn't care. Before delivering the dread sentence Mr Justice Scrutton, white-bearded and solemn, said in the course of his remarks – 'I think an exhortation to repentance would be wasted on you'.

Smith had hardly been removed from the dock ere he was busy with his appeal.

He felt confident that he would succeed in upsetting the death sentence. He came into the Appeal Court with his hair carefully brushed and his dark moustache waxed and curled, and, in fact, presented quite a jaunty appearance. His jauntiness vanished when the adverse decision was spoken. As the Lord

Chief Justice announced their concurrence with the verdict of the Old Bailey trial, Smith clutched the dock rail tightly till his knuckles shone white. Then he relaxed them, and was ushered below. His briskness had gone in a moment as if by magic. For the first time he saw the scaffold standing inevitable before him.

Up to now he had been kept in Pentonville Prison, but when the appeal was settled he was removed to Maidstone, where he was to be executed. His demeanour altered at once. While still at Pentonville – as I was told by an officer at Maidstone – he complained because one of the warders told to sit with him would not talk. Said he —

'He sits there all the time saying nothing. Anybody would think he was going to be hanged instead of me.' So they had to change this warder for one with greater conversational powers.

I was instructed to carry out the execution immediately the first trial ended. The appeal, of course, necessitated alteration of the date originally fixed upon (July 20), but in the end August 13, 1915, was decided as the day upon which the Brides' Baths Murderer should die. Accordingly I travelled south from Rochdale on the previous day.

The rule is that executioners must reach prison by four o'clock on the afternoon preceding the day on which the sentence is to be carried out, and must not leave the building until after it is all over. But through a mistake when I booked my ticket, I did not arrive at Maidstone Station until nearly five that afternoon, and both the Sheriff (Mr Bartlett) and the Under Sheriff (Mr Howlett) were waiting anxiously on the platform for me. They were openly relieved when I arrived, and advised me to get inside the prison as fast as I could. I had a shave first, and then entered the grim building under whose roof lay the doomed man. Nobody was about at the time, and so I entered quite unnoticed. At once I was taken by the Chief Warder to an interview with the Governor, who gave me necessary details about Smith's physical measurements. The condemned man, he said, was 5 ft. 7 ½ in. in height, and weighed 161 lb. I made a note of those figures, as they were to assist me in determining the length of the drop.

The proper Governor of Maidstone Prison was at the time on a visit to his son lying in a hospital in France, so Deputy Governor Wintle came from Liverpool Gaol to take charge. I had met this gentleman before when I hanged George Ball (alias Sumner), the lad who was the central character in the great Liverpool Sack Murder Mystery, and he recalled this occasion by remarking —

'I hope you will carry out this execution as well as you did Ball's.' [See Chapter 15.]

'How is Smith keeping up?' I asked.

'He seems a little depressed', the Governor answered. 'I am afraid he will require some assistance in the morning.' Hearing this I suggested that Smith should be given a good dose of brandy a minute or two before eight o'clock, but the Governor was not inclined to do this on his own responsibility. 'That is a matter left entirely to the doctor', he said, so, leaving the Governor, I went to examine the trap-doors in the death shed, resolving to see the doctor as soon as I could.

My assistant was already in the prison. His name was Edward Taylor, and he came from Brighton, this being his first appointment. As it happened, he was one of the many men who, from time to time all through my life, used to write to me, telling me they wanted to be hangmen, too, and would I help them? I always told them I had no power to give them appointments, but invariably sent them a courteous reply, informing them where to apply. This Mr Taylor was one of them, and he had followed up my advice and passed his examination until he was fully qualified.

When I got chatting with him I discovered a still further coincidence. It was, I found, from him that I had purchased my first bulldog, four years previously, and I may say here that I afterwards became fairly renowned in the canine world for the bulldogs I bred. I took Taylor along with me to put things right on the scaffold, and this accomplished, I arranged with the chief warder for a view of the notorious Smith.

It was quite a light summer's evening, so the chief said —

'I will get him out of his cell into the grounds so that you can see him properly.'

He found the chaplain, whispered a few words of instruction to him, and then took Taylor and I into the hospital, from one of the windows of which we were to gaze down into the grounds where Smith would be paraded before us without knowing I was watching him. What a shock I got when he came into view! You will all have seen the photos of him as a smart, well-dressed, and spruce, handsome man. He was like that at his trial. But now! – heavens, what an alteration!

His hitherto well-brushed hair had turned almost white, and was hanging unkempt over his shoulders. His face was drawn and haggard, and even his moustache drooped sadly and seemed to be changing colour. His back was bent, and he looked altogether like an old man. Indeed, I would have taken him for 63 instead of 43.

The chaplain sat on a seat with Smith, who was, of course, still in convict garb. His own clothes would be given him that night for him to wear at the end.

His position on the garden seat was not giving me a chance of seeing the back of his neck, as I desired, and so I sent a warder to fashion a pretext for walking Smith up and down in front of the window where I was stationed. This ruse succeeded, and I saw what I wanted. Then came my chance for a chat with the doctor. He volunteered the information that Smith's heart was diseased, adding – 'It would not surprise me if he collapses under the strain before he gets to the scaffold'.

I then offered my suggestion that a liberal dose of brandy should be given him in the morning, as I had frequently found this to have remarkable efficacy in bracing up the condemned persons. The doctor agreed, but I may as well say at this point that Smith never had it after all.

One of the warders took it to him at the prescribed time – a few minutes before the execution – but Smith waved it away. 'I do not require that', he declared in his lordly way, though it was obvious that he was badly in need of a stimulant. A few mornings before the end came he was confirmed by the Bishop of Croydon, although he was attended in his last moments by a Wesleyan minister.

While I was chatting with the officers on the last evening of Smith's life I learned many interesting things, among them being something of what transpired during the Bishop's visit. The murderer declared that the Bishop asked him if he had any confession to make, adding as an inducement to candour that if Smith desired it kept secret he (the Bishop) would regard his lips as for ever sealed. The impudent murderer replied – 'I have no confession to make, as I am innocent'.

In revealing this episode I do so with particular pleasure, because in many quarters I have heard and read it most definitely stated that Smith made a confession. He did not. I know for a positive fact that he told one of his attendants that he had nothing to tell, and that he wouldn't say anything in any case because of Miss Pegler. 'I do not care about myself', he told this officer, 'but I am considering those I am leaving behind'.

He told these things very freely to his attendants, and I spent many hours that evening listening to their stories of him. He told them, for instance, that his trial had cost him £1400 but he still had something left, In virtue of this he made his will, and one of the warders told me he signed it as a witness.

'There will be £150 for Miss Pegler when everything is settled', Smith had said.

Yet he refused to allow Miss Pegler to visit him. He said she wanted to come and see him, but he wanted no visitors.

The long last night passed at last, and the day of Smith's execution dawned brilliantly fine. When I got up to complete my preparations on the scaffold I heard that a letter had arrived for the doomed man with the address in printed characters as though to disguise the handwriting, but, I doubt very much whether it was given to him. Nothing from the outside world is allowed to distract a condemned man on the morning of his execution.

His nerves were now failing him. The air of calm impudence disappeared, and the man's inner cowardly self peeped forth. A breakfast of boiled eggs, bread and butter, and tea was placed before him, but he hardly touched it. Yet as I have already said, he declined to have the brandy.

The final moments arrived. I had arranged the rope for a drop of 6 ft. 8 in. My assistant and I walked through a strangely hushed prison to the corridor outside Smith's cell. On the way we met the Governor, who said to me:

'Will three minutes suit you, Mr Ellis?'

'One minute will be nearer the mark', I replied.

It was accordingly settled that he should give me the signal to go to Smith at one minute to eight. It would be about a minute and a half to eight when we arrived outside Smith's door, and then a curious thing happened.

Hearing our feet shuffling outside, the chaplain imagined the time had arrived, so he opened the cell door and came out. Smith followed him. The condemned man had reached the doorway before he was noticed, but an officer then stepped forward and gently pushed him back into his cell.

Smith was thus left alone in his cell for the first time since his condemnation, and I look upon the incident as one of the most remarkable in all my career. For a full half minute we, the officials of the law, stood outside in a bunch, while the Sheriff (Mr Bartlett) stood with his watch in hand ticking out the seconds of a man's life.

On the other side of the door for that same space of time stood Smith, the Brides' Bath Murderer, absolutely alone. If ever a man had an opportunity to search his soul and display penitence he had it then. I have often thought that it would surely be the most interesting thing in the whole of this remarkable case if one could learn what passed through his mind as he stood there alone after getting that glimpse of the officials outside waiting to come in and take him forth and hang him. The experience was absolutely unique in my career. Dead silence reigned during those thirty seconds of waiting. Then came the nod I was waiting for from Mr Bartlett. The time had come.

I pushed open the cell door and entered. Smith was standing with his back to me, and his hands clasped behind his back. He flinched slightly as I gripped his left wrist and put the pinioning strap over it, but he made no attempt to struggle, or even to move at all. I then fastened this wrist and the other together behind his back. Having loosened his shirt neck I departed from the cell, leaving Smith in charge of my assistant, and made with all speed for the scaffold.

The procession came forth behind me from the prison, and I stood awaiting it at the place of execution thirty yards distant. Many of those present were perhaps inclined to forget the man's awful crimes as he walked at a fair pace to his doom. But this compassion must have vanished when he presently showed that, despite the imminence of death, he was as impertinent as ever. He was facing me hardly a couple of inches off the trapdoors when he halted and exclaimed:

'I am innocent of this crime!'

The old loathing against the man was revived at once by those words. Perhaps that is why the prison authorities never allowed them to be made public before this. Maybe they preferred the public to think kindly of the man as having confessed his sins before expiating them. But in reality he neither confessed them nor showed any contrition for them. One might almost imagine he gloried in them.

I pulled him on to the chalk mark on the trapdoors and put the white cap over his head. While I was fixing the rope round he spoke again. 'I am innocent!' he lied once more. His last chance for righting himself with God was gone. I pulled the lever, and 46 seconds after leaving his cell Smith, the Brides' Bath Murderer, was dead. No man ever more richly deserved his fate.

Chapter 17

The Air Raid Murderer

(Louis Marie Joseph Voisin, Pentonville, 1918)

When a judge goes out of his way to hint that all the facts in connection with a murder case have not been made public, as Mr Justice Avery did in the trial that came as a sequel to the sensational Regent Square mystery, the public may be excused for feeling a degree of dissatisfaction. I am not going to pretend that I shall reveal these hidden facts. This much, however, I can safely say, that when I hanged Louis Marie Joseph Voisin there died the only man in the world who had any guilty share in the murder of Mme. Gerard. Incidentally, he showed himself in his last hour as precisely the kind of craven coward that one might have expected a man of his gross life and still more gross crime to be at heart.

I imagine there were few people who had any belief that the culprit would be arrested when the first sensational discovery of a woman's dismembered body was made public. There seemed almost nothing for the police to work upon. A male nurse at a nearby hospital, while passing along Regent Square, Bloomsbury, on the morning of Friday, November 2, 1918, saw inside the railings of the semi-public gardens a parcel that provoked his curiosity. He thought it was a soldier's kit bag at first, but when he put his hand through the railings and touched it the soft feel of its contents made him determined to find out what really were its contents. So he climbed the railings and here in his own words are the results of his investigation:

'The parcel', he said, 'was done up in sacking and tightly bound with a thin rope very firmly knotted. As I could not untie the knots I cut the rope with my knife. I was shocked to see the top of the trunk of a body. The head had been cut away close to the shoulders as if with a very sharp instrument. I then opened the package fully, removing an inner white sheet, in which the trunk of a woman was tightly wrapped. The body was clothed in a beautifully-made undergarment, with lace and blue ribbon round the upper part. On it lay a piece of torn brown wrapping paper, on which I read the words – "Blodie Belgian", written in pencil.

I threw the wrappings loosely over the body and blew my whistle for the police. A crowd quickly gathered. Before the police arrived I looked round wondering whether the missing parts lay near. Against a tree trunk I picked up a smaller parcel, which was tied up in much the same thorough way. I opened it with my knife, and discovered a leg and a foot. When the police came and I looked more closely, I observed that, besides the white sheet in which the trunk was wound, there were other pieces of torn sheeting, which seemed to have been used to staunch the flow of blood from the wounds. What impressed me was the clean nature of all the cuts. Speaking from personal experience, I hardly think a skilled surgeon could have made the amputation more deftly. I was astonished to detect that the outer wrappings of both parcels were only damp with the morning mist. I inferred from this that they had not lain there long. I remembered that a good deal of rain fell after midnight. The sheets inside both parcels were quite dry.'

Dr Gabe, the police surgeon, who saw the body where it lay, expressed the opinion that death had taken place within twenty-four hours.

What a sensation that discovery made. Never, I venture to state, since the days of Crippen's somewhat similar crime had so much speculation been aroused over a murder mystery, for it really seemed almost impossible that much progress would ever be made in solving it. The clues were of the slenderest description, and as the woman's head was missing, there were extraordinary difficulties in the way of establishing her identity.

The gruesome parcel had been placed in the garden within an hour of its discovery. That was clearly proved. And the body had been dissected by a surgeon or a butcher, and the victim had died from shock following upon loss of blood some twenty-four hours previously.

Those were the only direct clues as to the murder itself. But the wrappings round the parcels and the sheets in which the body was wrapped furnished assistance of a kind likely to be more valuable. There were three pieces of white fabric used, bearing the circular trade stamp – 'Argentina La Plata Cold Storage', which again hinted that a butcher was concerned in the affair. And – more important still – the body was wrapped in two fine sheets, one of which bore the laundry mark '11 H'.

A photograph of the latter appeared in the newspapers, and – not for the first time in criminal annals – this assistance by the press led to the subsequent solution of the whole mystery. That laundry mark was a small thing, but as is so often the case, it was just that little overlooked detail that laid the criminal by the heels. A laundry saw the photograph, recognised it, and communicated with the police. The missing link had been supplied. From that moment the chain of inquiries went forward unchecked, and that which a few days previously had seemed a hopeless mystery was quickly solved.

The first result of the information about the laundry mark was that the police discovered that the murdered woman was Mme. Emilienne Gerard, wife of a soldier in the French Army. She had been living in rooms in Munster Square, St Pancras, about a mile from the spot where the body was discovered, and had been missing for several days. The police communicated with the French military authorities, with the result that Paul Gerard, a soldier in the French Army in the western front, was brought to London to complete the identification.

The poor fellow wept bitterly when he saw his beloved wife's dismembered body in St Pancras Mortuary. Mme. Gerard had been a good-looking woman of thirty, inclined to plumpness, possessing abundant fair curly hair, and her landlady told an interviewer that she and her husband seemed very much attached to each other. This lady gave other information of a most valuable kind. Indeed, it led to the arrest of the murderer.

Mme. Gerard had a frequent visitor, who, she said, was her brother-in-law, and who used to call on her both before and after her husband went to join the French Army. He used to drive a funny-looking little trap drawn by a mule, which he drove from the back, as one drives a governess car. Two days after Mme. Gerard disappeared, he drove up in a more modern trap, and told us that madame had gone to the country for a fortnight. He also said that he was sending her a sack of potatoes. This hint was not lost on the police. They quickly found that Mme. Gerard's visitor, the man who drove 'a funny-looking little trap', was well-known in Upper Soho as Louis Voisin. He was 57 years of age, and lived in Charlotte Street, and he was one of the most striking figures in a peculiar district possessing many queer characters.

The 'funny-looking trap' which he owned was familiar to all around there. Voisin was said to have built it to his own design with his own hands. This vehicle was closed entirely in front, apparently, except for a hole through which the reins passed; it opened at the back like a governess car, but was enclosed on the top and sides. In fact, it was a sort of snuggery on wheels, and Voisin delighted in taking all kinds of folk for a spin in this weird affair.

Obviously this man knew something of Mme. Gerard in life, and Scotland Yard meant to find out if he knew anything of how she came by her death. So on the Saturday following the first discovery in Regent Square a number of officers called on him, and he was asked when he last saw the ill-fated woman. 'At Munster Square on Wednesday at her house', he replied, 'when she told me she was going to Southampton to see her friend off. Her name is Marguerite. I do not know her other name, I said "Good-bye" to them on Wednesday morning. Mme. Gerard said that she might stay a few days and asked me to pay her lodgings.'

So far there was nothing upon which any charge could be formulated against Voisin, however much suspicion may have pointed in his direction, but next day further facts came to light, and it was decided to question him further. He was taken to Bow Street, where he made a statement very much on the lines of what he had said the day previously.

Then came a dramatic development. Chief Inspector Wensley said to the interpreter: 'Ask him if he has any objection to writing the words "Blodie Belgian". These words, it will be remembered, were found on a piece of paper in the parcel containing Mme. Gerard's body. 'Not at all', replied Voisin, and he wrote the words down several times. At once it became apparent that the hand-writing was precisely the same as that found on the body. All doubts were now at rest. Voisin was told that he was under arrest.

Here it is necessary to go back a little bit. For twelve months Mme. Gerard had gone each day from her home in Munster Square to keep Voisin's house in order for him. But some months before the crime he met another woman named Berthe Roche (or Martin), and forthwith he dispensed with Mme. Gerard and installed Berthe Roche at Charlotte Street as his housekeeper.

This woman was suspected now of being concerned in the murder, and when Voisin was taken to Bow Street she accompanied him. Consequently when the police decided to charge Voisin with the murder they included Berthe Roche too, and the pair were told they were under arrest, and were placed in the cells. But the end of the sensation in this remarkable case had not yet been reached. A search was made of the Charlotte Street premises, and here the dead woman's head and the two missing hands were found in a brine tub! Some of Mme. Gerard's jewellery was also found in a secret drawer in Voisin's rooms.

Who now could doubt his guilt? It was even possible to form a reconstruction of the whole crime, which when it came to the jury had a most convincing quality. It may seem a long way from an air raid to the Regent Square mystery, but the two things were undoubtedly connected. For it was under cover of the disturbance caused by the bomb-dropping on that night of October 31 that Mme. Gerard was done to death.

The raid warnings were issued about 11.30 that night, and Mme. Gerard was heard moving about in her room at Munster Square at that time. Possibly, with a view to seeking the protection of Voisin, whose house had a cellar, Mme. Gerard went to Charlotte Street. According to Berthe Roche, when they were given the raid warning there, she left Voisin's room and sheltered with the other occupants of the house, and when she returned Voisin was asleep. This statement, however, contained discrepancies of a vital character, for it must have been during that period that Mme. Gerard arrived at the house and was murdered.

The question of motive is one that cannot be entered into, and even the suggested method of the murder has many puzzling features. According to Dr Spilsbury the unfortunate woman was struck many savage blows on the head, and yet so little strength was used that although the scalp was pierced in many places the skull was not even fractured. The woman practically bled to death, and the weapon as it rose and fell scattered blood all over the place. It was the unpleasant duty of the jury who heard the case to go to that loathsome cellar in Charlotte Street, and there they saw these bloodstains for themselves, and were shown how the woman was probably killed in the doorway, while the blood that poured from her wounds ran off down the drain.

An amazing feature of the case was that blood had been taken apparently to Mme. Gerard's house in Munster Square, and scattered about her room with the object of leading people to think that she had been murdered there. Voisin made a most remarkable 'explanation' of the whole affair when called upon to produce his defence. Having confirmed what Mme. Roche had said regarding his movements on Wednesday night during the air raid, he went on to say:

'Mme. Martin (Roche) is not concerned in this crime at all. The crime was committed at Mme. Gerard's place. I went there on the Thursday at 11 a.m., and when I arrived the door was closed but not locked. The floor and the carpet were full of blood. The head and hands were wrapped up in a flannel jacket, which is at my place now. They were on the kitchen table. That's all I can say. The rest of the body was not there. I was so astonished at such an affair I did not know what to do.'

'I remained five minutes stupefied. I did not know what to do. I thought that a trap had been paid for me. I commenced to clean up the blood and my clothes became stained with it. I looked to see whether there was anybody else in the house, but they had all gone out. As soon as I cleaned up the blood I left the head and hands in the things they were wrapped up in. I then put the lot in the small rug by the side of the bed.'

'There were bloodstained finger-marks on the handle of the jug. I then went back to my house, had lunch, and later returned to Mme. Gerard's room and took the packet to my place. I kept thinking this was a trap. I had no intention to do any harm to Mme. Gerard. Why should I kill her? I didn't want any money. Mme. Gerard owes me nothing, and I owe her nothing. I cannot see why I should do such a thing as that to Mme. Gerard. I wanted to see Mons. Gerard because I knew Mme. Gerard was mixed up with bad associates, and had taken people to her flat. I knew she had taken somebody there that night, and there are letters there to show that she had been meeting men.'

As will be seen, his story was an ingenious one, but the facts I have already detailed were sufficient to show it all up as a fabrication. I should also like to add that his hints with the object of casting aspersions on the dead woman's character were proved quite unfounded and false.

At any rate, he took care to run no risks that might have resulted from cross-examination, for he did not avail himself of his right to go into the witness box – a point that Mr Justice Darling emphasised in his summing up.

Quite early in the trial it became evident that there was no direct or positive evidence against Berthe Roche on the murder charge although, as Mr Justice Darling remarked, 'It is a case of very strong suspicion against her'. So the jury were ordered to acquit her on the capital charge, though she was held in custody to face a subsequential trial as accessory after the fact.

As for Voisin, the jury took but fifteen minutes to find him guilty, and when they returned with their verdict the Clerk of the Court, speaking in French, for Voisin could not converse in English, asked him if he had anything to say. Voisin tried to smile'I say I am innocent', he replied in French, and visibly braced himself for the death sentence.

Mr Justice Darling then adopted a curious procedure. He passed sentence as follows:

'You have been found guilty on incontestable evidence of the murder of Mme. Gerard and I have to pronounce sentence of death on you in the form prescribed by English Law. As you no not understand English I shall pass judgement in you in your own language, and I must then repeat it in English, as our law requires.'

The Judge then added – 'May the Lord have mercy on your soul'. The sentence in French was followed by the grim formula in English, and Voisin, who had only paled a little, without a glance round the court, disappeared down the stairs to the cells.

The condemned man's execution was fixed for February 5 at Pentonville Prison, and I was duly engaged to carry it out. But ten days prior to that I received notice from the Acting Under Sheriff (Mr. R. K. Metcalfe) that Voisin had appealed. The technical grounds of the appeal were, however, insufficient to secure any alteration in the sentence, so once more the machinery for carrying out the law's extreme punishment was put in motion, and I received a wire from Mr Metcalfe – 'Are you disengaged February 26?' to which I replied that I was.

But there was to be still another component. Mme. Berthe Roche was to be tried that week as accessory after the fact. And although an assurance was given that the condemned man was not to be called as a witness, the feeling was held that if he were executed on the arranged date (Tuesday 26 February) something might arise which would cause one side or the other to use the argument that the chief possible witness was dead.

Accordingly, Voisin was respited from the Tuesday to the Saturday (2 March), his accomplice's trial being heard on the intervening Thursday and Friday. The prosecution relied on a chain of acts by the woman Roche, all leading to shield Voisin, and the very definite fact that she had washed his shirt which was stained with human blood, and had done so in a manner that suggested she knew quite well whose blood it was and how the stains came there.

At the end of the trial after the verdict was delivered Mr Justice Avory asked a significant question. 'I presume', said he to Mr Muir, the prosecution counsel, 'there are other facts connected with this crime that have not been made public?' To which Mr Muir replied, 'That is so'.

The jury believed Berthe Roche to be guilty as an accessory after the fact, and their verdict to that effect produced a bitter outburst from the accused woman. 'I am innocent', she cried. 'I did not know Mme. Gerard'. She then broke down utterly, and rocked herself to and fro in the dock, and presently collapsed. Assisted to a seat at the side of the dock, she moaned and wailed at the top of her voice.

For several minutes the Judge waited patiently. Then, when she was more composed, he simply remarked: 'Mme. Roche, the sentence upon you is that you be kept in penal servitude for seven years.' She had to be carried to the cells, having been supported by two warders and two wardresses while sentence was passed.

Those were the days of food shortage and ration cards, and it was therefore quite in keeping with the spirit of the times that the Governor of Pentonville Prison should write me as follows:

'I beg to inform you that it will be necessary for you either to bring your own meat, bacon, sugar, butter, or margarine, for which you will receive the money equivalent, or bring your food cards, and the articles will be purchased here for you (the quantities would have to be on the rationed basis). If you have no difficulty in obtaining supplies I would advise you to adopt the former course.'

I decided to fall in with the suggestion to take my own food, but a surprise awaited me when I reached the prison on the afternoon of Monday 1 March. They had my tea ready for me, and gave me my other meals while I was there without any difficulty or inquiry for my food cards.

Just when I and my assistant had got nicely started on our tea the chief warder came to summon us. They were on the point of taking Voisin to be weighed, and it was thought this would be a good opportunity for me to have a surreptitious look at him. The weighing machine was set up in a sort of hall at the junction of a number of corridors of cells on the ground floor, and the chief warder stationed us behind two glass doors, about three or four yards from the apparatus.

Presently we heard a clatter of echoing footsteps. The noise came from two warders, who were walking one on each side of the condemned man. He himself moved along silently, for he was wearing slippers. What a heavy man he looked! He was not very tall – standing only 5 ft. 3 ½ in. – and he had an extraordinarily thick neck. The Governor and I commented on this. It made the man look even heavier than he actually was. To my mind, he was a dark, ugly-looking man.

Voisin looked depressed, but stepped calmly on to the machine. Then it was noticed that he was still wearing his slippers, so he was told to take them off. He did so, and the scale then registered 179 lb. against him.

The Governor had come out of his office while we stood there silently watching this scene, and he noticed that three or four of the warders were standing round Voisin in such a manner as to obstruct my view.

'The fools – they are standing right in front of him!' he muttered, and tapped on the glass with his keys. The warders took the hint and moved out of our line of vision, but Voisin paid no attention to the incident.

We went back to finish out tea. Shortly afterwards they took us to the scaffold so that I might see that everything was in order. There I met the acting Under-Sheriff (Mr Metcalfe), the Governor (Mr O. E. Davies), and the doctor (Dr Manders), and they asked me what drop I thought Voisin ought to have. Evidently they had already been discussing the subject, for when I suggested six feet, the doctor remarked, 'I said you would say that'. 'Well', I added, 'If I had things freely my own way, I would give a lot more than that, but as the drop I have suggested is already five inches over the Home Office scale I felt you would not agree to more than six feet.'

We talked the matter over amicably, and at length agreed on the drop I had suggested. That settled, I tied a sandbag (weighing approximately the same as Voisin) to the rope and dropped it through the trapdoors by a movement of the lever – just as would be done when Voisin himself would be attached to the noose. But when I went below to examine the rope, I found that the gutta-percha lining to a portion of the noose had cracked a considerable distance.

Coming up and reporting this, Mr Metcalfe ordered another rope to be brought. Examination showed that this rope too was useless for the same reason as the first. Both these ropes, I would add, had been used at former executions.

The Governor then decided to take no further risks, and told the foreman of the works to fetch a brand new rope. This rope stood all tests satisfactorily, and was left hanging in the pit with the sandbag suspended to it. The morning dawned bright and fair, and I arose at 6.30 – the execution being fixed for nine o'clock. I got everything on the scaffold in readiness by about seven o'clock and returned to my rooms to await the final call.

It was about ten minutes to the dreaded hour when I and my assistant joined the silent knot of officials in the corridor outside the condemned man's cell. But Voisin was anything but silent. He had refused to eat his breakfast, and we could hear him in his cell carrying on like one demented.

Now that he had to face the reality of death all his 'courage' oozed out of him and his true nature stood revealed.

While we stood there waiting with our feelings harrowed by the moans and cries emanating from the condemned cell, the doctor's dispenser arrived with a glass and a bottle of brandy, and a stiff dose of the stimulant was poured out and taken in to the doomed man.

I judged that Voisin did not at first take more than a sip of the brandy for I heard the doctor call out – 'Drink it all up'.

Things quietened down, and I got the signal to begin operations. I entered the condemned cell, and saw Voisin seated between two chaplains, who were both assiduous in the ministrations. Voisin was still quietly sobbing, and in his left hand he clutched his handkerchief, which was so wet with his tears that it resembled a dishcloth. My assistant gently disengaged this from Voisin's hand and threw it on the floor, so that I might get hold of this hand and pinion it at the back. By this time the priests had risen to their feet, and Voisin was, of course, also standing. But as the clergymen did not stand still Voisin moved also, and I had considerable difficulty in getting hold of his right hand to complete the pinioning.

The voices of the priests rose in prayer, and Voisin mumbled what I took to be responses in French. Within seconds I had him prepared and then left him in charge of my assistant while I hurried to the scaffold. Voisin followed in the short procession, and walked fairly well, considering his state only a few minutes previously. Immediately he reached the trapdoors I put the white cap over his head, and almost simultaneously his nerves again gave way. He leaned forward on me as if on the point of fainting, and it was no small task for a man of my slight build to hold up such a man as he. Signalling to two of the officers, I got Voisin's weight transferred to them.

My next duty was to adjust the noose round Voisin's neck, and this, again, proved no mean task. He had such a stout neck that he had hardly any projecting chin or jawbone, and I was afraid that the rope might slip over his head and cause such a scene as I dared not visualise. The only way out was to make the noose extra tight, and with this in view I pulled on it so much that I quite expected Voisin to protest that I was choking him. But he made no demur. He was too far gone. All he could do was to mumble away just as he had done all along. I hope he was praying for forgiveness for his sins.

He kept his head hanging down in utter dejection, and this increased the difficulty of my task. At length, however, I signalled to the others to stand clear. For a fraction of a second the murderer stood alone. Then my hand touched the lever. It was all over. Voisin died absolutely at once, and the Governor voiced his validation at the way in which the grim ceremony had gone off. 'Very quick!' he remarked to me though personally I felt that I had never been so slow in my life as during that trying effort to fasten the moose round the murderer's throat. However, I was afterwards told that only 30 seconds had elapsed from the moment I entered the condemned cell until Voisin's death, so no doubt my own nerves had misled me.

Chapter 18

The Worst I Ever Encountered

(Frederick Rothwell Holt, Strangeways, Manchester, 1920)

 It is the invariable rule in British prisons to judge convicts merely as 'prisoners', without any reference to the crime that sent them there. Thus the officials may class a petty thief as a bad prisoner and a murderer as a good prisoner. It all depends on their behaviour in prison.

So it was not because Frederick Rothwell Holt, the man who took the life of pretty Mrs Kathleen Elsie Breaks, of Bradford, on the sandhills near Blackpool, was condemned for a particularly mean murder that he was so hated in gaol. It was purely because he stirred up so much trouble and carried on so obnoxiously that everybody breathed a sigh of relief when all was over.

Never from the first moment of his arrest did he ever show the slightest consideration for the feelings of others. I don't know whether he imagined he was going to bluff his way through and convince the Judge and jury of his innocence, but he certainly behaved as if he thought he had only to get up in court and arrogantly declare his innocence and everybody would then fawn upon him. No doubt it was in this spirit that he treated the officials with whom he came in contact – as if they would shortly be very sorry for having kept him in custody, and would be releasing him with signs of abject apology. But perhaps one could not expect anything better from this man who made love to a pretty woman in most passionate fashion, ruined her married life, and then murdered her in a love embrace for the sake of money he had persuaded her to will to him.

Some of the details of the story are well worth recalling, because at the time a furious fight was waged to save the man from the consequences of his crime, and I was told after the execution that there were lots of people outside Strangeways Gaol Manchester, who thought it 'a shame' to hang Holt. I am afraid I could not agree with them. I have felt sympathy with many upon whom I have had to carry out the law's decree, but I must confess, I never felt the slightest pang over 'Eric' Holt.

Mrs Elsie Breaks, the woman whom he eventually murdered, had called him 'the whitest man I have ever known', which shows how cleverly he had masked his true character. For while he was making smooth love to her, he was secretly plotting how to kill her without chance of being brought to book as her murderer, and thus be able to enjoy the £4800 which he had induced Mrs Breaks to will to him.

This all came out when Holt stood his trial and I remember taking a very keen interest in all the strange facts of this most unusual type of crime. I believe that Holt marked Elsie Breaks down as a victim from the first moment that he met her. She was only 25 years of age then, and was a singularly beautiful girl, who had got utterly fed up with things in general. Holt was just the sort of fellow to appeal strongly to her at such a time, and when he found that she had fallen head over heels in love with him he at once made a diabolical scheme to enrich himself at the cost of her life.

First of all though he would get her insured in his favour, obtain her death on some fashion, and live comfortable for the rest of his life on the money he would draw. Knowing the sort of man he was I can quite easily imagine how very annoyed he must have been when he approached an insurance agent with a proposal to insure Mrs Breaks' life for £10,000, only to learn that such a policy could not be issued to him as he had no insurable interest in her. I can quite imagine, too, how Holt would think the situation over, absolutely determined to make money out of Elsie Breaks somehow. A chance remark by one of the insurance agents he had spoken to gave him a brain wave, and he at once set about persuading Mrs Breaks to do what he wanted – a by no means difficult task.

The upshot was this. He first got Mrs Breaks to insure herself for £5000, Holt paying the premium. Then he got her to make her will, leaving everything to him. That done, he took her to Blackpool, ostensibly for a breath of ozone, but really because he intended to murder her there.

A few days later some schoolboys walking along the sandhills between Blackpool and St Annes were poking into the sands with their sticks as they played about, when one of them brought a revolver to the surface. The boys had the good sense to take it to the police, who went to the spot, and found something much more dramatically interesting – namely, the concealed body of Mrs Elsie Breaks. By some really smart detective work the police not only traced the ownership of the revolver to Holt, but had him under lock and key within twenty-four hours. So all his brainy scheming to conceal his crime came to nothing, and although he was defended by Sir E. Marshall Hall, who tried to prove that Holt was insane, Holt was quite rightly found guilty and condemned.

Immediately following the trial, Messrs. Wilson, Wright, and Davies, of Preston, who act as Under Sheriffs for the county of Lancashire, made preparations for carrying out the death sentence, and wired me: 'Can you go to Manchester Monday 15 for 16 March?' I knew what that meant. It indicated that Holt's execution was to take place on the morning of the 16th, and, in accordance with the regulations, I would need to be inside Strangeways Prison by the afternoon of the previous day.

I had at that time just returned from a trip to Ireland which had rather unusual features, so perhaps it will not be out of place if I tell the story here.

Three men were sentenced to death in Londonderry for complicity in one of the murders that were so common in those troubled times in Ireland, and Mr Craig, the Under Sheriff, wrote me forthwith to engage my services. He also made arrangements for two other Englishmen to act as my assistants, and elaborate plans were laid to give us full protection.

Two detectives accompanied me from Rochdale to Manchester, and there we met my two assistants and several other detectives. They locked us in a carriage by ourselves, and phoned to the Liverpool police to send an escort to meet us and look after us during our several hours' wait before the departure of the Belfast boat.

We had a pleasant enough sea trip, but a surprise awaited us as we walked to the station to catch the train for Londonderry. The newsboys' placards announced 'Reprieve for Derry Condemned Men.' However, we had no option but to continue our journey, and on arrival there we met Mr Craig as we walked up the street towards the County House. He took us back to his office and explained that the men had been reprieved too late to stop us commencing our journey. He, however, very kindly agreed to pay us our full fees, and we thereupon recrossed the Irish Channel by the first available boat.

We had spoken to no strangers throughout the double trip, but it is amazing how Irishmen always knew folks' movements. Just before we left the boat at Liverpool a steward sidled up to me and murmured: 'They have not shot you, then?' 'No – not yet!' I replied, putting on a jocular manner. But it gave me a creepy feeling to find out that I had been known, and probably shadowed, despite all the efforts at secrecy.

I had other much more exciting experiences in connection with Irish executions but will reserve these for telling later on. This particular episode is mentioned here because it happened just before I got first intimation that Holt was to hang.

The date first arranged for was, however, not adhered to, as an appeal was lodged against the sentence, and when that was thrown out, and the execution fixed for April 13, every possible effort known to Holt's naturally distracted relatives was put forward in the hope of saving the doomed man. His excellent record gained him the sympathy of many members of the general public, who were also influenced by the fact that Holt's mother had died in a lunatic asylum. Thousands of signatures were obtained to the petition for his reprieve.

While all this was going on, Holt was in Strangeways Prison, giving everybody as much trouble as he could, and showing not the slightest spark of gratitude for the almost superhuman efforts of his family to ward off execution. He seemed to accept it as nothing more than his due, and he was so wrapped up in himself and so regardless of those outside who loved him and pined for news of him that from the day his appeal was dismissed he never again wrote a single letter to any of his broken-hearted people. The Governor asked him one day if he was not going to send out a visiting permit to his father. Holt replied with a surly 'No', so the Governor, nettled by the man's selfish thoughtlessness, said – 'Well, I am going to send permits to your father myself, and allow him to visit you whenever he wishes'. Holt merely grunted an 'All right', and made no effort to be gracious to his weeping relatives when they came to see him.

'We'll have trouble with this man in the morning', prophesied the Governor when I went to see him in his room shortly after my arrival at the prison on the afternoon of 12 April 1920. 'Holt has fairly got the wind up.' 'Give him a stiff dose of brandy', I advised, but I was told that Holt had already declared that he would take nothing of that kind. Chatting with the warders afterwards, I found that throughout the prison Holt was most cordially disliked. I do not remember any such atmosphere surrounding a condemned man in all my career.

The poor doomed creatures are usually regarded with large-minded sympathy by the prison officials, who are much more human in their attitude than is generally believed by the outside public. But no one had a good word to say for 'Eric' Holt. He began his trick right away when he came back to Strangeways after his trial. As a condemned convict he had to change from his own clothes into the broad-arrowed prison garb, whereupon he raised a protest of a curious kind. It was not so much the ignominy of the hideous dress that he objected to, but the fit! 'Why cannot I be measured for the suit as I always am for my clothes? Why must I wear a ready-made?' he exclaimed with heat.

The matter rankled with him for some time and gave the officers a good foretaste of the kind of thing they would have to put up with from him continuously from that day to the morning of his execution. The warders who have to sit in company with a condemned man have a very difficult task. They must never leave him day or night, and they are supposed to talk with him and keep him cheerful. But Holt was a morose fellow, who would never initiate a conversation with them. He had but one topic of conversation, and that was women. Silent on all other subjects, he would yet talk very freely about anything that related to the feminine sex.

On my first evening in the prison I went to test the scaffold, and as usual fastened the rope noose round the neck of a bag of sand and dropped it as if it had been a body. This is always done to take the 'stretch' out of the rope, and the sandbag is always left dangling from the previous evening until the morning of the execution. In this instance when the bag of sand was dropped the gutta-percha eyelet on the noose-end of the rope broke through. So we pulled up the bag and fitted on a new eyelet. But when this was put to the same test it broke, too, and it was only with much difficulty and some ingenuity that the contrivance was fixed up well enough to ensure that there would be no serious accident in the morning.

'Now let me see Holt', said I, and was taken to an open window overlooking the prison yard, where, I was told, Holt would be at exercise. When he came in sight I thought I must be looking on at a man in training for some athletic event. Holt's tall figure – he stood just over six feet in his stockings – strode along between two warders, who had all their work cut out to keep up with him.

During the hearing of the case I had heard a lot of talk about suggestions that Holt was insane. So I looked closely at him to see if I could see any signs of madness in his face. I saw none. Holt's features expressed only cunning self-love, and there were no signs that he was on the road to madness. 'Mad?' ejaculated one of the warders, to whom I spoke about Holt, 'He isn't mad. He's done nothing but complain since he came in. We shall be glad when everything is safely over.'

That was the feeling everywhere behind the prison walls – a remarkable contrast to the opinions held outside. The general public seemed most unduly concerned about this man's execution, and as a matter of fact a special guard was placed round the gaol because of certain information that came to the knowledge of the authorities. They learned that an attempt to get Holt out of prison was being framed up, so for over a week before the execution extra placement were placed on duty outside the prison, while a strengthened patrol also guarded the interior whenever Holt was out at exercise. But nothing actually happened to cause the authorities any uneasiness.

I retired to rest that night wondering if the fears about the morning would come to anything, though I was quite determined in my own mind to be kind with Holt, but to permit no nonsense, for his own sake, as I always felt that it was more humane to get the whole thing over quickly than to increase the mental agony of the poor, doomed creature by giving them too long to brood over what was coming or get excited about it. At 7.10 next morning I was already up and in the execution shed putting everything in order. The sandbag that hung on the rope all night was hauled up and taken off, the rope coiled handily over the beam, and the trap-doors pulled up and closed so that the required touch on the lever would release them when the proper time came. Inside a quarter of an hour all was ready, and I went back for a wash and brush up.

My watch stood at four minutes to eight o'clock when I joined the waiting crowd of silent officials in the corridor near the condemned cell. They had had so much to put up with from Holt during his incarceration in Strangeways that they were all worrying inwardly as to how the fellow was going to behave. But I was not under this disadvantage, and so my mind was quite clear. It was told me afterwards that Holt had eaten very little breakfast and had said to the officers who were keeping vigil with him: 'I am innocent It will all be found out after I am gone.'

But nobody attached any importance to this statement.

At a minute to eight the Governor gave me a significant nod. I knew what that meant. Stepping forward, I pushed open the condemned cell door. The final moments had arrived. Holt was standing within, almost directly opposite the door, and facing it is if he wanted to see me at the first possible moment. In his mouth a cigarette hung loosely, as if he had placed it there mechanically and without any real desire for it. The chaplain stood near by with his head bent over a Prayer Book, but Holt's whole attitude seemed to ignore the clergyman's presence, and I learned afterwards that he had positively refused to listen to the minister's efforts to make him realise the necessity of making preparations for the end. Holt had waved him aside almost churlishly, and declared he had no use for that sort of thing.

My first move was to get behind Holt to pinion his arms, I got hold of his left hand quite gently and was just on the point of slipping the strap over it when Holt jerked himself free. 'Hullo!' thought I. 'Here's the trouble beginning after all!' Holt glared at me with fury in his face and barked out harshly 'Is this necessary?' I replied quietly, for I had no wish to fan the flame of the man's obvious temper. But that did not satisfy him. With a scornful grunt he wheeled round and faced the Acting Chief Warder, who was standing by, and again, repeated his question, 'Is this necessary?' The officer said 'Yes', and with that Holt clenched his fists in anger, looked as if he meant to make a fight of it, and then suddenly thought better of it. I again seized his left hand, and this time Holt submitted quietly.

Fastening the strap round his wrist, I brought his other hand across too, and before he could make up his mind for further obstreperousness they were both fixed together behind his back. Then my hands went up to his shirt neck to loosen it, and his face gazed down into mine with anger as I did so. But he said nothing more, and I left him in my assistant's care while I walked forward to the execution shed to await his coming. He walked very quickly towards the scaffold, still paying not the slightest heed to the ministrations of the chaplain, and I could see a baleful glare in his eyes as he approached where I was standing at the scaffold. I will give him that due. It was something much more malignant, as if he was thinking of something unspeakable.

When he got to the edge of the trap-doors he voluntarily stopped and looked at me. What his idea was I cannot even guess, but the officers round about were apprehensive of more trouble. My assistant, however, gave him a gentle but firm push forward, and now that Holt was within my reach I whipped the white cap out and made to put it over his head. At that moment Holt opened his mouth to speak, and, thinking the man had at last seen the need of repentance, I paused for a fraction of a second. But repentance was a long, long way from Holt's heart. He was simply raising his voice in still another of his many protests. 'You are not going to put that on!' he almost commanded, indicating the white cap in my hands. 'Oh, yes, I must', I replied, suiting the action to the words, though I had to stand on my toes to get it on to his head that towered so far above mine. When I was putting the cap on him he glared at me. Queer eyes he had, too! I remember them now. 'Don't forget' he said to me, 'I'll see you again.' Then on went the noose, and I darted to the lever before Holt could think of any further awkwardness.

It may not seem kind to say it, but a positive sigh of relief came from the officers when they saw Holt go down. 'Well, that's the last of him', said one of them to me afterwards, 'and I am not sorry.' And that aptly expressed the general feeling among these men who in a general way I have always found to be strongly sympathetic towards a condemned prisoner. Even the Governor – a splendid type of kind, gentlemanly official – felt the same about it. He told me quite frankly that if there had been another week to wait before the execution they would have collapsed with the worry Holt had caused them.

He then extended a kindness to me that was characteristic of him. Next morning my Assistant [Tom] Pierrepoint and I were due in far-off Newcastle upon Tyne to carry out the death sentence upon Henry Perkins, a very different type of man, who was believed to have been responsible for a murder nineteen years previously in Kettering. He knew that I was due the same afternoon at Cardiff where I was required to hang a black man from Zanzibar named Tom Caler. To fulfil this engagement I would have to catch the 9.30 train from Manchester which if the Governor had stuck to the usual rule, would have been impossible. Instead he not only gave me permission to go at once, but also paid for a taxi to take me to the station. Strangely enough, he had done me a similar favour many years previously, when he was Governor of Worcester Gaol, where I had gone for the execution of William Yarnold, a strangely likeable fellow, who stabbed his wife in the back, but whose provocation had been so sore that everybody hoped he would be reprieved.

On that occasion the Governor had come to our rescue by letting us leave the prison almost immediately after Yarnold's execution and paid our cab fare to the railway station. He repeated this act of thoughtfulness on the morning of Holt's execution and thus I was able to get to Cardiff in good time.

The man upon whom I carried out the law's sentence at Cardiff may have come from another country and followed another faith but it is the matter in which he went to his doom that contrasted oddly with Holt's attitude. Tom Caler committed what Mr Justice Salter called 'two of the most cruel and barbarous murders in the annals of crime' by cutting the throats of a woman and her baby in a house in Christina Street, Cardiff. But when he came face to face with death as a penalty for his crimes he did everything he could to show proper penitence and did his best to put himself right before he crossed over.

Holt, the well-educated Englishman, of careful Christian upbringing, declined the aid of a clergyman when his extreme hour arrived, but Caler, was praying sincerely, when I entered his cell to prepare him for execution. He had a copy of the Koran in his hands, which I had to gently take from him and he murmured prayers right up to the moment when he died. Compare that with Holt's defiantly callous behaviour and you will understand why I describe him as probably the most disliked condemned prisoner of modern times.

Chapter 19

The Boy on the Gallows

(Henry Julius Jacoby, Pentonville, 1922)

One bright afternoon in 1922 I rang the bell at the grim entrance gate at Pentonville Prison. The dread duty that called me there all the way from my Lancashire home seemed all out of keeping with the cheerful sunlight that was even softening the harsh outlines of the gloomy prison buildings.

The particular task that awaited me within was one of the very, very few cases in all my years of experience that really worried me. I felt that in this instance British justice – usually so magnanimous – had not erred on the side of mercy.

A few minutes after my arrival in the prison I was conducted to a spot from which I could obtain that glimpse of the condemned person which a hangman is bound to take if he is to calculate the required length of the 'drop' accurately. They took me to a window in what is known as the Magistrates' Room which overlooked the exercise yard. Peering through furtively, I saw a most extraordinary thing. He whom the Law had declared must die in a little more than twelve hours time was playing cricket! And what a child he looked. For I was gazing down upon Henry Jacoby, the pantry boy, whose murder of Lady White in an exclusive West End private hotel mystified the whole of Britain until he lifted the veil himself.

His crime was obviously the unreasoning frightened act of one whose mental growth had not even kept pace with his tender years – for he was only eighteen – but the authorities, who would reprieve Ronald True*, who was lying in that same prison at that time, refused to give an extension to the life of Jacoby.

When I saw the youth playing cricket, an old tin can stuck against a large door served for wickets, and a piece of rough, hewed wood was his bat. And there Henry Jacoby played his last game, with a uniformed warder acting as

---

* Editor's note: Ronald True had been found guilty of bludgeoning and murdering London prostitute, Olive Young, by asphyxiation. A member of a wealthy, titled family they had the money and connections to ensure he had superb legal representation. True was granted a reprieve following a psychiatric examination that concluded True was legally insane. He was removed to Broadmoor where he remained until his death from a heart attack in 1951.

bowler. Whatever feelings I had about this case were doubly confirmed as I stood and watched that amazing scene. Jacoby was laughing and chattering and enjoying himself as only a youth can who has not a care in the world. I thought then that it was wrong to hang that child.

In saying that I do not desire to abate one jot all the sympathy due to the bereaved relatives of the murdered lady. Nothing can excuse such a fearful crime as was committed that night in the Spencer Hotel in Portman Street. Perhaps the real reason for the attitude of the Home Office was contained in the remark made to me by a prominent prison official next morning after it was all over but I'll come to that later.

The crime that brought youthful Jacoby to the gallows was one which in its early days attracted the attention of numerous famous criminologists besides those connected with the police force. For in the bare elements the murder of poor Lady White presented as complete and insoluble a mystery as ever a novelist invented.

The victim, who was the widow of a former chairman of the London County Council hadn't a known enemy in the world. She had not been robbed, in spite of the fact that many articles of valuable jewellery were lying exposed on her dressing table. Yet she was found dying on her bed in a quiet, exclusive hotel by her maid one morning, the injuries to her skull being so dreadful that she could not be removed. She died without regaining consciousness.

Not only was there no apparent motive for the deed, but experts disputed among themselves as to how her assailant gained entrance and egress without leaving the slightest trace. In a private hotel of this class there is no free passage in and out. All doors are locked almost as much by day as by night. Not one of these doors showed the slightest sign of having been tampered with. The same applied to all the windows. Neither was there a single finger print anywhere to guide the Scotland Yard men who were early on the job for hunting down the assassin. The thing was positively uncanny, and afforded an open field for every imaginable conjecture.

Suddenly the whole affair took a most amazing turn. One phrase of three words uttered by a pantry boy in the hotel dispelled the whole atmosphere of mystery. 'I did it' nonchalantly remarked Henry Jacoby. Following which he proceeded without the slightest hesitation to tell the whole tragic story:

'I sat on my bed until about ten minutes to two. I made up my mind to go upstairs to the visitors bedrooms to try to get some money – to steal it, if there was any there. It occurred to me to prepare for emergency in case I got caught up there, so I thought I would take a hammer with me...When I reached the bedroom corridor of the first floor I tried the door facing the staircase. It was locked. I then tried the next door No. 14. It was shut but not locked. The corridor was in darkness. I quietly opened the door and walked in, left the door ajar, turned my torch on, saw two beds and some person in one near the window. The person awoke and I saw it was a woman. She gave a slight shriek and I got the wind up and hit her on the head with the hammer.

My torch was in my left hand, showing a beam of light. I was standing between her bed and the window near her head. She partly raised herself in the bed when she screamed and at that moment I struck the blow. I struck her at least twice, because after I struck her the first time, I heard her moaning and struck her again. I left the room and went back to my bed. I took the hammer back to my bedroom with me and considered what I was doing with it, and a few minutes later I went and washed it under a tap in the basement. The hammer was covered with blood. I washed all the blood off and wiped it with my handkerchief.'

There were many who held that the boy at the time he committed the crime was incapable of forming any intention, and struck the woman in sheer terror. If this were so he should have been found guilty of manslaughter and not murder. The verdict, however, was held to be one of murder and so far as the law was concerned Jacoby was guilty of the capital offence.

Personally, I did not like the task that was placed in my hands, though to tell the truth, I at first did not think the authorities would allow this boy to go to the scaffold.

On Whit Sunday (4 June 1922) I had a letter from Mr Metcalfe, the London Under Sheriff. It was headed 'Henry Jacoby' and ran:

'As there is no reprieve for the above convict, please be at Pentonville Prison as arranged on Tuesday next and four o'clock.'

Following this, the typewritten portion of the letter, Mr Metcalfe had added in his own hand writing – 'to prevent any misunderstanding'. I knew what that meant. I took it as a hint that it had finally been decided to carry the grim drama through despite anything the public might desire. After that touching game of cricket Jacoby went indoors and sat down to write a few final letters. To his solicitors he wrote: 'The only way I can show my gratitude is by keeping a stiff upper lip and going through it bravely'.

I got to the scaffold in full readiness and tested it in the presence of the prison governor, the deputy Governor, the doctor and Captain Hare, son of Sir John Hare the famous actor, who was there in some official capacity which was not explained to me. It might be of interest if I add that the rope which I tested was unique, in as much as it was fitted with certain improved gutta-percha fittings according to a suggestion I had previously made to the Home Office.

That evening I had a chat with the chaplain – a Church Army officer – and made a suggestion that would, I felt, help in shortening this miserable drama in the morning. I put it to him that when we led the little tragic procession to the scaffold he should walk straight on across the trap doors instead of stopping and stepping aside when he got there. 'Oh no' he protested, 'I really couldn't do that'. I naturally respected his objection but pointed out to him that if he stepped aside Jacoby would probably turn around to look for him and this would occasion delay. But if he walked across the drop the lad's eyes would look straight ahead and I could do my part and have him down so much quicker. After considering the matter from this point of view the chaplain kindly consented to do as I asked.

Jacoby rose quite blithely on the morning of his execution, and in accordance with his own request a glass of brandy was taken to him. Outside his cell there gathered, just before eight o'clock, a small, silent knot of high officials, in the midst of which the Governor stood with his watch in his hand. The others also took out their watches and compared times with him. When they had agreed that it had gone a minute to the hour, the Governor nodded to me and said in a low, tense voice – 'Get it over Ellis'.

At that I pushed open the cell door and entered with one hand behind my back holding the pinioning strap. Jacoby was sitting on the edge of his bed talking to the chaplain, as he saw me enter he arose and shook hands with the cleric. He looked more a child than ever, but he stood bravely still as I pinioned his wrists behind him. 'Look straight at me when you get there laddie' I muttered 'and it will soon be over'. He did not answer me but I could see he understood me. Leaving him I hurried off to the scaffold. Almost at once Jacoby followed me out of the condemned cell but when he caught sight of the Governor he stopped short. 'I want to thank you and the officers for the kindness you have shown me', he said in a fairly firm voice. It was an episode that almost moved everybody to tears. Then the boy moved on and walked straight to the drop. He never showed the slightest sign of faltering and was easily the most collected being in the prison yard.

The rest was soon over. Henry Jacoby was dead within ten seconds of his involuntary pause outside the condemned cell. 'Ellis you go quicker every time' remarked the Governor afterwards, to which I replied, 'The quicker the better for the poor creatures, sir'. Then there arose a general conversation about the unfortunate boy who had just died. I gave it as my emphatic opinion that it was wrong to hang the child, to which came the reply that there had been so many recent murders by youngsters that something had to be done to stop it. I caught my train home to Rochdale. Two mornings later the postman brought me official notification of Ronald True's reprieve.

Chapter 20

The Hay Poisoner

(Major Herbert Rowse Armstrong, Gloucester, 1922)

It may seem curious for me to say that my most lasting impression of the execution of Major Armstrong, the poisoner, concerns what I took at the time to be a personal insult. Yet that's the truth, and perhaps it has some public interest because it arose out of the fact that Armstrong was a University man and a solicitor. They seemed to forget that he was a murderer of an absolutely despicable order. I suppose people will fancy I am not a squeamish sort of man, and I expect they imagine that, to me, a murderer is just somebody to be hanged. I would like to disabuse the public of that notion. Like them, I follow the newspaper reports of these cases purely as any ordinary citizen who is anxious to settle in his own mind whether the accused person is innocent or guilty. And in this case I felt not only that the evidence proved Armstrong to be guilty, but also that he was a vile sort of man, who did not deserve the pity one sometimes accords an ill-educated man who perhaps takes another person's life in a moment of inflamed passion.

The first words used to me by officials when I reached Gloucester Prison on the afternoon before the execution were to the effect that he hoped I would be as gently as possible with Armstrong, as he was not an ordinary man. To say that I was astonished is to put it mildly. The suggestions seemed to be in the first place that I was in the habit of dealing cruelly with condemned prisoners, and secondly that in any case Armstrong was entitled to special treatment. Can you wonder that I was very resentful of such imputations? 'If I don't know my business after 21 years' experience', I retorted, 'it is time I got out of it'. Evidently, however, the official did not realise how he had offended me. 'Ah', said he, 'but you won't have sent away a man like him in all your 21 years' experience. He is not of the ordinary type.' I was prepared to dispute this.

Sir Roger Casement and Dr Crippen had appeared to me as gentlemen of standing quite as high as Armstong, if not higher. And I added: 'I have never knocked anyone about in all my life. My idea has always been to get things over as quickly as possible, which seems to me to be the best way for all concerned'.

The official made no reply to that. I may say that the incident was closed later on by what was tantamount to an apology.

For the sake of those who may have forgotten the details of the affair I will just run through its outstanding features as they appealed to me at the time. The case that grew into such a sensational affair began in quite a small way, with Armstrong merely charged with the attempted murder of another solicitor. But there was a 'something' in the atmosphere even at that early stage that convinced me we were going to get some extraordinary revelations before long. We got them right enough! It appeared that the first suspicions about Armstrong grew out of the illness of this solicitor friend of his, a man named Martin who also lived in the little town of Hay, in Herefordshire.

Something made his doctor suspect that he was a victim of arsenical poisoning, though he did not seem to have taken any arsenic knowingly. Then someone remembered a box of chocolates that had been sent to Mr Martin, and when these came to be examined they were found to be punctured with small holes, and contained arsenic. Another incident that was remembered at this time was when Mr Martin had gone at Armstrong's invitation to have tea with him, and Armstrong had picked out a particular buttered scone and given it to his guest with the remark, 'Excuse fingers'. Mr Martin had been ill after this in the same way as when he partook of the chocolates. When the worried medical man in charge of Mr Martin heard in a quiet way that Armstrong had been buying a lot of arsenic from a local chemist he wrote to the authorities, and Scotland Yard thought his fears so well founded that Chief Inspector Crutchett was sent down to make discreet inquiries.

Inspector Crutchett worked on the case for six weeks before he made a definite move. I can well understand why he was so cautious, for he had a very clever fellow to beat, and one who was so highly connected that a weakly-supported criminal charge would have stood no chance against him. Major Herbert Armstrong was a Cambridge University man, and a fine athlete in his youth. After serving in the Royal Engineers during the war he returned to his big practice as a solicitor in Hay, where he was actually Clerk to the Magistrates. So you can guess how carefully Crutchett had to go about his investigations.

When at last the detective felt confident, the bomb exploded under Armstrong, though it had a sort of time fuse attached to it. He was charged at first with attempting to murder Mr Martin, and then when he was safely in prison a certain churchyard grave was opened, and an examination was made of the body therein. Then newspaper readers were provided with a new sensation. Major Armstrong was called on to face a more serious charge – the murder of his wife!

This lady had died about twelve months earlier, and Major Armstrong was apparently already completing his arrangements for marrying another lady – a mysterious Mrs X, who created a lot of unsatisfied curiosity during the trial. You won't want me to go over all the details of long-drawn-out proceedings, but I must confess I read every word of them at the time. There was something very fascinating about this man Armstrong.

He was a regular Jekyll and Hyde, from what I could make out, for although openly he was a jolly and popular man of breeding, in secret he was a degenerate, and determined poisoner. In fact, although he was only charged with the murder of his wife, I happen to know that if that case had failed there was enough evidence about the deaths of certain other people to have him hanged three times. And this was the man they wanted me to be specially tender with. Well, I had no intention of doing anything less than my duty in the most humane way, but I certainly resented the suggestion that this foul man who murdered his wife was a being to stand in awe of. Certainly if money and influence could have saved a man from the scaffold, Herbert Armstrong would never have paid the penalty for his crimes.

Sir Henry Curtis Bennett put up a masterly defence, and I remember reading with wonderment of how Armstrong faced eight hours' cross-examination by Sir Ernest Pollock, the then Attorney-General, and never flinched once or said a wrong thing. When the verdict went against Armstrong an appeal was at once lodged, and I believe legal men all over the kingdom watched these proceedings closely, because of the strong objection Sir Henry Curtis Bennett had made to the acceptance of the evidence about the attempt on Mr Martin's life. This great barrister actually made a twelve hours' speech and if he had won his point the conviction would have been quashed, and Armstrong, a proved murderer, would have gone free. But the Appeal Court Judges threw out the appeal.

Even then Armstrong's powerful friends were not disposed to give in, and there was some talk of trying to take the case to the House of Lords. That idea was defeated, and so the final efforts to save the murderer's life were directed towards trying to get the Home Secretary to grant a reprieve.

Everything that money could do was done. Meanwhile the authorities made their arrangements for the execution. At first there was some uncertainty as to who was to be responsible, although the trial took place at the expense of the county of Herefordshire. The Hereford Prison had been closed for some time, and Armstrong had been kept in Gloucester Gaol throughout his trial.

The question was whether responsibility fell on the Sheriff of Herefordshire, where the crime was committed, or the Sheriff of Gloucestershire, wherein stood the prison where the execution would take place. It was decided that the matter must be undertaken by the Herefordshire Sheriff, Mr Francis R. James, who at once engaged my services. He wrote to me on May 17, 1922, as follows:

Dear Sir,
I have provisionally fixed the 31st inst. For the execution of Armstrong at
Gloucester Prison, and I shall be glad if you will hold yourself in readiness for
that date.
   It is possible there may be an appeal to the House of Lords, but I shall not
know before Monday or Tuesday whether this will be allowed or not.
   I will write you directly I hear definitely. – Yours truly,
   Francis R. James

It was fully another week before the idea of this appeal to the highest Court in the land was abandoned, whereupon I got this telegram:

'No appeal. Therefore date fixed, thirty-first. James.'

This date was a little bit awkward for me, as I was also required to carry out an execution on May 30 at Manchester. But I knew I could rely upon the unfailing courtesy of the Strangeways officials to let me get away in good time to catch my train for Gloucester, so as to reach there according to the regulations on the afternoon before the execution.

Perhaps the Manchester execution is worth a line or two at this point, for the man, Hiram Thompson, was one of the most callous creatures I ever met in all my long career. He was callous over his crime – the brutal murder of his wife in their home at Bamber Bridge, near Preston – callous afterwards when arrested, for he almost went the length of boasting about it; callous at his trial, when he stood with folded arms while the Judge sentenced him to death; and callous to a degree on his last morning on earth when I executed the sentence of the law upon him.

One of the dramatic points about this affair was that one of the two warders whose duty it was to keep the condemned man company was an old friend of Thompson's named Sharrocks. Warder Sharrocks told me he and Thompson went to school together as boys, and knew the murdered woman well. Naturally he was much affected at meeting his old school chum again in such dreadful circumstances. But Thompson himself never turned a hair. He refused to lodge an appeal against his conviction, telling the governor, when he asked him his intentions – 'It's no use appealing. This is only a one-man boat'. When the last moments arrived and I went in to pinion him, this man, from whom the governor had rather feared trouble, sat there calmly smoking his pipe and looking perfectly happy and contented! Then, as he walked out smartly to the scaffold, he called out a cheery 'Good morning!' to the prison officers.

Afterwards I was told that he had slept so well on his last night that he had to be shaken into wakefulness at 6 a.m. And then he actually grumbled because he had not been awakened earlier, and told the officers that he had slept better in prison than he ever did at home! With everything safely over at Strangeways, I went across the city to London Road Station and booked to Gloucester by the ten o'clock train. I have a valued friend living in Birmingham, so when the train reached that place about noon he met me there by arrangement and took me to his home at Small Heath to have dinner with his wife. They knew me well enough not to attempt to make me talk about the business I was going South for, but all the same they could not help talking about Armstrong. The case had really made in immense impression on the general public, and my friends, like most other people, regarded the murderous solicitor as a man of whom the world would be well rid.

We spent a very pleasant time together, and shortly after two o'clock I left Birmingham and resumed my journey to Gloucester, which I reached at 3.29 p.m. A taxi quickly bore me to the prison gate, where the warder who opened the small door in it asked me my name, and promised to send word to the governor that I had arrived. Then ensued the little episode which I told you about at the beginning of this article. However, my ruffled feelings were smoothed a little presently when a warder came in with an evening paper, from which I learned that I had backed a 'dead-heater' (Trumpeter) at Epsom at the comfortable odds of 100 to 8.

A rest and a smoke in the room allotted to me (where I was joined by my assistant, Edward Taylor, who had just arrived), and soon an officer came to tell me that I could now have a chance of seeing Armstrong. He led the way through a cellar filled with stacks of timber, until we came to the office of the foreman of the works. 'You will be able to see Armstrong by getting on this stool', he said, handing it to me. 'He will come out of that door.' Pointing to the entrance to a small yard. I waited several minutes but there was no sign of the condemned man, So, to help me to get on with my business, I asked if anyone could tell me Armstrong's age, height, and weight. To my astonishment they said he had not been weighed for two or three weeks. This meant another trouble in my path. I told them it was vital that a condemned man's weight should be ascertained no further back than two days prior to his execution, and I added emphatically that I would not accept the responsibility for the carrying out of Armstrong's execution unless he was weighed that evening.

Just when the argument had reached this point Armstrong came in sight on his way to exercise. He was carrying a book in both hands, and two officers strode along behind him. Never have I been so surprised at a man's appearance. 'This is never Armstrong!' I exclaimed, but was assured that it really was the notorious poisoner. The papers had been full of his photographs for weeks, and I had seen most of them. Yet I could never have recognised the man in the yard had I not known from the circumstances that it really was Armstrong. Maybe his unshaven face had something to do with it. I don't know. The newspaper portraits showed him as a pretty smart-looking fellow. But the man before me was as miserable-looking a specimen as you could never expect to see.

Having seen Armstrong and observed the points necessary to aid me in fixing the length of drop, I went to look at the scaffold. But before doing so I again insisted upon Armstrong being weighed, as I presumed that the fact that he had not been put on the scales was another of those strange evidences of subdued respect for this man, whom I could not work up any sympathy for, speaking personally. But I really was sorry for his children, and it made me feel a little softer towards Armstrong when I heard how concerned he was for the future of his innocent youngsters. His regard for them was the man's one redeeming feature.

The warders told me that he had been what they called a good prisoner and a tremendous reader. He did not talk a great deal, but he could not hide his strong belief that Sir Henry Curtis Bennett would win the appeal against his sentence. Armstrong did not attend the Court of Criminal Appeal when the case came up, but he paced his cell in very agitated fashion while he waited for news of the result. Gradually his nerves settled down, and he was earnestly reading a book when the news percolated into the prison that the application for an appeal had been dismissed.

One of his attendant warders who had been out of the cell for a short time and gathered this news returned with the intention of breaking its purport to the condemned man. But he found it too difficult a task to put into words. He was more upset than Armstrong was! For the poisoner glanced at the warder, guessed the truth from the expression on his face – and calmly resumed his reading! But he lost a lot of his calmness when, as a consequence of his rejected appeal, he was ordered to change from his own blue suit into the ordinary prison dress. The hideous arrow-marked clothes seemed to bring home the truth to him as nothing else had done. He almost collapsed then, and it was now quite clear that he had never expected the failure of his appeal.

No doubt it was this incident that gave rise to the rumour outside the prison walls that Armstrong had fallen critically ill from sheer terror of his approaching death on the scaffold. These stories, of course, only came to my knowledge after it was all over. They were not true, but I expect they arose out of the undoubted fact that Armstrong fell to pieces for a time after the dismissal of his appeal – a fact that somebody must have got a hint about. Just before I reached the prison on that Tuesday afternoon before the execution Armstrong received his last visitors. They were his solicitor, Mr Matthews, of Hereford, the Rector of Cusop, the Vicar of Hay, and a gentleman friend of the family. To the first three gentlemen he declared – 'I am innocent of the crime for which I have been condemned'.

To the last-mentioned friend of the family he explained that he would dearly have liked to see his children once more, but he had denied himself that because he did not want them to have a mental picture of the prison imprinted upon their memories. I prefer to remember this last thoughtfulness for his children rather than his calculated lie about his innocence. There was also, I believe, a rumour that the famous Mrs X, had visited his in prison. But I heard nothing of any such caller on the condemned man.

When Armstrong had been weighed, as I had requested, he tipped the scales at 115 lb. – very light for a man of his height (5 ft. 6 ½ in.) and years (52). I therefore decided to give him one of the longest drops of my career – 8 ft, 8 in. – a length that would have startled some of my predecessors, who were afraid to give long drops. Armstrong retired to his bed that night with a good stiff 'nightcap' of whisky but it did not give him the peaceful sleep he desired. I was told afterwards that he turned and tossed, and often got up and paced his felt slippers up and down the floor of the big, condemned cell he occupied. No doubt his mind dwelt in anticipation upon the dread ordeal that he was to go through in a few hours in the chamber just beyond the thin partition that ran along one side of his cell.

In this respect, at least, I gave Armstrong a measure of pity for I can well believe that an educated man must suffer more from his imagination that the more stolid type with undeveloped brains. I have a fancy, too, that remorse was at last troubling the man. Once just after midnight, he fell into a snatch of sleep, from which he awoke, crying, 'What's the time?' On being told, he uttered a stifled moan, and muttered, 'It's hard to wait to die'.

Early on his last morning he was up and dressed – this time in his own clothes. But it came as a slight shock to him when he found they did not give him his collar. The significance of this was not lost upon him and he went out to exercise in the yard looking shaky and unsteady on his feet.

I, too, had arisen early to take advantage of Armstrong's absence to get everything ready on the scaffold. Much as I detested the criminal, I felt that it would be too much like deliberate torture to let him hear us making noises as we made the necessary preparations. Soon everything was ready in the execution chamber, so I went and had a shave and brush-up. About 7.40 the Under-Sheriff sent for me, and asked if all was in order. 'Yes sir', I replied. Then he spoke to me about the expenses of my journey and said he would pay me directly after it was all over if it had gone off all right.'I shall not witness the execution, as

I do not wish Armstrong to know I am here', said Mr James. 'You see, I knew him well before this trouble arose.' The hour set for the execution now drew on quickly, and when five minutes to eight arrived I went to the corridor outside the condemned cell and there met the chaplain, the governor, and several other officers. They all looked very anxious.

Wondering how Armstrong was keeping, I peered in through the inspection hole. He was standing up, chatting quite composedly with one of the warders.

At two minutes to eight the governor gave a nod. The door was opened, and the chaplain, the Rev. W. C. Macklin, entered, closely followed by the governor. They both said 'Goodbye' to Armstrong, and came out looking very much affected. As the governor came out he signalled to me to go in. I did so, and found Armstrong still standing in the same position as when I looked in several minutes earlier.

I got hold of his left hand and put on the pinioning strap, and while I was doing so he said, 'Good-bye!' to me. 'Good-bye', I returned, and added (making my voice sound as reassuring as possible) – 'Please look straight at me when you get there and it will soon be over'. He answered quietly, 'I will'. I then handed him over to the care of my assistant, while I walked quickly forward straight to the scaffold.

After I got there I looked round, expecting him to be almost there, too. Instead I saw him still standing in his cell talking to someone. Then the chaplain began to walk towards the scaffold, and Armstrong followed him. But the slow pace of the clergyman seemed to fret the doomed man's nerves, for I could see Armstrong looking towards me over the chaplain's shoulders, and he seemed to be trying to pass him. To give Armstrong his due, he went bravely to his death. He strode along with erect body, just like a soldier. Immediately he reached my side I whipped the white cap over his head and fastened the noose. Just as I flew to the lever I heard his last words – 'I am coming, Katie!' So his mind had gone back to his murdered wife as he stood on the brink of eternity. Next moment he was down and he died instantly.

A few minutes later I saw the Under-Sheriff in his office, and when the doctor came in Mr James asked him if everything was correct. Dr Bell assured him that it was so, and the Under-Sheriff made out my cheque, saying – 'I will send a good report about you to the Home Office'.

At nine o'clock I went to the scaffold to take down Armstrong's body, which had now hung the full hour insisted upon by law. 'Don't you trouble about that', said the foreman of works. 'We will take him down.' I thanked him, and accepted his kind offer.

A fair crowd was outside waiting to see us come out, but we doubled round a corner and gave them the slip by pretending to make for the Great Western

Railway Station and going, instead, through the subway to the Midland Railway Station. Walking round to the front entrance booking office I had a pleasant surprise, for I ran into an old friend of mine, the well-known Rochdale Hornets player, Jack Robinson. He had heard I was in Gloucester, where he was living, and had come to the station in the hope of meeting me, and we had a very pleasant half-hour together. At 10.15 I left Gloucester and got home about 4.10, quite glad to be entirely finished with this thoroughly unpleasant affair.

Chapter 21

My Dreadful Scene with Edith Thompson

(Edith Jessie Thompson, Holloway, 1923)

It is easy for me to select the most nerve-racking execution I ever participated in. The scenes that marked the carrying out of the death sentence upon Mrs Edith Thompson are indelibly imprinted upon my memory. Somehow rumours of what had happened leaked out publicly, and roused such a fierce storm of controversy that the general clamour very nearly stampeded the Government into doing away with the death penalty at once. Yet I venture to claim, in all modesty, that if the suggestions I put forward that morning had been strictly adhered to, both Mrs Thompson and those who were forced to witness that dreadful last scene would have been spared much of the anguish they had to endure.

The question of whether a woman should be hanged at all is hardly one that I care to pronounce an opinion upon. This I can honestly aver, however – that almost to that last I believed Edith Thompson would be reprieved, and it may astonish those who choose to regard a hangman as an inhuman monster when I add that I genuinely hoped she would be saved from the rope. Not that I had any respect for Mrs Thompson herself. She had shown herself to be utterly false to her marriage vows, had apparently deliberately plotted against her husband's life, and then when Nemesis placed her in a felon's dock she was not sporting enough to stand true to her lover, young Bywaters, and was concerned only with saving her own neck. Nevertheless, only in a legal sense was she a murderess, for she had no actual part in committing the crime. Moreover, she was a woman, and there was something distasteful to me in hanging even a bad woman in such circumstances.

There have been two other occasions in my career when I have been concerned in the execution of women. The first was in 1903, when I assisted Billy Billington at the double execution of John Gallagher and Emily Swann at Armley Gaol, Leeds, for the calculated and brutal murder of the woman's husband. The other was twenty years later, when Mrs Susan Newell paid the penalty in Duke Street, Prison, Glasgow, for doing to death a twelve-year-old newsboy. Both these women were of a very coarse type, very different from Mrs Thompson, though

I do not put this distinction forward as necessarily telling in her favour. Still, it undoubtedly had weight with thousands who did not worry themselves unduly about the execution of the other two women, but who held up their hands in horror when Mrs Thompson was sent to the scaffold.

Her crime will be so fresh in the memory of readers that it is hardly necessary for me to describe it fully. A brief resume of its dramatic outline will, I think, be sufficient. Edith Jesse Thompson had been married about seven years when the tragedy came that swept her husband, her lover, and herself to death. For almost the whole of those seven years she and Percy Thompson had lived the ordinary uneventful lives of a normal husband and wife. There had been no children of the marriage, and consequently Mrs Thompson continued in her post as book-keeper and manageress of a London millinery establishment, where she earned £6 a week, plus fairly valuable bonuses. This and Percy Thompson's £6 a week as a shipping clerk meant that the unencumbered couple were able to live very comfortably in their Ilford home.

Reading between the lines of what I read about her at that time, it seemed to me that Mrs Thompson looked upon herself as a woman with a capacity for deep passion which she was forced to bury beneath the mask of humdrum life with an unimaginative husband. Then came a fateful holiday in the Isle of Wight when she was thrown into contact with Frederick Bywaters, a steward on the P. & O. liner Morea. Straight away Edith Thompson plunged into the passion that she had dreamed about for so long. The woman of 28 and the youth of 20 became secret lovers.

Percy Thompson had no suspicions at that time about his wife's faithfulness, and so we find young Bywaters actually being received into the Thompson household for several weeks as a trusted, paying guest. Then the young fellow went a-voyaging, and he and Edith Thompson bridged the gap of their parting by passionate correspondence without equal in any case that has ever come under my notice during my whole career. Bywaters had so lost his head over his friend's wife that he kept all her letters – a piece of foolishness that I always regarded as his crowning mistake and one that might be said to have led the woman to the scaffold. For those burning epistles contained numerous passages referring to Mrs Thompson's abortive attempts to cause her husband's death, so that she might openly be united with her illicit lover!

One evening Mr and Mrs Thompson – who were outwardly on the happiest terms with each other – went to a theatrical show in the West End of London. One their way home they were walking towards their house in Ilford when, in the darkness, a weird tragedy was enacted.

A passer-by heard Mrs Thompson suddenly scream out, 'Oh, whatever shall I do? My husband has fallen and cut his head!' A doctor came in the scene, and by the flickering light of a match examined the huddled body on the pavement and pronounced Percy Thompson dead from a haemorrhage. Not until a later examination in the mortuary was it discovered that the man had been murdered —that he had been three times so savagely stabbed that he must have died at once.

This point once established, the police moved swiftly. They interrogated the hysterical widow. She professed herself unable to throw any light on how her husband had been killed. Whose had been the hand that came out of the dark and stabbed her husband at her side she knew not.

But in a street drain near the fatal spot a heavy knife, still stained with blood, had been found. The knife was Fred Bywater's. So he was arrested, and in his rooms those extraordinary letters of Edith Thompon's were found. She was, therefore, arrested too, and the pair faced trial for conspiring together to murder Percy Thompson. There was a five-days' legal battle over them at the Old Bailey. The jury, consisting of eleven men and one woman, took two and a quarter hours to agree upon their verdict. When it came it brought death to both white-faced occupants of the dock.

At once the British public accomplished a remarkable volte-face. Up till then Mrs Thompson had been universally execrated. No one could say things harsh enough about this real life vampire, who was regarded as having been Bywaters' evil genius. She had been not merely an adulteress, but, as shown by her letters, had secretly made various attempts to poison her husband, and had undoubtedly urged on her lover to kill the man whose wedding ring decorated her finger. But no sooner was she sentenced to death than an immediate revulsion of feeling shook Great Britain from one end to the other. At first people told each other that the sentence was a mere matter of form – that no woman had been hanged for murder for fifteen years, and that it was unthinkable that a woman should ever again be sent to the scaffold.

Then others argued that it would be entirely unjust to reprieve the woman and hang the man, while it would be still more unjust to allow such a fearful crime as they had committed to go unpunished. Meanwhile the authorities went quietly ahead. Immediately after Mrs Thompson and Bywaters were condemned the solicitors who act as Under-Sheriffs for the County of Essex wrote me with regard to their execution. And at that stage, I might add, it was intended to hang Bywaters on one morning and Mrs Thompson on the next. This arrangement was afterwards changed and it was decided to get both executions over on the same morning. However, my first letter in connection with the case was in the following terms:

Sheriff's Office,
Chelmsford.
Dear Sir, – Re execution of Frederick Edward Francis Bywaters and Edith
Jessie Thompson. The above named convicts were sentenced to death yesterday,
the male prisoner at Pentonville and the female prisoner at Holloway.

Subject to an appeal, we have provisionally fixed Tuesday the 2nd January at 9
a.m., for the execution of the male prisoner at Pentonville, and Wednesday, the
3rd January at 9 a.m., for the execution of the female prisoner at Holloway. We
should be much obliged if you would let us know whether you can carry out these
two executions, and if so, you will be in attendance at Pentonville on Monday,
the 1st January, at 4 p.m. In the event of an appeal, perhaps you will kindly let
us know whether you have any other engagements for January.
  We are,
  Yours faithfully,
  GEPP & SONS.

I wrote an acceptance, but I may as well frankly admit that I, too, at that time
never dreamed Mrs Thompson would hang. I rather shared the sentimental
leanings of the general public in the direction of mercy towards the woman merely
because of her sex, and I really believed the authorities would bow before the
storm and save her from the gallows. Disillusionment came quickly. About ten
days after the Old Bailey trial ended the Court of Criminal Appeal considered
the case of the two condemned persons and dismissed their application. Then
arose a change in the execution arrangements, and I found myself in a quandary.
Mr Gepp wrote me:

It is possible that both executions will take place on the same day, in which event
it will be necessary to employ two executioners. We should be glad to know whether
you would be prepared to act at the execution of Mrs Thompson on Tuesday,
the 9th January, at Holloway, or on Friday, the 5th January, at the same place.

This was the first real hint I had received that it was really likely that Edith
Thompson was to be sent to the scaffold. I had never at any time held any desire
to hang a woman, and for that reason, when Mrs Thompson was condemned
to death, I nursed the strong hope that she would be reprieved.

Now I was faced with the task of deciding whether I would accept a request
that I should act as executioner of one who was undoubtedly a murderess in
spirit if she did not actually plunge the knife into her husband's body, but who
was, after all, a woman. What ought I to do? The question troubled me for

hours. In the end I decided that it was my duty to obey instructions. Apart from that, I knew that the Home Office had implicit faith in my capacity to carry out such an affair with the minimum amount of risk of anything going wrong, and I felt that it was my duty to the poor doomed wretch to help her through her ordeal with all the swift humanity that my twenty years' experience had taught me how to bestow. So I sent my acceptance in spite of the fact that I knew the general public would regard my act as that of a morbid, depraved man.

I was not long left in any doubt as to the attitude of the people towards myself, they seemed to think if I refused the job that the State would never find anyone else to do it – a colossal mistake. You would be surprised at the constant succession of letters I got from men of all grades of respectability all over the kingdom who hankered for the hangman's post, and later on I may have something else to say on this subject.

Anyway, the public poured out the vials of its wrath upon my head, and the anonymous letter fiends got very busy indeed. One man sent me a sheet of foolscap decorated on one side in the following fashion:

BE A MAN
AND
NOT A MACHINE.
REFUSE
TO HANG EITHER
'VENGEANCE IS MINE – I WILL REPAY.'
LAW IS NOT ALWAYS JUSTICE.
THINK
(FROM AN EX-SOLDIER.)

This was drawn out carefully in ink, all the words being in capitals as if to disguise the author's writing. But he must have changed his mind afterwards, for he wrote in the back this further message in lead pencil in undisguised handwriting:

EXPLANATION.
Bywaters is a victim of sympathy drawn into it through that agent in the first instance.

Mrs Thompson's fall is through vanity, which is no credit, and, next to greed, the worst sin in the world – but as she did not actually do the crime, and being a woman, should, like Bywaters, be reprieved.

Many others of a similar nature came to me over this case – generally addressed 'Care of the Governor, Holloway Prison, London'. One indignant person cut Mrs Thompson's photo out of a newspaper, and added this note:

Dear Sir, - Be a man and don't hang a woman, You know you have to die yourself in a few years. Just think.

Still another writer was thoughtful enough to send his message on a picture postcard showing the entrance to Dartmoor Prison. This is how he phrased his protest:

If you go and pull that lever and take a woman's life, Government ain't to answer for it. God'll send the bill to you. 'Nemesis.'

Naturally these things had no effect on my decision to do my duty as I saw it. My contention was always that I had no greater personal responsibility in conducting a condemned criminal to the scaffold that was borne by the Judge who pronounced that death sentence. Gradually it grew more and more doubtful whether the Home Secretary would be swayed by the hysterical agitation of those folk who not so long before had been among the most downright in their expressions of detestation of this woman's evil life.

Two assistants were engaged in addition to myself, and a few days before the fateful Tuesday morning I received a letter from Mr Gepp containing the pregnant phrase, 'There is no reprieve'. I learned after I reached the prison that Mrs Thompson never really believed she was going to be hanged until the last fatal hour was almost upon her. 'I am not going to die', she often said to the wardress whose melancholy duty it was to keep her company. 'My reprieve will come. But, oh! This dreadful waiting.' And, steadfast in this opinion, this extraordinary woman wrote blithely to her friends outside, discussing books she had read and her mother's birthday, etc. Never did she thoroughly realise that her days were numbered.

Even on the very afternoon that I arrived in the prison to prepare for the following morning's execution she was still confident. Her mother and father, sister, and brother were there to see her, and by sheer force of personality she implanted that same idea in their heads that she would be saved. In point of fact, she chattered quite cheerfully with them, and parted from them without even bidding the customary good-byes. But I am anticipating somewhat. Let me now go back a day or two. When I first had that hint – 'No reprieve'. – I was myself just a little bit taken aback. But my hand was now on the plough, and my proper course lay clear before me.

I saw in advance some of the unusual difficulties that would beset the execution of a woman. One of these concerned the question of leg pinioning. In the case of a man his ankles are strapped together at the last moment on the trap doors, but one could hardly deal with a woman in this way. So I wrote to the Under-Sheriff telling him that it would be necessary to procure a longer strap, which I proposed to fasten round the bottom of her skirts.

I discovered afterwards that on receipt of my letter the Holloway Prison engineer was sent over to Pentonville to see if they had a suitable long strap. They hadn't. So someone spliced a special strap which proved quite suitable. It may be interesting to my readers to learn that on this occasion of Mrs Thompson's execution I had my first experience of an aeroplane journey. For some time I had longed to go up in an aeroplane, for although I am not a physically strong man I have always been keen on trying everything that's going that has a sporting kick to it. Hence, when Edith Thompson's execution drew near, I resolved to make my first acquaintance with air travel by flying from Manchester to London. Behold me, therefore, on the morning of Monday, January 8, 1923, leaving my home in Rochdale and journeying by train into Manchester.

When I got out to the aerodrome it seemed that I was the only intending passenger, and the booking-office clerk made various comments about unsatisfactory flying weather, etc. I expect he was trying to test my nerve. However, I paid my fare, which was £2 5s. and was given a blue paper 'Airway Ticket No. M240', bearing my name and date of passage. I don't think the man recognised my name; anyway, he made no comment. The seat he showed me into was a very comfortable one, and presently there I was away up in the air swooping southwards. It was a great experience, and I never felt any nervousness. Now and then the machine did a bit of what the pilot called 'banking', and that made you think things quickly. But apart from that there was nothing to make anybody worry, and the sight of those railway stations and little towns flat out underneath us was worth it all. We arrived at Croydon Aerodrome ten minutes in front of scheduled time, and an official came and told me to go to the hotel until the motor-car arrived to convey me to the city.

Time passed, and I was beginning to get rather irritated at the delay. So I went to inquire about that motor. It then appeared that as I was the only passenger they were reluctant to run a special car into London. Just when it looked as if we were going to have a few words on the subject another car came in from the city bringing a passenger for the flight back to Manchester so I hopped into this car and was whipped up to London in fine style. Some time later I was thrilled at learning that this same machine as I had flown in was smashed while on the journey back from London to Manchester, both passengers and pilot being killed. It would be about three o'clock in the afternoon when I reached the neighbourhood of Holloway Gaol in company with one of my assistants named Phillips whom I had met by arrangement in the city.

There was a big crowd round the gates, which a number of policemen were having a little difficulty in keeping orderly. What these people expected to see beats me, but if they were looking for the executioner they missed him completely. For Phillips and I had given our names in at the gates and been admitted before the crowd had a chance to recognise us. Even the press photographers did not spot us. I saw five of them with their backs to me busy taking snaps of the crowd, while the one for whom they were no doubt waiting slipped quietly inside the prison.

By the way, I think I can correct a mistake concerning the numerous armed policemen whose presence around the prison gave rise to so many rumours. I saw it stated in several papers that they were there as a measure of precaution over Mrs Thompson's execution. That was not the case. They were there because of a Sinn Fein woman lying in one of the cells. She was in on a charge of secreting arms at Woolwich, and the Scotland Yard folk confidently expected a raid with the object of attempting to rescue her. Hence the armed policemen.

Within a few minutes of my arrival, the other assistant, Baxter, turned up, and a little later the Under-Sheriff, Mr Gepp, reached the prison. He and the governor, Dr John Hall Morton (who acted as both prison governor and medical officer), came at once to the scaffold, where I had already gone to try the lever and see that the trapdoors were working properly. Mr Gepp asked me if I would like any more assistants in addition to my own two men, Phillips and Baxter.

'No', said I, 'I think we shall be able to manage.'

However, the Under-Sheriff had already arranged with the authorities at Pentonville to send over two officers to help in the morning, and he assured me that as they had already been present at several executions I would be able to reply upon their nerves standing the strain. At the moment, I must confess, I saw very little necessity for these extra men, but later events were to prove them extremely useful. Our conversation turned upon other aspects of the morrow's task. Turning to the Governor I advised him to give Mrs Thompson a good stiff dose of brandy about five minutes before the fatal hour. You may call that giving 'Dutch courage', but I know this, it has never failed in helping poor condemned wretches over those last terrifying moments. In fact, to my mind, that is the secret of the whole thing, and is the general explanation of the commonly-used phrase, 'the condemned man walked firmly to the scaffold'.

While I am on the subject, let me clear up another false idea that people have about executions. When the Mrs Thompson affair was safely over one of the prison officials, who realised what an awful ordeal I had been through, said to me – 'Mr Ellis, excuse the question, but do you have anything to help you carry out a job of this sort?'

I pretended not to understand him, so he said more frankly —

'I always thought you have some secret drink which you made yourself!'

No doubt there are lots of people like him who fancy that a hangman has either to get half drunk or doped before he can do his duty. To him and to others who may have wondered on this matter I give the same reply, that on the morning of an execution the only form of strong drink I have ever touched is – tea!

But to return to the discussion between the Governor, Under-Sheriff, and myself. My suggestion about the brandy was adopted, but, unhappily, as I shall show presently, it was not carried out in the proper fashion. Hence the terrible scene that we were to face next morning.

'How is Mrs Thompson bearing up?' I asked, to which Dr Morton replied:

'She is a most puzzling woman. Sometimes she is quite cheerful for hours and then she will have a sham faint. But to-day she really was unconscious, and I begin to fear we shall have serious trouble with her in the morning. I fully expect we shall have to use the chair, which I have ordered to be put in readiness in the shed.'

Mentally I hoped we would be able to do without using that chair, which would have necessitated sitting the condemned woman in it on the trapdoors, a plan that might lead to all sorts of unpleasant complications.

Dr Morton was, I found, a very courteous gentleman, ever ready to listen to my suggestions with an open mind, which I might say is not an invariable characteristic of prison governors.

'What shall you do if she swoons?' he asked. 'Pinion her in her cell', I replied, 'and put the strap round her skirts at the same time. My two assistants would then carry her to the shed and hold her up while I do the rest. They will be more used to that sort of thing than the warders from Pentonville.' Thus it was arranged. A little later in the evening I met Miss Elizabeth Crisnin, a superintendent of the prison and had a chat over old times, for we had met before at Lancaster and at Maidstone Prisons. She confessed that the strain of looking after Mrs Thompson was extremely trying. The woman, she said, was most considerate to the wardresses, who had the task of sitting with her, but now and again she would have emotional breakdowns. I told Miss Crisnin that I would need to get a good glimpse of Mrs Thompson as soon as possible so as to get a general idea of her physique. Miss Crisnin replied my best chance would be when they took Mrs Thompson from her present quarters to the condemned cell, and promised to send for me then.

About 8.20 that evening a wardress came for me, and I accompanied her to a passage ending in a glass door that faced the prison centre. 'She will come down that long corridor and up that flight of steps', the wardress said, pointing across, and then leaving me. In a minute or two she returned, and although she was a well-disciplined wardress she showed certain signs of mental distress. 'She's coming!' she whispered. 'They are having to hold her up.' A few moments later I was looking at the woman whose name had been so much bandied about. And a pitiable sight she presented. She seemed to be in a state of partial collapse, and yet it seemed to me as if she were trying her level best to bear up and trying to make her brain do that which her body was unable to do.

She looked fairly tall for a woman. As a matter of fact, she was 5 ft. 7 ¾ in. in height according to prison measurement. It might be interesting to add at this point, too, that she had actually gained 11 lb, in weight during the weeks while she lay under sentence of death, having gone up to 9 st. 4 lb. But when she first came under my gaze she looked anything but robust, and though I detested her crime I could not help pitying her. She was clothed in the ugly, arrow-marked prison dress which had often brought protests from her. One of the wardresses told me that Mrs Thompson absolutely loathed the costume she was forced to wear. 'Why should I be forced to wear this degrading garb?' she cried. 'Shall I ever wear my furs again?' As they brought her along the corridor towards the room which she was only to leave to face death a most unpleasant incident occurred. Mrs Thompson suddenly caught sight of me through the glass door as I peered at her.

All through my career it has always been one of my aims to spare the condemned criminal from the shock of seeing me until the final moments arrive, for my civilian dress in a place where everybody wears uniform tells the poor wretches that they are under the observation of the hangman.

This only adds to the already heavy load on their nerves, so that although it was absolutely necessary for me to see them the evening before execution I tried to be as unobtrusive as possible. So you can understand how upset I was when I saw Mrs Thompson's white face turned in my direction and realised that she had recognised me. I expected this to complete her collapse. Instead, it had just the opposite result. The marvellous woman lifted her head proudly, straightened her sagging body and stalked onwards with new dignity.

When I observed where the condemned cell was I foresaw another possibility of trouble for Mrs Thompson. It was only a few yards from her apartment to the execution shed itself, and it was obvious to me that the poor woman could not fail to hear our preparations in the morning when we would have to haul up the sandbag that hangs overnight on the rope and fix up the trapdoors. It seemed so cruel that she should hear this that I went to the Governor and asked him if it would not be possible to remove her from her cell while we were getting ready. Dr Morton was full of sympathy, and said he had thought over the same problem himself, but he could not see any way out of it. The only thing I could do was to promise to work as quietly as possible. 'What do you propose giving her Ellis?' Dr Morton asked me. I told him I had decided upon 6 ft. 10 in. Which was 10 inches less than the Home Office Regulations suggest for the same height and weight. Dr Morton was surprised at this. 'I understand you generally give more than the regulation, why are you doing otherwise in this case?' he asked. 'Because we are dealing with a woman, a matter of physical difference the Home Office scale does not recognise', I pointed out. The Governor accepted my explanation and not long after I and my assistant retired for the night to the quarters assigned to us.

The morning of the execution broke dismal, rainy weather fully in keeping with the task before us. Baxter, Phillips and myself rose about 6.30 and had a drink of hot tea. Then we moved towards the execution shed for the final arrangements. While my assistants were getting the necessary tackle I went to the door of the condemned cell and looked through the inspection hole. It was then 7.40am and Mrs Thompson was still in bed, apparently asleep, for all was quiet within, and the solitary gas jet shed a dim light on the dreamy gaol furnishings.

After putting in a quarter of an hours work on the scaffold I returned to the condemned cell and peeped in again. Mrs Thompson was now awake and standing at the foot of the bed where the two wardresses were helping her to dress. Amazing to relate, Mrs Thompson was perfectly cheerful and actually laughing at the jests of the officers whose job it was to keep her mind off what was coming at nine o'clock.

They were fastening her stocking suspenders, and I heard one of the wardresses remark – 'I don't want to fasten them too tight for you, my dear'. Mrs Thompson made some joking reply that I could not catch and turned her head towards the door, though of course it was impossible for her to see me. I was surprised and considerably relieved to notice how calm she was and not wishing to pry upon the woman while she was dressing, I retired, glad that I could tell my assistants and the officers present that I believed all would go well, as Mrs Thompson was bearing up so well.

Events were to turn out very, very different from what I anticipated. The execution shed was not quite ready. Its only item of furniture beside the grim cross beam and coil of rope and the lever beside the trap doors was a chair. This was not for the doomed woman, but for the chaplain. The reverend gentleman had previously made a point of seeing me and asking if I could accommodate him with a chair as he was subject to fits of dizziness.

My assistants and I filled the remaining period of waiting in our own room. Then at 8.55 we went to the prison centre to meet the Governor, as had been previously arranged between us. There were other officers there also and they all looked very haggard. We made a gloomy, silent crowd as we stood there waiting, with the Governor holding his watch in his hand measuring out the fast flying minutes of Mrs Thompson's life.

About three minutes to nine an eerie sound reached us. It was a low moan from the condemned cell. It startled me perhaps more than it did the others. The officers were apparently aware already that Mrs Thompsons nerves had given way. But my last glimpse of her had been so reassuring that this new development came as a great shock. It came to my knowledge afterwards that Mrs Thompson managed to nibble a piece of buttered toast and an apple after she was dressed and remained quite composed and in good spirits until quite near the hour fixed for her execution. Why she had so suddenly fallen to pieces I could not understand, but in view of the arrangements made between the Governor and I the previous evening I still believe that she would pull herself together in the final moments. This however was not to be. Instead we were to witness a scene that will never fade from my memory, although I may not be able to describe it adequately here.

At one minute to nine we walked to the condemned cell. Waiting for the signal, I stepped inside. Mrs Thompson was in a state of complete emotional collapse, and had absolutely lost all control of herself. When I entered, the chaplain was striving to help her with consoling words, the two wardresses were seconding his efforts bravely. Indeed, I've often wondered since then how those two female officers stood the terrific ordeal, for there were strong men peering in from the corridor who afterwards confessed that they had great difficulty themselves in refraining from breaking down.

Understanding my beckoning nod, the chaplain left Mrs Thompson's side and the wardresses practically lifted the sobbing woman to her feet, for she was totally unable to stand unaided. My own feelings defy description. The woman's cries and semi-demented body movements almost unnerved me, but I told myself that my only human course was to work swiftly and cut Mrs Thompson's agony as short as possible. So pulling myself together I quickly pinioned her hands behind her back.

By this time the poor woman's cries were being blotted out by the unconsciousness which now mercifully descended upon her and from which she never again emerged. She sank back into her chair and realising that there was nothing for it but to put into operation the emergency measures which I had hoped would never be needed, I called forward my two assistants and also the Pentonville warders. I instructed Phillips and Baxter to strap her skirts round her ankles and that they must carry Mrs Thompson to the scaffold with the help of the two warders. I then left the agonising scene and hurried through to the scaffold.

In a few minutes I saw them coming bearing Mrs Thompson. She looked as if she was already dead. The door through which those four men had to carry her inert body was an extremely narrow one. How they all got through with their burden I have never been able to understand.

My back was to them as they approached but as soon as they reached the trap doors, I put the white cap on her head and face and slipped the noose over all. It was a pitiable thing to see the woman being held up on her feet by four men. Her head had fallen forward on her breast and she was utterly oblivious to all that was going on. Without giving time for anything further to happen, I sprung to the lever. One flick of the wrist and Mrs Thompson disappeared from view. She died instantaneously and painlessly. I saw her afterwards when I assisted the matron in the unpleasant task of putting her in her coffin, and her face was calm and composed as if she were peacefully asleep.

When all was over the Under Sheriff came to me and said he was quite satisfied with the way the execution was carried out and I felt this was some consolation for the worrying time we had been through. The Governor later on said something similar. But personally, I was more than puzzled at Mrs Thompson's sudden change from her earlier high spirits and put a question to Dr Morton, which elicited the explanation of the mystery. I asked him if Mrs Thompson had had the brandy I recommended. He replied that she had been having sips of brandy from 8 o'clock onwards.

There can be no doubt that Dr Morton took that course in a genuine desire to ease Mrs Thompson's last moments, but I shall always maintain that if instead of having sips of brandy beforehand, she had been given one stiff glassful at 5 minutes to nine, when she first began to lose control of herself, she would have been saved the terrible sufferings of the 5 minutes of dreadful misery. In conclusion, I would like to say that I have described those tragic scenes so fully not because I want to harrow people feelings but because I feel that the public is entitled to the full truth about this affair.

Appendix 1

The Execution Protocol

John Ellis' time as assistant and executioner began when prisons still allowed reporters in to observe the executions. He was one of the last to be trained in the art of hanging at Newgate Prison and was assistant to executioner William Billington at the last execution carried out there. The gallows were then removed to Pentonville Prison.

Ellis began work as executioner when many county prisons had condemned cells some distance from their execution sheds or 'death chambers' where their gallows were installed. This would also mean the condemned would be taken in procession from the condemned cell down echoing corridors and even across the prison yard where the execution shed awaited them. Ellis saw many of these prisons either cease as 'hanging prisons' or have their gallows installed within the prison in a dedicated 'execution suite' that would have consisted of the condemned cell with adjoining 'death chamber'.

Despite executions being completely behind doors, crowds would still gather outside the prison gates but the only indication they received that the execution was taking place was the tolling of the prison bell immediately before the execution, the raising of a black flag to signify the execution had been carried out, the 'Declaration of the Sheriff' stating he and others had witnessed the execution and a certificate from the prison surgeon confirming the death of the condemned, which would then be displayed on the exterior of the entrance doors of the prison. The execution protocol observed at this time was fine-tuned and explicitly described in the Rules and Standing Orders for the Government of Local Prisons.

The execution protocol begins with the receipt of the prisoner under sentence of death. The Governor was duty bound to notify the High Sheriff who was responsible for carrying out the sentence and the Secretary of State on the day the sentence was pronounced with any special recommendation of the jury being fully set out in his correspondence. A detailed newspaper report of the trial from a reliable rather than sensational newspaper would be attached along with a copy of the entry relating to the prisoner in the confidential before-trial calendar. Any observations relating to matters of importance which may have been suggested to the Medical Officer by the evidence given at the trial or by information obtained subsequently from the Director of Public Prosecutions would also be forwarded as soon as possible, as would be the notification of the date set for the execution.

The Governor would also contact the Prison Commissioners asking to be furnished with the list of candidates reported as competent for the office of executioner, with information as to the conduct and efficiency of each of them and the regulations to be observed in carrying out the sentence. On receipt of these papers, the Governor would transmit the list of candidates to the High Sheriff together with the memoranda issued by the Secretary of State in reference to executions, specifically the conditions to which any person acting as executioner or assistant executioner should conform.

When practicable permanent warders would be assigned to watch the prisoner and unless absolutely necessary no one would be engaged temporarily and no others would be permitted to come into contact with the condemned. The condemned would also be allowed private exercise and dietary allowances as the Governor or Medical Officer may direct. A chaplain would have free access to visit and to be called for by the condemned. Any other visitor would only have access to the condemned after having obtained an order from the Governor or a Prison Commissioner.

The Governor would then have to ensure the scaffold and all necessary appliances were in good order. He would have obtained the necessary equipment upon request from the stock held at Pentonville Prison. The items would be sent in two boxes, one small box containing the chains for adjusting the rope, the rest of the equipment in what looked like a long wooden tool box fastened with a sturdy retaining bar and padlock. Inside this larger box was:

1. The rope.
2. The pinioning apparatus.
3. The cap.
4. A bag capable of containing sand to the same weight as the prisoner in clothes. The bag was made to an approved pattern with a very thick neck, well-padded on the outside with soft canvas to obviate any damage to the rope. The instructions sternly pointed out 'No unnecessary experiments should be carried out either with the rope or bag'.
5. A piece of chalk (to mark the rope or floor with a 'T' to position the feet of the condemned as necessary).
6. A few feet of copper wire.
7. A rule, or graduated pole, six feet long.
8. A piece of pack thread (just strong enough to support the excess coils of the rope without breaking).
9. A tackle to raise the bag of sand, or the body, out of the pit.

A week before the execution the rope was tested by a competent officer in accordance with directions so that in case of any defect a new one may be obtained. The Governor was authorised to pay the engaged executioner £10 (£5 for the performance of his duty and £5 if his conduct and behaviours were satisfactory) and assistant executioner the sum of £2 2s to cover all charges for each attendance along with reasonable travelling expenses; normally a Third Class railway fare and such cab fares shown to be absolutely necessary. The Governor would also provide proper food and lodging for the executioner and assistants while they were required in the prison.

The Governor would also ensure the Medical Officer, Sheriff, Chaplain and Coroner were provided with the correct papers to sign and confirm the judgement of death had been executed upon the offender; the same papers were displayed upon the prison door after the execution. He would also ensure the persons required or entitled to attend the execution were attended to.

On his arrival at the prison the day before the execution, the executioner was furnished by the Governor and Medical Officer with all necessary information as to the height and weight of the culprit, his general condition, age and whether he was likely to offer any resistance. The executioner would observe the prisoner from an unseen location, often while he took some exercise, then armed with all this information the executioner would calculate the length of the drop required according to the 'Table of Drops' and his own experience. The Governor and Medical Officer might recommend a departure from the table if, after careful examination, it appeared there were special reasons for such a departure. If the executioner disagreed with the other officials he would be entitled to ask that the amendment to his calculations be annotated and signed by the officials that demanded it.

As the appointed time for the execution approached, in some prisons about 30 feet of coconut matting would be laid outside the condemned cell to avoid the sound of approaching booted feet over the iron grid floor. The executioner and his assistant with two warders in escort would gather in front of the condemned cell door. The Prison Governor, Medical Officer and Sheriff would wait outside the door of the lobby area; the Chaplain was usually inside the condemned cell with the prisoner. The Governor would check his watch and as the chimes of the prison clock marked the hour so the life of the condemned would be tolled out also.

Upon a given signal at the appointed time, all would enter their relevant doorways. The Governor and officials would move through the lobby area and flatten themselves against the wall of the execution chamber. The executioner would lead in, the condemned normally sat with his back to the entrance door at this time. He would often stand up automatically and before he had a chance to turn around his hands would be pinioned by the executioner. Meanwhile the other door in the condemned cell (which if the condemned had asked, they would have been told it led to store room) opened into the lobby area and the prisoner was led through by the executioner followed by the assistant and the warders. If the condemned offered resistance or was in a state of collapse he would be supported onto the gallows by the warders. Two sturdy planks crossed the pit for them to stand on and ropes with hefty knots hung down for the warders to hang onto and steady themselves as the gallows traps opened. Many of those present were surprised at the size of the pit; in many prisons the gallows were large enough to take two or three condemned at a time, so when the traps did drop open it appeared 'as if the floor disappeared'.

The *Memorandum of Instructions for carrying out the details of an Execution* lays out the entire Home Office approved procedure for carrying out an execution from the testing and preparation of the gallows and rope to how the execution proper should be carried out. Each copy of the memorandum was headed 'Confidential' and pointed out 'By order of the Secretary of State, this document is to be treated as most strictly confidential'. Originally printed in this form in December 1891, it was reprinted throughout John Ellis's time as hangman. It was issued to the executioner on appointment and a copy would be kept by the prison governor. If a county Sheriff was supplied a copy of the memorandum he was requested to return it to the prison governor from whom he had received it after the execution had been carried out and his duties discharged. What follows is a loyal transcription of that memorandum.

Memorandum of Instructions for carrying out the details of an Execution

1. The apparatus for the execution may be tested in the following manner:

   The working of the scaffold should first be tested without any weight. Then a bag of sand of the same weight as the culprit should be attached to the rope, and so adjusted as to allow the bag a drop equal to, or rather more than, that which the culprit will receive so that the rope may be stretched with a force of about 1,000 foot-pounds. The working of the apparatus under those conditions should then be tested. The bag must be of the approved pattern, with a thick well-padded neck, as to prevent any injury to the rope and leather. As the gutta-percha round the thimble of the execution ropes hardens in cold weather, care should be taken to have it warmed and manipulated immediately before the bag is tested.

2. After the completion of this testing the scaffold and all appliances should be locked up and the key kept by the Governor or other responsible officer until the morning of the execution; but the bag of sand should remain suspended all the night preceding the execution, so as to take the stretch out of the rope.
3. The executioner and any persons appointed to assist in the operation should make themselves thoroughly acquainted with the working of the apparatus.
4. The lever should be fixed as to prevent any accident while the preliminary details are being carried out.
5. Death by hanging ought to result from dislocation of the neck. The length of the drop is determined according to the weight of the culprit.
6. The required length of drop is regulated as follows:

At the end of the rope which forms the noose the executioner should see that 13 inches from the centre of the ring are marked off by a line painted around the rope; this is to be a fixed quantity, which, with the stretching of this portion of the rope, and the lengthening of the neck and body of the culprit, will represent the average depth of the head and circumference of the neck after constriction.

About two hours before the execution the bag of sand should be raised out of the pit, and be allowed another drop so as to completely stretch the rope. Then while the bag of sand is still suspended, the executioner should measure off from the painted mark on the rope at the end of this length. A piece of copper wire fastened to the chain should then now be stretched down the rope till it reaches the chalk mark, and should be cut off there so that the cut end of the copper wire shall terminate at the upper end of the measured length of drop.

The bag of sand should then be raised from the pit and disconnected from the rope. The chain should now be adjusted at the bracket that the lower end of the copper wire shall reach to the same level from the floor of the scaffold as the height of the prisoner. The known height of the prisoner can be readily measured on the scaffold by a graduated rule of six feet long. When the chain has been raised to the proper height the cotter must be securely fixed through the bracket and chain. The executioner should now make a chalk mark on the floor of the scaffold, in a plumb line with the chain, where the prisoner should stand.

These details should be carried out as soon as possible after 6 o'clock, so as to allow the rope to regain a portion of its elasticity before the execution, and, if possible, the gutta percha on the rope should again be warmed.

7. The copper wire should now be detached, and after allowing sufficient amount of rope for the easy adjustment of the noose, the slack of the rope should be fastened to the chain above the level of the head of the culprit with a pack-thread. The pack-thread should be just strong enough to support the rope without breaking.

8. When all the preparations are completed the scaffold should remain in charge of a responsible officer while the executioner goes to the pinioning room.

9. The pinioning apparatus should be dexterously applied in some room or place convenient to the scaffold.

10. On reaching the gallows the duty of the executioner should be as follows:

    (1) Place the culprit *exactly* under the part of the beam to which the rope is attached.

    (2) Strap the culprit's legs tightly.

    (3) Put on the white linen cap.

    (4) Put the rope round the neck quite tightly (with the cap between the rope and the neck), the metal eye being directed forwards, and placed in front of the angle of the lower jaw, so that with the constriction of the neck it may come underneath the chin. The noose should be kept tight by means of a stiff leather washer, or an india rubber washer, or a wedge.

    (5) Go *quickly* to the lever and let down the trap doors.

11. The culprit should hang one hour, and then the body should be *carefully* raised from the pit. The rope should be removed from the neck, and also the straps from the body. In laying out the body for the inquest the head should be raised three inches by placing a small piece of wood under it.

Many executioners also took great pride and considered it most humane to carry out their duties as quickly as possible. It was quite common for them to leave only the merest tip of the safety pin in the lever socket to enable a rapid knock to release it and allow the lever to be pushed and release the trap doors. In most cases the execution, from the moment of entry to the condemned cell to the condemned dropping into the pit, took less time than the steady chimes of the prison clock to mark the hour – about 20 to 30 seconds.

Immediately after the inquest, a record of the execution would be entered in the prison executions register with a copy sent to the Commissioners. Appliances would be carefully examined and any damage which may have occurred, reported and repaired. The rope and pinioning apparatus was to be kept in a warm, dry place and all the leather lubricated with Vaseline or pure petroleum ointment before being returned in their transit box to Pentonville.

Regulations were keen to point out 'The Governor will not allow casts to be taken of the heads of criminals who have been executed' and made it clear that the name of any executioner or assistant 'who did not give satisfaction or whose conduct is in any way objectionable, so as to cast discredit on himself, either in connection with the duties or otherwise, will be removed from the Home Office list of approved executioners and assistants'.

In an attempt to prevent the selling of souvenirs and ropes used in executions, or part thereof, as had been a very lucrative sideline for Victorian hangmen, regulations also made it clear:

'The apparatus approved for use at executions will be provided at the prison. No part of it may be removed from the prison, and no apparatus other than approved apparatus must be used in connection with any execution.'

The burial of executed criminals was to be carried out by the authorities of the prison where the execution took place. An allowance of 5s each was allowed for two prison officers to perform the special duties in connection with an execution, removing the body, placing it in a coffin then carrying it to, and placing it in the grave, then filling it in. And so would end the tale of the condemned; laid in a grave with a plain stone set in the wall above their initials and date of execution carved thereon or perhaps with no marker at all, their place of burial only marked on a map and retained by the Prison Clerk or Engineer.

Appendix 2

The Table of Drops

SCALE SHOWING THE STRIKING FORCE OF FALLING BODIES AT DIFFERENT DISTANCES.												
Distance Falling in Feet Zero	8 Stone	9 Stone	10 Stone	11 Stone	12 Stone	13 Stone	14 Stone	15 Stone	16 Stone	17 Stone	18 Stone	19 Stone
	Cw. Qr. lb.	Cw Qr. lb.	Cw. Qr. lb.	Cw. Qr. lb.	Cw. Qr. lb.	Cw. Qr. lb.	Cw. Qr. lb.	Cw. Qr. lb.	Cw. Qr. lb.	Cw. Qr. lb.	Cw. Qr. lb.	Cw. Qr. lb.
1 Ft.	8 0 0	9 0 0	10 0 0	11 0 0	12 0 0	13 0 0	14 0 0	15 0 0	16 0 0	17 0 0	18 0 0	19 0 0
2 ,,	11 1 15	12 2 23	14 0 14	15 2 4	16 3 22	18 1 12	19 3 2	21 0 21	22 2 11	24 0 1	25 1 19	26 3 9
3 ,,	13 3 16	15 2 15	17 1 14	19 0 12	20 3 11	22 2 9	24 1 8	26 0 7	27 3 5	29 2 4	31 1 2	33 0 1
4 ,,	16 0 0	18 0 0	20 0 0	22 0 0	24 0 0	26 0 0	28 0 0	30 0 0	32 0 0	34 0 0	36 0 0	40 0 0
5 ,,	17 2 11	19 3 5	22 0 0	24 0 22	26 1 16	28 2 11	30 3 5	33 0 0	35 0 22	37 0 16	39 2 11	41 3 15
6 ,,	19 2 11	22 0 5	24 2 0	26 3 22	29 1 16	31 3 11	34 1 5	36 3 0	39 0 22	41 2 16	44 0 11	46 2 5
7 ,,	21 0 22	23 3 11	26 2 0	29 0 16	31 3 5	34 1 22	37 0 11	39 3 0	42 1 16	45 0 5	47 2 22	50 1 11
8 ,,	22 2 22	25 2 4	28 1 14	31 0 23	34 0 5	36 3 15	39 2 25	42 2 7	45 1 16	48 0 26	51 0 8	53 3 18
9 ,,	24 0 11	27 0 12	30 0 14	33 0 23	36 0 16	39 0 18	42 0 19	45 0 21	48 0 22	51 0 23	54 0 25	57 0 26
10 ,,	25 1 5	28 1 23	31 2 14	34 3 4	37 3 22	41 0 12	44 1 2	47 1 21	50 2 11	53 3 1	56 3 19	60 0 9

Appendix 3

Roll of Executions Credited to John Ellis

The number of executions credited to John Ellis is 203; when listed and numbered they actually amount to 204.

1. 7 December 1901 – John and John Robert Miller, Newcastle (Thomas Billington exe. and John Ellis asst.).
2. 18 March 1902 – Richard Wigley, Shrewsbury (Henry Pierrepoint exe. and John Ellis asst.).
3. 6 May 1902 – George Woolfe, Newgate (William Billington exe. and John Ellis asst.).
4. 16 December 1902 —William Brown, Wandsworth (Henry Pierrepoint exe. and John Ellis asst.).
5. 30 December 1902 – George Place, Warwick (Henry Pierrepoint exe. and John Ellis asst.).
6. 7 July 1903 – Charles Howell, Chelmsford (William Billington exe. and John Ellis asst.).
7. 14 July 1903 – Samuel Dougal, 'Moat Farm Murderer', Chelmsford (William Billington exe. and John Ellis asst.).
8. 11 August 1903 – William Tuffen, Wandsworth (Henry Pierrepoint exe. and John Ellis asst.).
9. 2 December 1903 – Charles Whittaker, Manchester (John Billington exe. and John Ellis asst.).
10. 15 December 1903 – William Haywood (Henry Pierrepoint exe. and John Ellis asst.).
11. 29 December 1903 – John Gallagher and Mary Swann, Leeds (William Billington exe. and John Ellis asst.).
12. 29 March 1904 – Henry Jones, Stafford (John Billington exe. and John Ellis asst.).
13. 2 August 1904 – George Breeze, Durham (William Billington exe. and John Ellis asst.).
14. 16 August 1904 – Samuel Holden, Birmingham (William Billington exe. and John Ellis asst.).
15. 21 December 1904 – Eric Lange, Cardiff (William Billington exe. and John Ellis asst.).

16. 29 March 1905 – John Hutchinson, Nottingham (John Billington exe. and John Ellis asst.).

17. 25 April 1905 – John Foster, Cork (William Billington exe. and John Ellis asst.).

18. 23 May 1905 – Albert and Alfred Stratton, Wandsworth (John Billington exe.; Henry Pierrepoint and John Ellis assts.).

19. 20 June 1905 – Alfred John Heal, Wandsworth (John Billington exe. and John Ellis asst.).

20. 1 August 1905 – Ferat Ben Ali, Maidstone (Henry Pierrepoint exe. and John Ellis asst.).

21. 15 August 1905 – Arthur Devereux, Pentonville (Henry Pierrepoint exe. and John Ellis asst.).

22. 7 November 1905 – William George Butler, Pentonville – (Henry Pierrepoint exe. and John Ellis asst.).

23. 5 December 1905 – William Yarnold, Worcester (Henry Pierrepoint exe. and John Ellis asst.).

24. 6 December 1905 – Henry Perkins, Newcastle (Henry Pierrepoint exe. and John Ellis asst.).

25. 27 December 1905 – Frederick William Edge, Stafford (Henry Pierrepoint exe. and John Ellis asst.).

26. 28 December 1905 – George Smith, Leeds (Henry Pierrepoint exe. and John Ellis asst.).

27. 29 December 1905 – John Silk, Derby (Henry Pierrepoint exe. and John Ellis asst.).

28. 27 February 1906 – Jack Griffiths, Manchester (Henry Pierrepoint exe. and John Ellis asst.).

29. 13 November 1906 – Frederick Reynolds, Wandsworth (Henry Pierrepoint exe. and John Ellis asst.).

30. 27 December 1906 – Walter Marsh, Derby (Henry Pierrepoint exe. and John Ellis asst.).

31. 1 January 1907 – John Davies, Warwick (John Ellis exe. and William Willis asst.).

32. 2 April 1907 – Edwin James Moore, Warwick (John Ellis exe. and William Willis asst.).

33. 16 July 1907 – William Edward Slack, Derby (Henry Pierrepoint exe. and John Ellis asst.).

34. 13 August 1907 – Richard Brinkley, Wandsworth (Henry Pierrepoint exe. and John Ellis asst.).

35. 12 May 1908 – James Ramsbottom, Manchester (Henry Pierrepoint exe. and John Ellis asst.).

36. 4 August 1908 – Thomas Siddle, Hull (Henry Pierrepoint exe. and John Ellis asst.).
37. 19 August 1908 – Edward Johnstone, Perth (John Ellis exe. and William Willis asst.).
38. 15 December 1908 – Harry Taylor Parker, Warwick (Henry Pierrepoint exe. and John Ellis asst.).
39. 30 December 1908 – Noah Percy Collins, Cardiff (Henry Pierrepoint exe. and John Ellis asst.).
40. 12 March 1909 – Thomas Meade, Leeds (Henry Pierrepoint exe. and John Ellis asst.).
41. 30 March 1909 – Edmund Walter Elliott, Exeter (John Ellis exe. and William Willis asst.).
42. 8 May 1909 – William Joseph Foy, Swansea (Henry Pierrepoint exe. and John Ellis asst.).
43. 3 July 1909 – John Edmunds, Usk (Henry Pierrepoint exe. and John Ellis asst.).
44. 6 July 1909 – Alexander Edmunstone, Perth (John Ellis exe.).
45. 17 August 1909 – Madan Lal Dhingra, Pentonville (Henry Pierrepoint exe. and John Ellis asst.).
46. 7 December 1909 – John Freeman, Hull (Henry Pierrepoint exe. and John Ellis asst.).
47. 22 February 1910 – Joseph Wren, Manchester (Henry Pierrepoint exe. and John Ellis asst.).
48. 1 March 1910 – George Henry Perry, Pentonville (Henry Pierrepoint exe. and John Ellis asst.).
49. 24 March 1910 – Thomas Clements (William Butler), Usk (Henry Pierrepoint exe. and John Ellis asst.).
50. 14 July 1910 – Frederick Foreman, Chelmsford (Henry Pierrepoint exe. and John Ellis asst.).
51. 9 August 1910 – John Alexander Dickman, Newcastle (John Ellis exe. and William Willis asst.).
52. 15 November 1910 – Thomas Rawcliffe, Lancaster (John Ellis exe. and William Willis asst.).
53. 22 November 1910 – Henry Thompson, Liverpool (John Ellis exe. and William Willis asst.).
54. 23 November 1910 – Hawley Harvey Crippen, Pentonville (John Ellis exe. and William Willis asst.).
55. 24 November 1910 – William Broome, Reading (John Ellis exe. and William Willis asst.).

56. 21 December 1910 – Noah Woolf, Pentonville (John Ellis exe. and Thomas Pierrepoint asst.).

57. 4 January 1911 – William Scanlan, Cork (John Ellis exe. and William Willis asst.).

58. 31 January 1911 – George Newton, Chelmsford (John Ellis exe. and William Conduit asst.).

59. 9 May 1911 – Thomas Seymour, Liverpool (John Ellis exe. and Thomas Pierrepoint asst.).

60. 24 May 1911 – Michael Collins, Pentonville (John Ellis exe. and Thomas Pierrepoint asst.).

61. 20 June 1911 – Arthur Garrod, Ipswich (John Ellis exe. and William Willis asst.).

62. 19 July 1911 – William Palmer, Leicester (John Ellis exe. and George Brown asst.).

63. 17 October 1911 – Francisco Godhino, Pentonville (John Ellis exe. and Albert Lumb asst.).

64. 17 October 1911 – Edward Hill, Pentonville (John Ellis exe. and Albert Lumb asst.).

65. 15 November 1911 – Frederick Henry Thomas, Wandsworth (John Ellis exe. and Thomas Pierrepoint asst.).

66. 6 December 1911 – Michael Fagan, Liverpool (John Ellis exe. and William Willis asst.).

67. 12 December 1911 – Walter Martyn, Manchester (John Ellis exe. and George Brown asst.).

68. 12 December 1911 – John Tarkenter, Manchester (John Ellis exe. and George Brown asst.).

69. 14 December 1911 – Henry Phillips, Swansea (John Ellis exe. and William Willis asst.).

70. 15 December 1911 – Joseph Fletcher, Liverpool (John Ellis exe. and George Brown asst.).

71. 19 December 1911 – George Parker, Maidstone (John Ellis exe. and no asst. recorded).

72. 21 December 1911 – Charles Coleman, St Albans (John Ellis exe. and William Willis asst.).

73. 6 March 1912 – Myer Abramovitch, Pentonville (John Ellis exe. and Albert Lumb asst.).

74. 19 March 1912 – John Williams, Knutsford (John Ellis exe. and Albert Lumb asst.).

75. 18 April 1912 – Frederick Henry Seddon, Pentonville (John Ellis exe. and Thomas Pierrepoint asst.).

76. 23 July 1912 – Arthur Birkett, Manchester (John Ellis exe. and Albert Lumb asst.).

77. 1 October 1912 – Sargent Philip, Wandsworth (John Ellis exe. and Thomas Pierrepoint asst.).

78. 10 December 1912 – William Henry Beal, Chelmsford (John Ellis exe. and William Willis asst.).

79. 18 December 1912 – Alfred Lawrence, Maidstone (John Ellis exe. and William Willis asst.).

80. 7 January 1913 – Albert Rumens, Lewes (John Ellis exe. and Thomas Pierrepoint asst.).

81. 29 January 1913 – George McKay (alias John Williams), Lewes (John Ellis exe. and William Willis asst.).

82. 4 February 1913 – Eric James Sedgewick, Reading (John Ellis exe. and George Brown asst.).

83. 25 February 1913 – George Cunliffe, Exeter (John Ellis exe. and George Brown asst.).

84. 8 July 1913 – Henry Longden, Pentonville (John Ellis exe. and William Willis asst.).

85. 9 July 1913 – Thomas Fletcher, Worcester (John Ellis exe. and Thomas Pierrepoint asst.).

86. 13 August 1913 – James Ryder, Manchester (John Ellis exe. and no asst. recorded).

87. 14 August 1913 – Hugh McLaren, Cardiff (John Ellis exe. and William Willis asst.).

88. 2 October 1913 – Patrick Higgins, Calton, Edinburgh (John Ellis exe. and William Willis asst.).

89. 26 November 1913 – Augustus Penny, Winchester (John Ellis exe. and Albert Lumb asst.).

90. 27 November 1913 – Frederick Robertson, Pentonville (John Ellis exe. and William Willis asst.).

91. 17 December 1913 – Ernest Kelly, Manchester (John Ellis exe. and no asst. recorded).

92. 26 February 1914 – George Ball (alias George Sumner), Liverpool (John Ellis exe. and William Willis asst.).

93. 10 March 1914 – Josiah Davis, Stafford (John Ellis exe. and George Brown asst.).

94. 12 March 1914 – James Honeyands, Exeter (John Ellis exe. and William Willis asst.).

95. 24 March 1914 – Robert Upton, Durham (John Ellis exe. and William Willis asst.).

96. 25 March 1914 – Edgar Bindon, Cardiff (John Ellis exe. and George Brown asst.).

97. 14 May 1914 – Joseph Spooner, Liverpool (John Ellis exe. and William Willis asst.).

98. 16 June 1914 – Walter White, Winchester (John Ellis exe. and Thomas Pierrepoint asst.).

99. 28 July 1914 – Herbert Brooker, Lewes (John Ellis exe. and Thomas Pierrepoint asst.).

100. 11 August 1914 – Peter Evelyn Clifford, Lewes (John Ellis exe. and Thomas Pierrepoint asst.).

101. 4 November 1914 – Charles Frembd, Chelmsford (John Ellis exe. and no asst. recorded).

102. 10 November 1914 – John Eayres, Northampton (John Ellis exe. and William Willis asst.).

103. 12 November 1914 – Arnold Warren, Leicester (John Ellis exe. and William Willis asst.).

104. 23 December 1914 – George Anderson, St Albans (John Ellis exe. and William Willis asst.).

105. 11 August 1915 – Frank Steele, Durham (John Ellis exe. and Robert Baxter asst.).

106. 13 August 1915 – George Joseph Smith, Maidstone (John Ellis exe. and Edward Taylor asst.).

107. 17 August 1915 – George Marshall, Wandsworth (John Ellis exe. and George Brown asst.).

108. 16 November 1915 – William Reeve, Bedford (John Ellis exe. and no asst. recorded).

109. 1 December 1915 – John Thornley, Liverpool (John Ellis exe. and George Brown asst.).

110. 1 December 1915 – Young Hill, Liverpool (John Ellis exe. and William Willis asst.).

111. 1 January 1916 – Lee Kun, Pentonville (John Ellis exe. and George Brown asst.).

112. 8 March 1916 – Frederick Holmes, Manchester (John Ellis exe. and Edward Taylor asst.).

113. 29 March 1916 – Reginald Haslam, Manchester (John Ellis exe. and Edward Taylor asst.).

114. 3 August 1916 – Sir Roger David Casement, Pentonville (John Ellis exe. and Robert Baxter asst.).

115. 16 August 1916 – William Allan Butler, Birmingham (John Ellis exe. and Edward Taylor asst.).

116. 6 September 1916 – Daniel Sullivan, Swansea (John Ellis exe. and George Brown asst.).
117. 12 December 1916 – Frederick Brooks, Exeter (John Ellis exe. and William Willis asst.).
118. 19 December 1916 – James Howarth Hargreaves, Manchester (John Ellis exe. and William Willis asst.).
119. 20 December 1916 – Joseph Deans, Durham (John Ellis exe. and George Brown asst.).
120. 21 March 1917 – Thomas Clinton, Manchester (John Ellis exe. and no asst. recorded).
121. 29 March 1917 – Leo O'Donnell, Winchester (John Ellis exe. and Robert Baxter asst.).
122. 10 April 1917 – Alec Bakerlis, Cardiff (John Ellis exe. and Edward Taylor asst.).
123. 17 April 1917 – William Robinson, Pentonville (John Ellis exe. and Robert Baxter asst.).
124. 16 May 1917 – Thomas McGuiness, Duke Street, Glasgow (John Ellis exe. and Robert Baxter asst.).
125. 16 August 1917 – William Hodgson, Liverpool (John Ellis exe. and Edward Taylor asst.).
126. 19 December 1917 – Thomas Cox, Shrewsbury (John Ellis exe. and William Willis asst.).
127. 12 February 1918 – Arthur Stramrowsky, Wandsworth (John Ellis exe. and George Brown asst.).
128. 21 February 1918 – Joseph Jones, Wandsworth (John Ellis exe. and William Willis asst.).
129. 2 March 1918 – Louis Voisin, Pentonville (John Ellis exe. and Edward Taylor asst.).
130. 5 March 1918 – Verney Asser, Shepton Mallet (John Ellis exe. and William Willis asst.).
131. 9 April 1918 – Louis Van Der Kerkhove, Birmingham (John Ellis exe. and George Brown asst.).
132. 17 December 1918 – William Rooney, Manchester (John Ellis exe. and no asst. recorded.).
133. 19 February 1919 – Joseph Rose, Oxford (John Ellis exe. and Edward Taylor asst.).
134. 10 July 1919 – Henry Perry (aka Beckett), Pentonville (John Ellis exe. and William Willis asst.).
135. 22 July 1919— John Crossland, Liverpool (John Ellis exe. and Robert Baxter asst.).

136. 31 July 1919 – Thomas Foster, Pentonville (John Ellis exe. and Edward Taylor asst.).

137. 8 August 1919 – Henry Gaskin, Birmingham (John Ellis exe. and William Willis asst.).

138. 7 October 1919 – Frank Warren, Pentonville (John Ellis exe. and George Brown asst.).

139. 11 November 1919 – James Adams, Duke Street, Glasgow (John Ellis exe.).

140. 26 November 1919 – Ernest Scott, Newcastle (John Ellis exe. and Edward Taylor asst.).

141. 26 November 1919 – Ambrose Quinn, Newcastle (John Ellis exe. and Robert Baxter asst.).

142. 3 December 1919 – Djang Djing Sung, Worcester (John Ellis exe. and Edward Taylor asst.).

143. 6 January 1920 – Hyman Perdovitch, Manchester (John Ellis exe.; Robert Baxter and Edward Taylor assts.)

144. 6 January 1920 – David Caplan, Manchester (John Ellis exe.; Robert Baxter and Edward Taylor assts.)

145. 23 March 1920 – William Hall, Durham (John Ellis exe. and Robert Baxter asst.).

146. 13 April 1920 – Frederick Rothwell Holt, Manchester (John Ellis exe. and William Willis asst.).

147. 14 April 1920 – Thomas Caler, Cardiff (John Ellis exe. and William Willis asst.).

148. 11 May 1920 – Herbert Salisbury, Liverpool (John Ellis exe. and Robert Baxter asst.).

149. 11 May 1920 – William Waddington, Liverpool (John Ellis exe. and Robert Baxter asst.).

150. 26 May 1920 – Albert James Fraser, Duke Street, Glasgow (John Ellis exe. and William Willis asst.).

151. 26 May 1920 – James Rollins, Duke Street, Glasgow (John Ellis exe. and William Willis asst.).

152. 16 June 1920 – Frederick Storey, Ipswich (John Ellis exe. and Robert Baxter asst.).

153. 22 June 1920 – William Aldred, Manchester (John Ellis exe. and William Willis asst.).

154. 27 July 1920 – Arthur Goslett, Pentonville (John Ellis exe. and Edward Taylor asst.).

155. 11 August 1920 – James Ellor, Liverpool (John Ellis exe. and Edward Taylor asst.).

156. 1 November 1920 – Kevin Barry, Dublin (John Ellis exe. and no asst. recorded).

157. 30 November 1920 – Cyril Saunders, Exeter (John Ellis exe. and William Willis asst.).

158. 30 December 1920 – Samuel Westwood, Birmingham (John Ellis exe. and no asst. recorded).

159. 31 December 1920 – Charles Colclough, Manchester (John Ellis exe. and William Willis asst.).

160. 2 March 1921 – George Bailey, Oxford (John Ellis exe. and Edward Taylor asst.).

161. 14 March 1921 – Patrick Moran, Mountjoy Prison, Dublin (John Ellis exe. and William Willis asst.).

162. 14 March 1921 – Bernard Ryan, Mountjoy Prison, Dublin (John Ellis exe. and William Willis asst.)

163. 14 March 1921 – Patrick Doyle, Mountjoy Prison, Dublin (John Ellis exe. and William Willis asst.).

164. 14 March 1921 – Thomas Bryan, Mountjoy Prison, Dublin (John Ellis exe. and William Willis asst.).

165. 14 March 1921 – Francis Flood, Mountjoy Prison, Dublin (John Ellis exe. and William Willis asst.).

166. 14 March 1921 – Thomas Whelan, Mountjoy Prison, Dublin (John Ellis exe. and William Willis asst.).

167. 5 April 1921 – Frederick Quarmby, Manchester (John Ellis exe. and William Willis asst.).

168. 25 April 1921 – Thomas Traynor, Mountjoy Prison, Dublin (John Ellis exe.).

169. 24 May 1921 – Thomas Wilson, Manchester (John Ellis exe. and Edward Taylor asst.).

170. 7 June 1921 – Edmund Foley, Mountjoy Prison, Dublin (John Ellis exe. at 7.00am).

171. 7 June 1921 – Patrick Maher, Mountjoy Prison, Dublin (John Ellis exe. at 7.00am).

172. 7 June 1921 – William Mitchell, Mountjoy Prison, Dublin (John Ellis exe at 8.00am).

173. 16 August 1921 – Lester Hamilton, Cardiff (John Ellis exe. and Seth Mills asst.).

174. 22 December 1921 – Edward O'Connor, Birmingham (John Ellis exe. and Robert Wilson asst.).

175. 21 February 1922 – William Harkness, Duke Street, Glasgow (John Ellis exe. and Robert Baxter asst.).

176. 23 March 1922 – William Sullivan, Usk (John Ellis exe. and Thomas Phillips asst.).

177. 24 March 1922 – Edward Ernest Black, Exeter (John Ellis exe. and Seth Mills asst.).

178. 7 April 1922 – Percy James Atkins, Nottingham (John Ellis exe.).

179. 11 April 1922 – Frederick Keeling, Pentonville (John Ellis exe. and Seth Mills asst.).

180. 18 April 1922 – Edmund Tonbridge, Pentonville (John Ellis exe. and Robert Baxter asst.).

181. 30 May 1922 – Hiram Thompson, Manchester (John Ellis exe. and William Willis asst.).

182. 31 May 1922 – Herbert Rowse Armstrong, Gloucester (John Ellis exe. and Edward Taylor asst.).

183. 7 June 1922 – Henry Julius Jacoby, Pentonville (John Ellis exe. and Thomas Phillips asst.).

184. 10 August 1922 – Joseph O'Sullivan (John Ellis exe.; Edward Taylor and Seth Mills assts.).

185. 10 August 1922 – Reginald Dunne, Wandsworth (John Ellis exe.; Edward Taylor and Seth Mills assts.).

186. 11 August 1922 – Elijah Pountney, Birmingham (John Ellis exe. and Robert Baxter asst.).

187. 17 August 1922 – Simon McGeown, Crumlin Road Prison, Belfast (John Ellis exe. and William Willis asst.).

188. 19 August 1922 – Thomas Henry Allaway, Winchester (John Ellis exe. and Edward Taylor asst.).

189. 5 September 1922 – William Yeldham, Pentonville (John Ellis exe. and William Willis asst.).

190. 19 December 1922 – William Rider, Birmingham (John Ellis exe. and William Willis asst.).

191. 3 January 1923 – George Frederick Edisbury, Manchester (John Ellis exe. and Robert Wilson asst.).

192. 9 January 1923 – Edith Thompson, Holloway (John Ellis exe. and Robert Baxter asst.). (Bywaters was hanged by William Willis assisted by Seth Mills at Pentonville.)

193. 28 March 1923 – George Perry, Manchester (John Ellis exe. and no asst. recorded).

194. 5 April 1923 – Bernard Pomroy, Pentonville (John Ellis exe. and Edward Taylor asst.).

195. 10 April 1923 – Frederick George Wood, Liverpool (John Ellis exe. and Thomas Phillips asst.).

196. 11 June 1923 – John Henry Savage, Calton, Edinburgh (John Ellis exe. and William Willis asst.).
197. 4 July 1923 – Rowland Duck, Pentonville (John Ellis exe. and Robert Wilson asst.).
198. 24 July 1923 – William Griffiths, Shrewsbury (John Ellis exe. and Seth Mills asst.).
199. 8 August 1923 – Albert Burrows, Nottingham (John Ellis exe. and William Willis asst.).
200. 10 October 1923 – Susan Newell, Duke Street, Glasgow (John Ellis exe. and William Willis asst.).
201. 30 October 1923 – Philip Murray, Calton Edinburgh (John Ellis exe. and William Willis asst.).
202. 1 November 1923 – Frederick Jesse, Wandsworth (John Ellis exe. and Robert Baxter asst.).
203. 29 November 1923 – William Downs, Mountjoy Prison, Dublin (John Ellis exe.).
204. 28 December 1923— John Eastwood, Leeds (John Ellis exe. and Seth Mills asst.).

Select Bibliography and Further Reading

Doughty, Jack, *The Rochdale Hangman*, (Jade, 1998).

Eddleston, John J., *The Encyclopaedia of Executions*, (Blake, 2012).

Ellis, John, *Diary of a Hangman*, (Forum, 1996).

Fielding, Steve, *The Executioner's Bible*, (Blake, 2007).

Fielding, Steve, *The Hangman's Record*, (Vol. 2) 1900–1929 (Chancery, 1995).

Honeycombe, Gordon, *Murders of the Black Museum*, (Hutchinson, 1982).

McLaughlin, Stewart, *Execution Suite: A History of the Gallows at Wandsworth Prison 1878–1993*, (HMP Wandsworth, 2004).

Pierrepoint, Albert, *Executioner Pierrepoint*, (Harrap, 1974).

Storey, Neil R., *Victorian Prisons and Prisoners*, (History Press, 2010).

Acknowledgements

The author would like to record his personal thanks to the following:

First and foremost I would like to thank my friend and fellow historian, Joolz Bailey, for her work on the transcription of the original texts in the John Ellis scrapbook. I would also like to thank the following for their sage advice, contributions and encouragement for this book: Stewart P. Evans, Rob Clack, James Nice, Stewart McLaughlin, Johanne Edgington, Nigel Preston, Eve and Steve Bacon. I would like to say a huge thank you to the many legal professionals, crime historians, past and present police and prison officers and archivists who have kindly assisted me in my research over the years. I also extend my gratitude and appreciation to my commissioning editor and all the team at Pen & Sword books. Last but by no means least I give heartfelt thanks to my darling Irish cailín Jenny and my family for their enduring love and support.